CAPTAIN AMERICA

ALLIES & ENEMIES

CAPTAIN AMERICA: ALLIES & ENEMIES. Contains material originally published in magazine form as CAPTAIN AMERICA AND THE FALCON #1, CAPTAIN AMERICA AND THE FIRST THIRTEEN #1, CAPTAI AMERICAN A CROSSBONES #1, CAPTAIN AMERICA AND BATROC #1 and CAPTAIN AMERICA AND THE SECRET AVENGERS #1. First printing 2011. ISBN# 978-0-7851-5502-7. Published by MARVEL WORLDWIDE, INC., a subsidiary of MAR ENTERTAINMENT, LLC. OFFICE OF PUBLICATION: 135 West 50th Street, New York, NY 10020. Copyright © 2011 Marvel Characters, Inc. All rights reserved. $16.99 per copy in the U.S. and $18.50 in Canada (GST #R12703289 Canadian Agreement #40668537. All characters featured in this issue and the distinctive names and likenesses thereof, and all related indicia are trademarks of Marvel Characters, Inc. No similarity between any of the nam characters, persons, and/or institutions in this magazine with those of any living or dead person or institution is intended, and any such similarity which may exist is purely coincidental. **Printed in the U.S.A.** ALAN FI EVP - Office of the President, Marvel Worldwide, Inc. and EVP & CMO Marvel Characters B.V.; DAN BUCKLEY, Publisher & President - Print, Animation & Digital Divisions; JOE QUESADA, Chief Creative Officer; JIM SOKOLOW Chief Operating Officer; DAVID BOGART, SVP of Business Affairs & Talent Management; TOM BREVOORT, SVP of Publishing; C.B. CEBULSKI, SVP of Creator & Content Development; DAVID GABRIEL, SVP of Publishing Sale Circulation; MICHAEL PASCIULLO, SVP of Brand Planning & Communications; JIM O'KEEFE, VP of Operations & Logistics; DAN CARR, Executive Director of Publishing Technology; JUSTIN F. GABRIE, Director of Publishing & Edito Operations; SUSAN CRESPI, Editorial Operations Manager; ALEX MORALES, Publishing Operations Manager; STAN LEE, Chairman Emeritus. For information regarding advertising in Marvel Comics or on Marvel.com, please c tact Ron Stern, VP of Business Development, at rstern@marvel.com. For Marvel subscription inquiries, please call 800-217-9158. . **Manufactured between 3/31/2011 and 4/19/2011 by QUAD/GRAPHICS, DUBUQUE, IA, U**

10 9 8 7 6 5 4 3 2 1

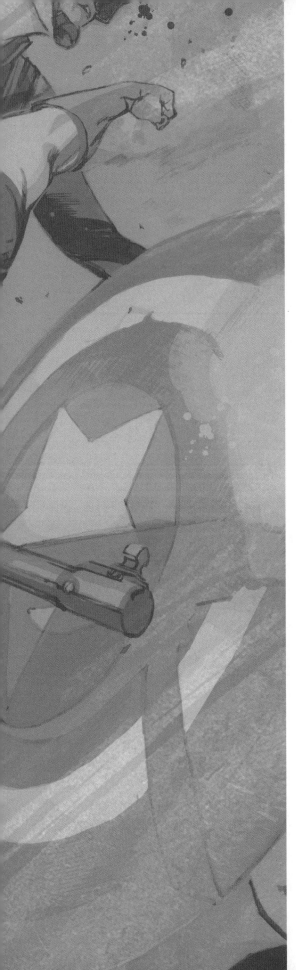

CAPTAIN AMERICA AND THE FALCON
WRITER: ROB WILLIAMS
ARTIST: REBEKAH ISAACS
COLORIST: ANDREW DAHLHOUSE
LETTERER/PRODUCTION: VC'S JOE CARAMAGNA
ASSISTANT EDITOR: RACHEL PINNELAS
EDITOR: TOM BRENNAN

CAPTAIN AMERICA AND THE FIRST THIRTEEN
WRITER: KATHRYN IMMONEN
ARTIST: RAMON PEREZ
COLORIST: JOHN RAUCH
LETTERER: JARED K. FLETCHER
PRODUCTION: DAMIEN LUCCHESE
EDITOR: RACHEL PINNELAS
SUPERVISING EDITOR: TOM BREVOORT

CAPTAIN AMERICA AND CROSSBONES
WRITER: WILLIAM HARMS
ARTIST: DECLAN SHALVEY
COLORIST: MATTHEW WILSON
LETTERER: JARED K. FLETCHER
PRODUCTION: MAYELA GUITIERREZ
ASSISTANT EDITOR: RACHEL PINNELAS
ASSOCIATE EDITOR: TOM BRENNAN
EDITOR: BILL ROSEMANN

CAPTAIN AMERICA AND THE SECRET AVENGERS
WRITER: KELLY SUE DECONNICK
ARTIST: GREG TOCCHINI
COLOR ARTIST: PAUL MOUNTS
LETTERER: DAVE LANPHEAR
PRODUCTION: TAYLOR ESPOSITO
EDITOR: LAUREN SANKOVITCH

CAPTAIN AMERICA AND BATROC
WRITER: KIERON GILLEN
ARTIST: RENATO ARLEM
COLORIST: NICK FILARDI
LETTERER: BLAMBOT'S NATE PIEKOS
PRODUCTION: DAMIEN LUCCHESE
EDITOR: CHARLIE BECKERMAN

COVER ARTIST: GREG TOCCHINI

CAPTAIN AMERICA CREATED BY JOE SIMON & JACK KIRBY

COLLECTION EDITOR: MARK D. BEAZLEY EDITORIAL ASSISTANTS: JAMES EMMETT & JOE HOCHSTEIN
ASSISTANT EDITORS: NELSON RIBEIRO & ALEX STARBUCK EDITOR, SPECIAL PROJECTS: JENNIFER GRÜNWALD
SENIOR EDITOR, SPECIAL PROJECTS: JEFF YOUNGQUIST SENIOR VICE PRESIDENT OF SALES: DAVID GABRIEL
SVP OF BRAND PLANNING & COMMUNICATIONS: MIKE PASCIULLO BOOK DESIGN: JEFF POWELL
EDITOR IN CHIEF: AXEL ALONSO CHIEF CREATIVE OFFICER: JOE QUESADA
PUBLISHER: DAN BUCKLEY EXECUTIVE PRODUCER: ALAN FINE

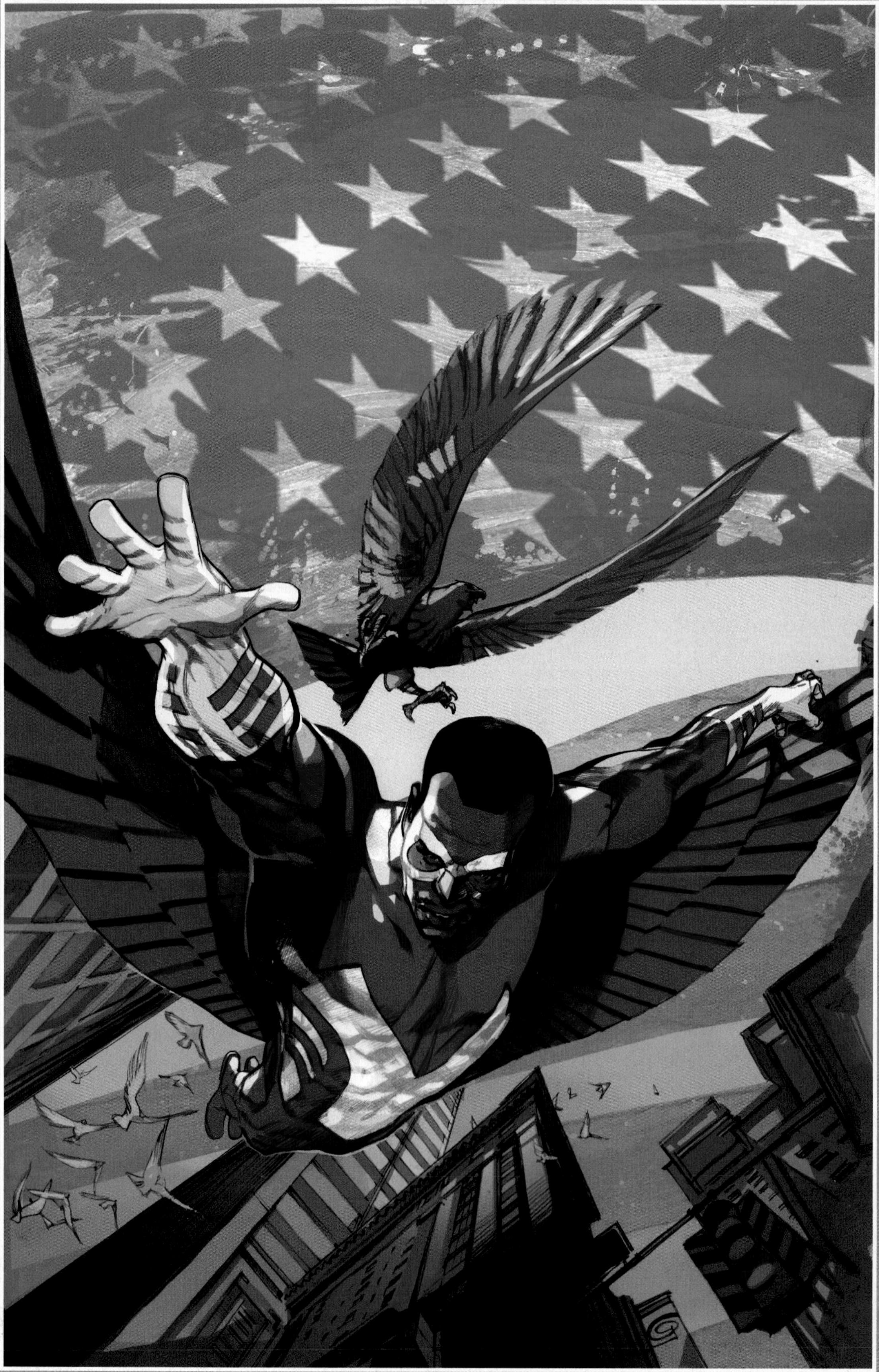

CAPTAIN AMERICA AND THE FALCON

CLASSIFIED

PROFILE #: 15313010
REAL NAME: Samuel Wilson
AKA: The Falcon

Sam "Snap" Wilson was a small time hood headed nowhere. Raised by loving parents in Harlem, Sam wasn't always on the wrong path. His father was a prominent minister and both parents encouraged him to pursue a good education and his interests. A childhood fascination with birds led him to build a pigeon coop on the roof of their apartment building. But when he encountered violence, drugs and racism in his teen years, he became jaded and began running with gangs.

While on a flight to South America for a "big score," Wilson's plane crashed on the island hideaway of The Red Skull, Nazi adversary of the super-soldier Captain America. Skull used the Cosmic Cube, a cosmic weapon capable of bending space and time, to give Wilson a mental link with birds and a suit that enabled him to fly. Sam took on the name the Falcon and quickly turned against the Red Skull, aligning with Captain America.

Captain America trained Falcon as a crime fighter – Wilson even joined Cap on his team of heroes, the Avengers. But Wilson made his biggest impact on his community, returning to school, becoming a social worker, and working to make life better in his neighborhood...

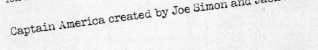

SPIKES

Writer
Rob Williams

Art
Rebekah Isaacs

Colorist
Andrew Dalhouse

Letters/Production
VC's Joe Caramagna

Cover Artist
Greg Tocchini

Assistant Editor
Rachel Pinnelas

Editor
Tom Brennan

Editor in Chief
Axel Alonso

Chief Creative Officer
Joe Quesada

Publisher
Dan Buckley

Exec. Producer
Alan Fine

Captain America created by Joe Simon and Jack Kirby

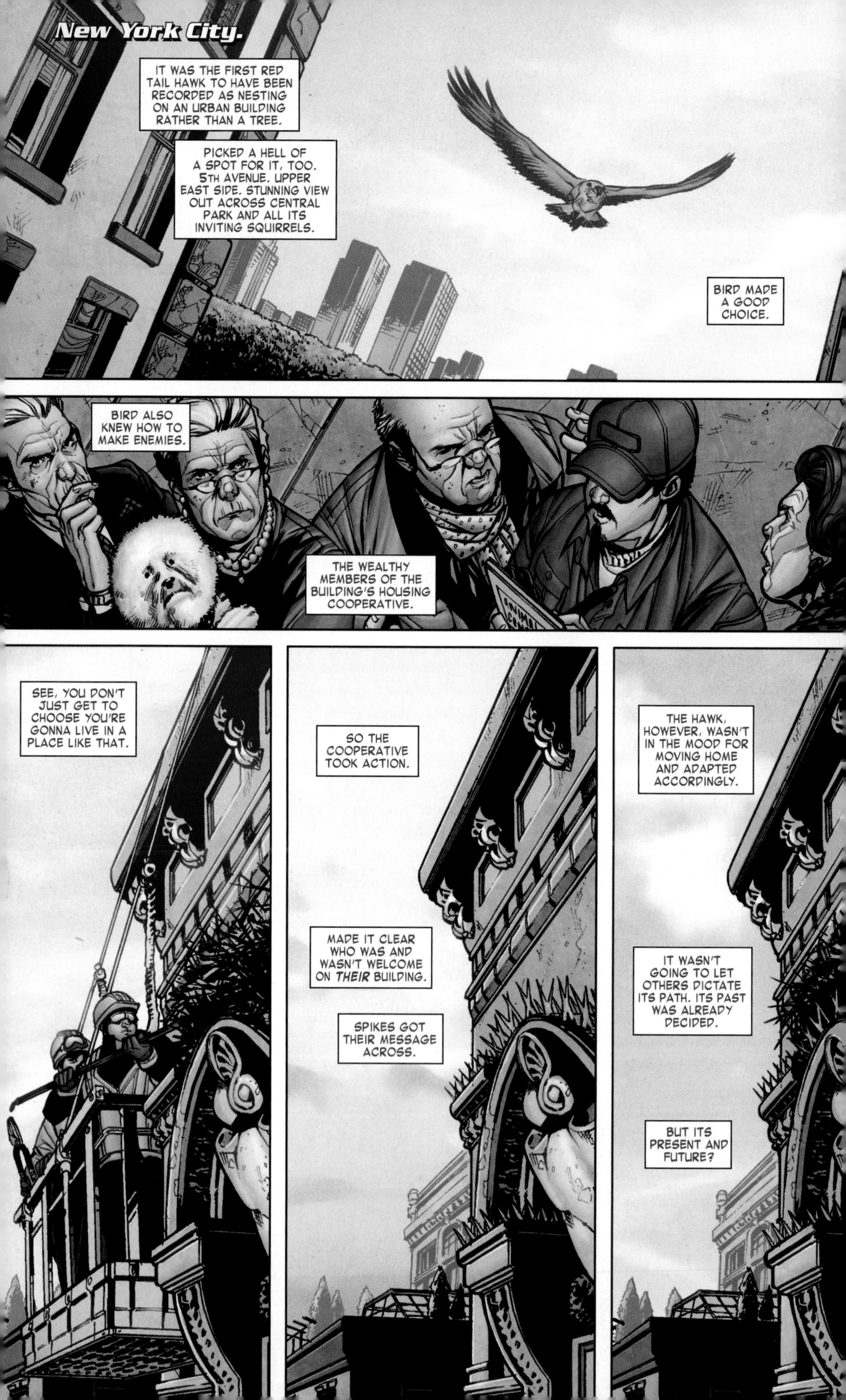
New York City.
IT WAS THE FIRST RED TAIL HAWK TO HAVE BEEN RECORDED AS NESTING ON AN URBAN BUILDING RATHER THAN A TREE.
PICKED A HELL OF A SPOT FOR IT, TOO. 5TH AVENUE. UPPER EAST SIDE. STUNNING VIEW OUT ACROSS CENTRAL PARK AND ALL ITS INVITING SQUIRRELS.
BIRD MADE A GOOD CHOICE.
BIRD ALSO KNEW HOW TO MAKE ENEMIES.
THE WEALTHY MEMBERS OF THE BUILDING'S HOUSING COOPERATIVE.
SEE, YOU DON'T JUST GET TO CHOOSE YOU'RE GONNA LIVE IN A PLACE LIKE THAT.
SO THE COOPERATIVE TOOK ACTION.
MADE IT CLEAR WHO WAS AND WASN'T WELCOME ON *THEIR* BUILDING.
SPIKES GOT THEIR MESSAGE ACROSS.
THE HAWK, HOWEVER, WASN'T IN THE MOOD FOR MOVING HOME AND ADAPTED ACCORDINGLY.
IT WASN'T GOING TO LET OTHERS DICTATE ITS PATH. ITS PAST WAS ALREADY DECIDED.
BUT ITS PRESENT AND FUTURE?

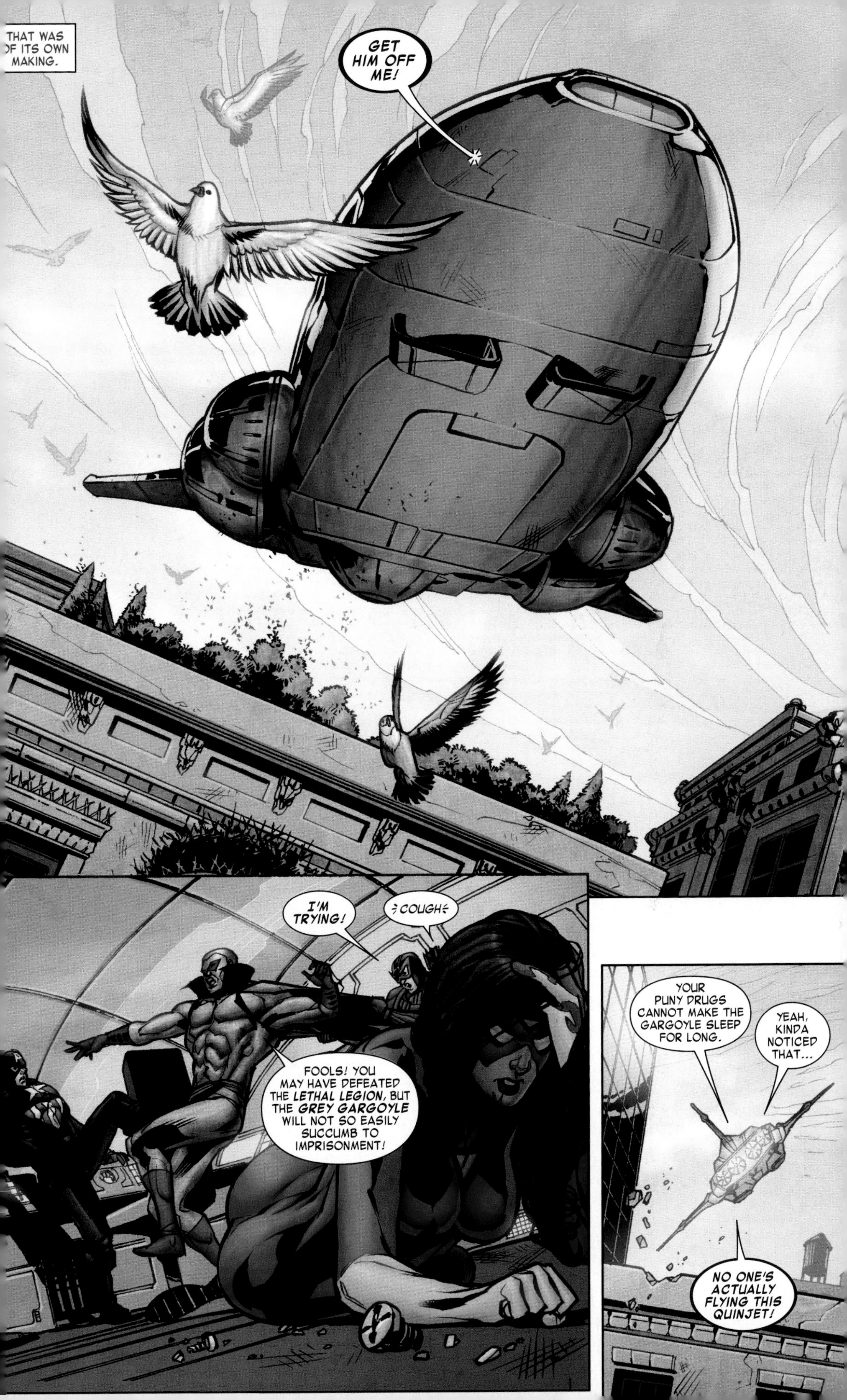
THAT WAS OF ITS OWN MAKING.
GET HIM OFF ME!
I'M TRYING!
COUGH
FOOLS! YOU MAY HAVE DEFEATED THE LETHAL LEGION, BUT THE GREY GARGOYLE WILL NOT SO EASILY SUCCUMB TO IMPRISONMENT!
YOUR PUNY DRUGS CANNOT MAKE THE GARGOYLE SLEEP FOR LONG.
YEAH, KINDA NOTICED THAT...
NO ONE'S ACTUALLY FLYING THIS QUINJET!

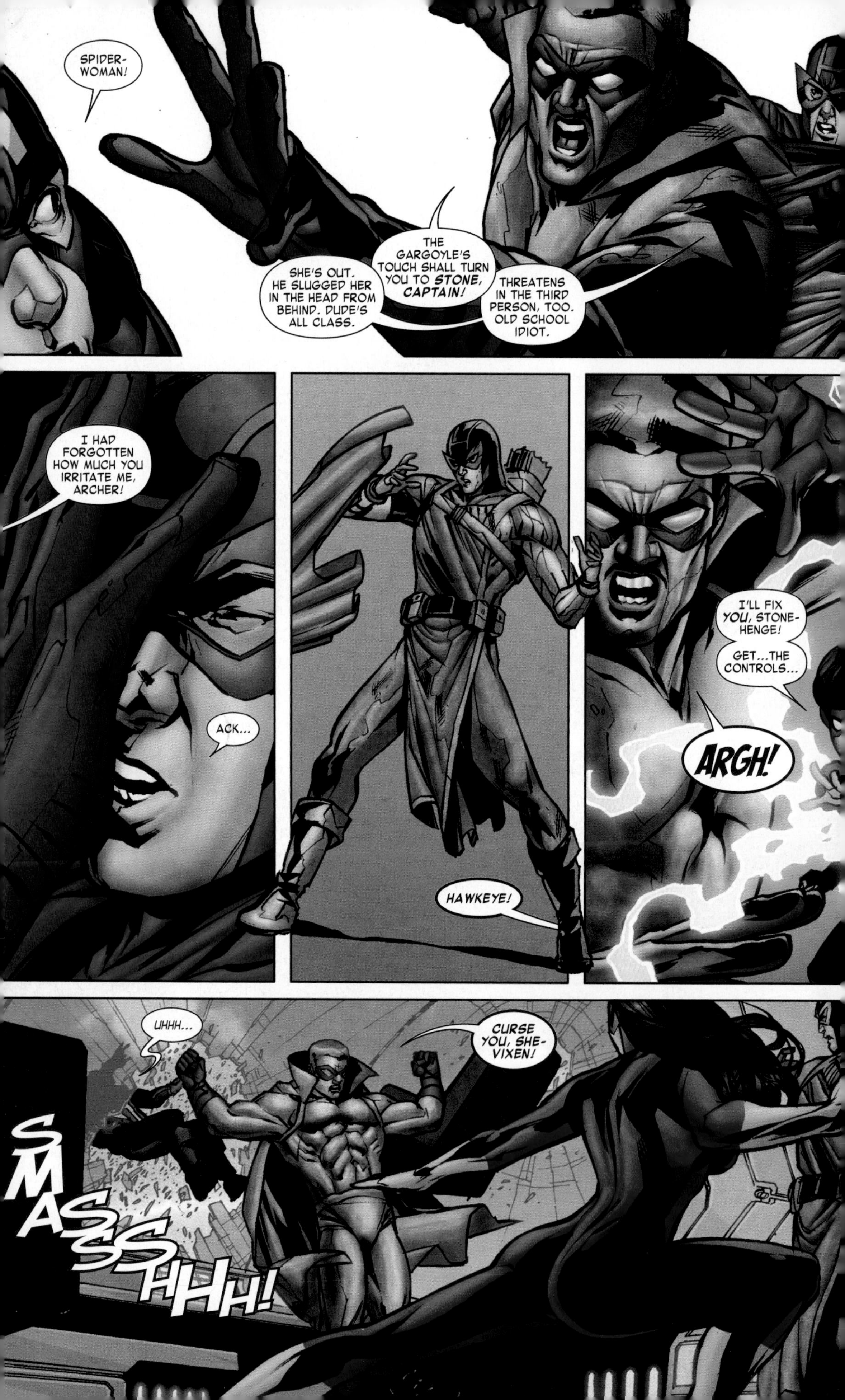
SPIDER-WOMAN!
THE GARGOYLE'S TOUCH SHALL TURN YOU TO STONE, CAPTAIN!
SHE'S OUT. HE SLUGGED HER IN THE HEAD FROM BEHIND. DUDE'S ALL CLASS.
THREATENS IN THE THIRD PERSON, TOO. OLD SCHOOL IDIOT.
I HAD FORGOTTEN HOW MUCH YOU IRRITATE ME, ARCHER!
ACK...
HAWKEYE!
I'LL FIX YOU, STONE-HENGE!
GET...THE CONTROLS...
ARGH!
UHHH...
CURSE YOU, SHE-VIXEN!
SMASSHHHH!

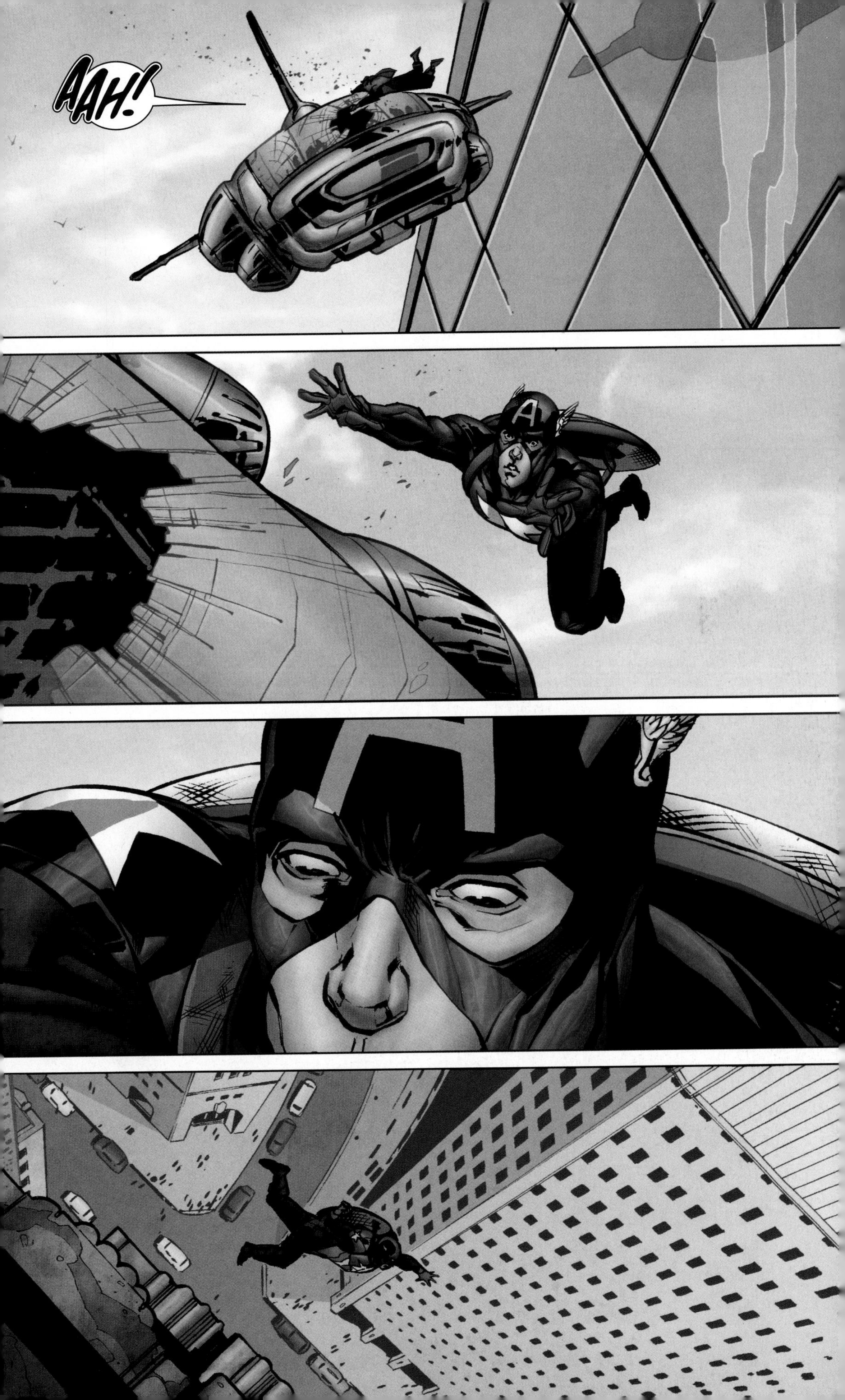
AAH!

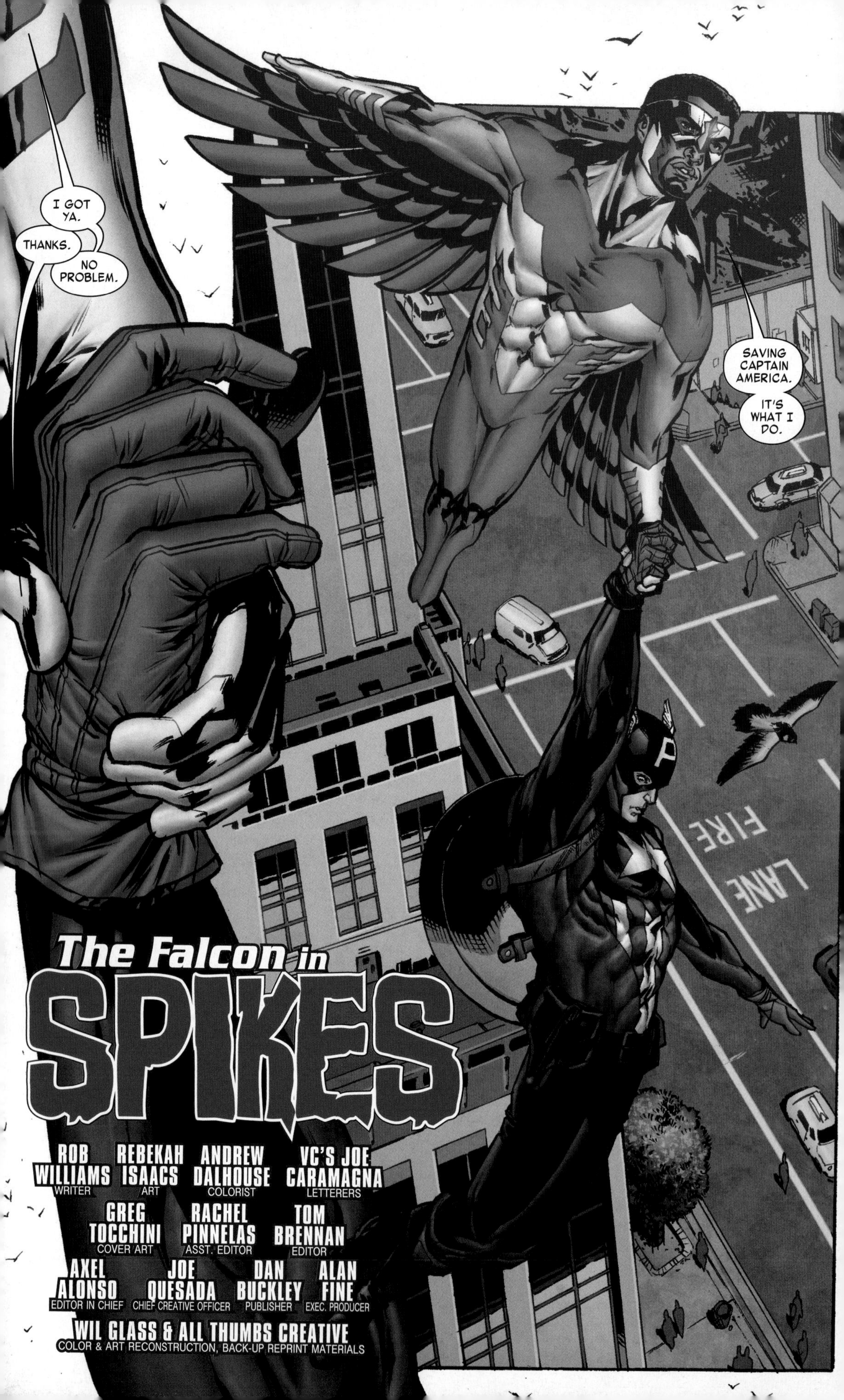
I GOT YA.
THANKS.
NO PROBLEM.
SAVING CAPTAIN AMERICA.
IT'S WHAT I DO.
FIRE LANE
The Falcon in
SPIKES
ROB WILLIAMS WRITER
REBEKAH ISAACS ART
ANDREW DALHOUSE COLORIST
VC'S JOE CARAMAGNA LETTERERS
GREG TOCCHINI COVER ART
RACHEL PINNELAS ASST. EDITOR
TOM BRENNAN EDITOR
AXEL ALONSO EDITOR IN CHIEF
JOE QUESADA CHIEF CREATIVE OFFICER
DAN BUCKLEY PUBLISHER
ALAN FINE EXEC. PRODUCER
WIL GLASS & ALL THUMBS CREATIVE
COLOR & ART RECONSTRUCTION, BACK-UP REPRINT MATERIALS

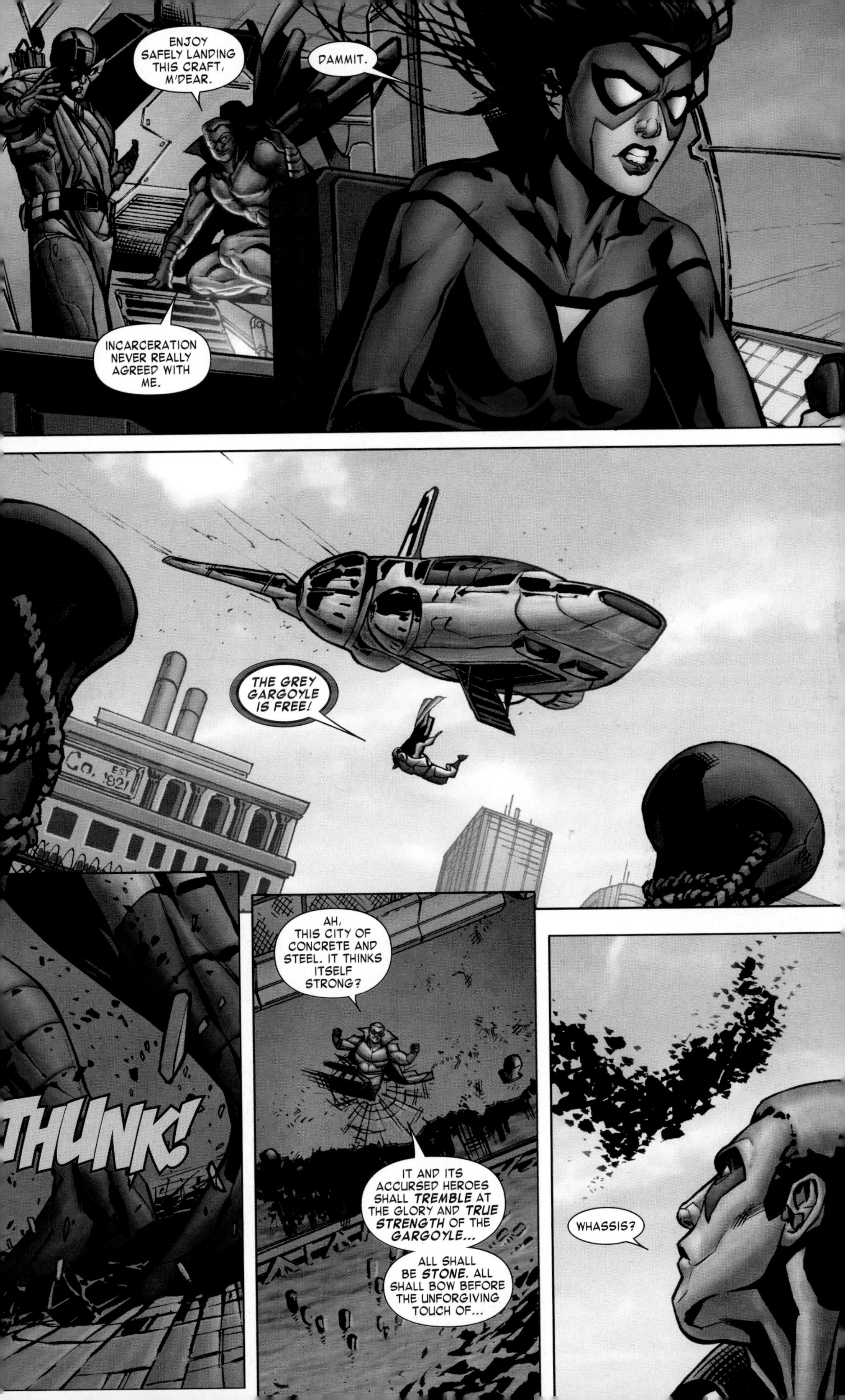
ENJOY SAFELY LANDING THIS CRAFT, M'DEAR.
DAMMIT.
INCARCERATION NEVER REALLY AGREED WITH ME.
THE GREY GARGOYLE IS FREE!
CO. EST 1821
THUNK!
AH, THIS CITY OF CONCRETE AND STEEL. IT THINKS ITSELF STRONG?
IT AND ITS ACCURSED HEROES SHALL *TREMBLE* AT THE GLORY AND *TRUE STRENGTH* OF THE *GARGOYLE*...
ALL SHALL BE *STONE.* ALL SHALL BOW BEFORE THE UNFORGIVING TOUCH OF...
WHASSIS?

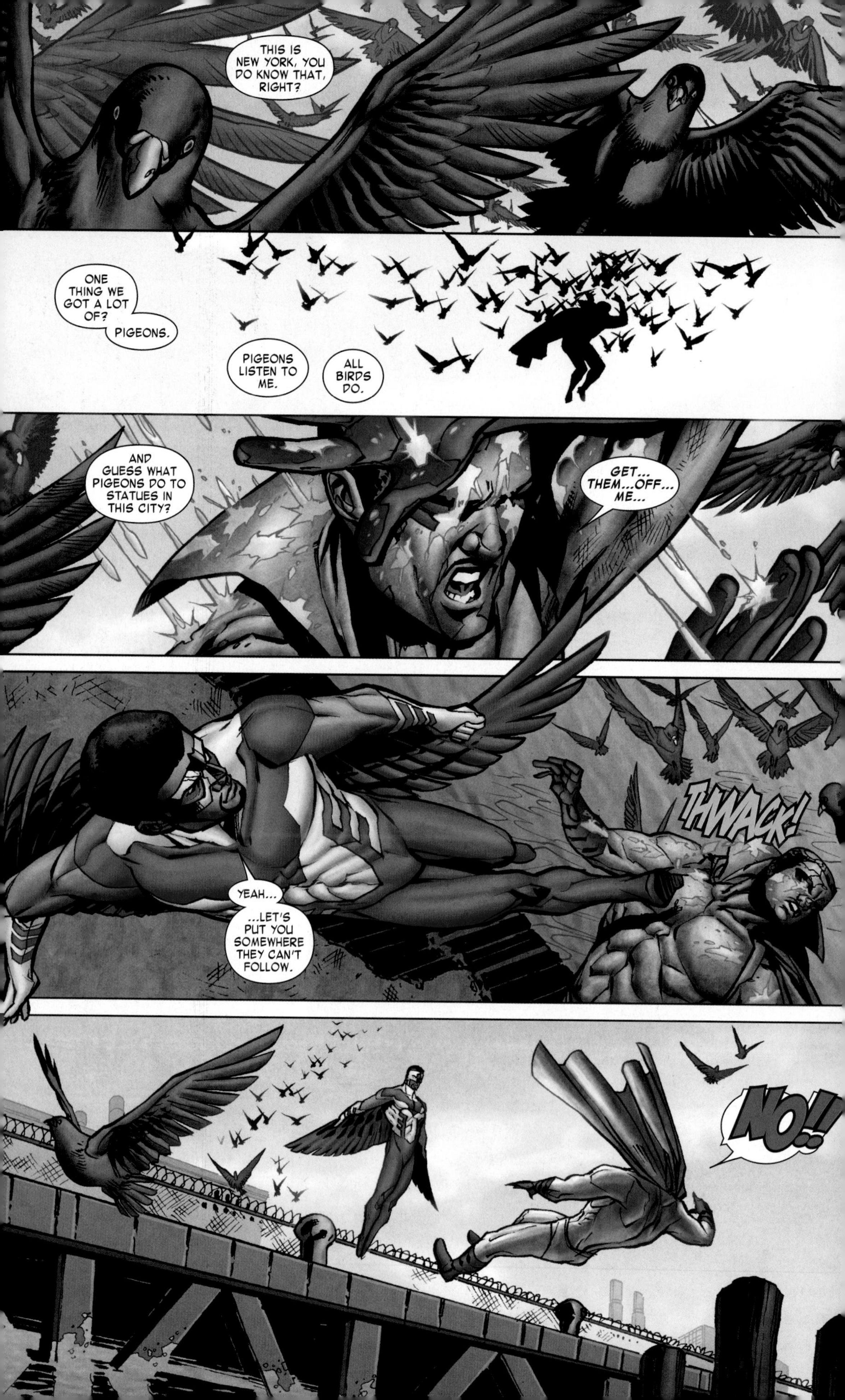
THIS IS NEW YORK, YOU DO KNOW THAT, RIGHT?
ONE THING WE GOT A LOT OF?
PIGEONS.
PIGEONS LISTEN TO ME.
ALL BIRDS DO.
AND GUESS WHAT PIGEONS DO TO STATUES IN THIS CITY?
GET... THEM...OFF... ME...
THWACK!
YEAH...
...LET'S PUT YOU SOMEWHERE THEY CAN'T FOLLOW.
NO!!

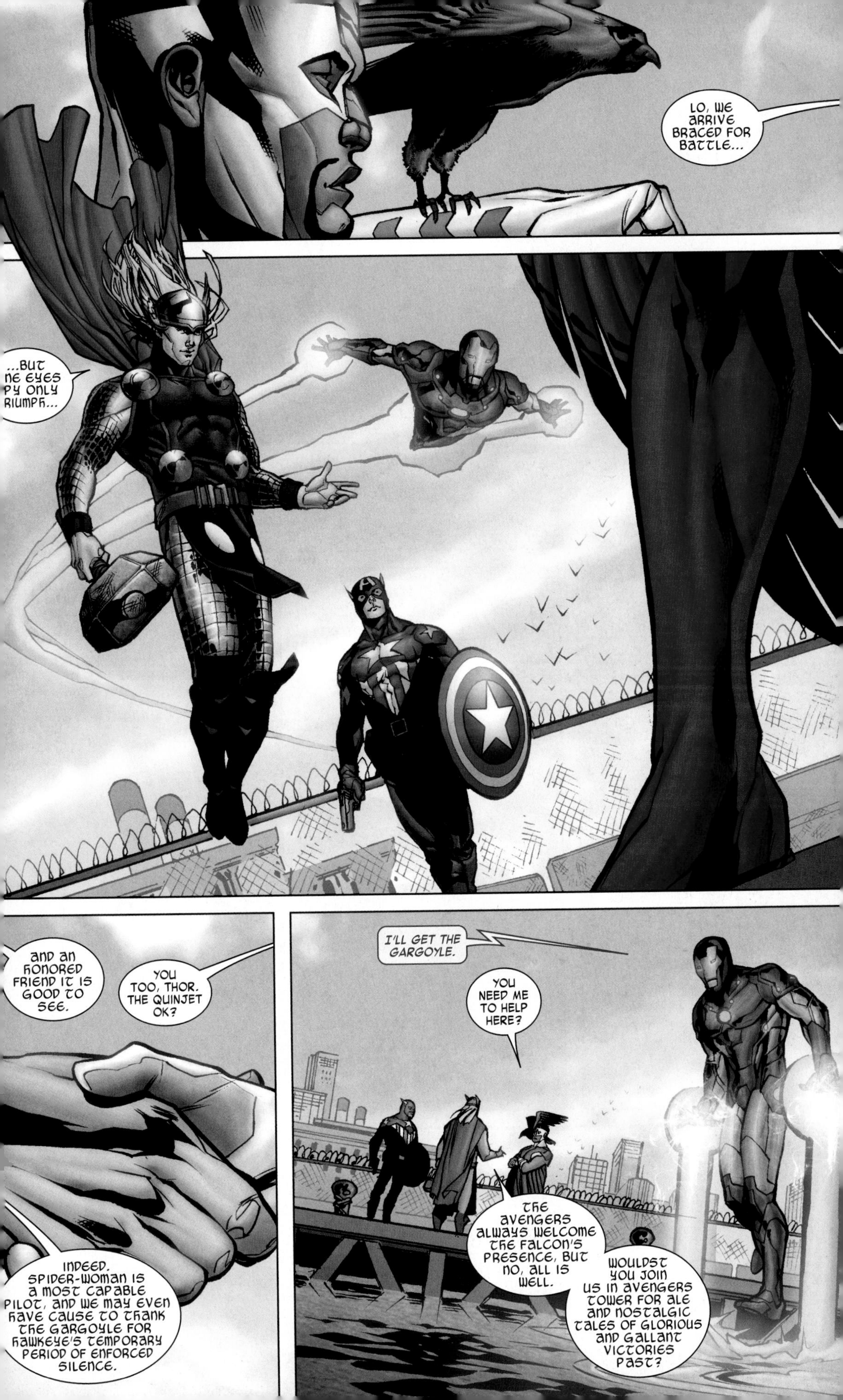
LO, WE ARRIVE BRACED FOR BATTLE...
...BUT ...NE EYES ...PY ONLY ...RIUMPH...
AND AN HONORED FRIEND IT IS GOOD TO SEE.
YOU TOO, THOR. THE QUINJET OK?
INDEED. SPIDER-WOMAN IS A MOST CAPABLE PILOT, AND WE MAY EVEN HAVE CAUSE TO THANK THE GARGOYLE FOR HAWKEYE'S TEMPORARY PERIOD OF ENFORCED SILENCE.
I'LL GET THE GARGOYLE.
YOU NEED ME TO HELP HERE?
THE AVENGERS ALWAYS WELCOME THE FALCON'S PRESENCE, BUT NO, ALL IS WELL.
WOULDST YOU JOIN US IN AVENGERS TOWER FOR ALE AND NOSTALGIC TALES OF GLORIOUS AND GALLANT VICTORIES PAST?

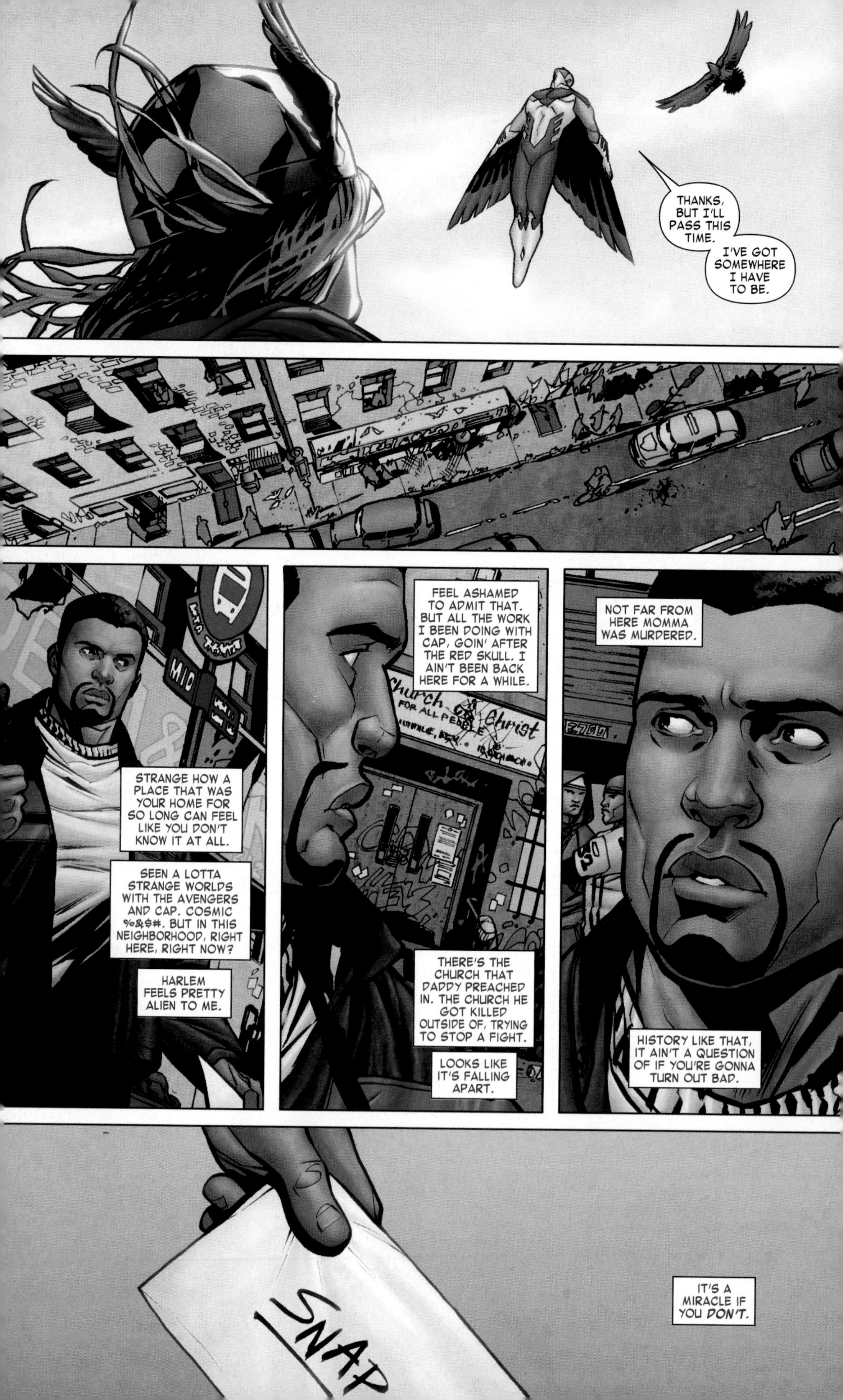
THANKS, BUT I'LL PASS THIS TIME.
I'VE GOT SOMEWHERE I HAVE TO BE.
STRANGE HOW A PLACE THAT WAS YOUR HOME FOR SO LONG CAN FEEL LIKE YOU DON'T KNOW IT AT ALL.
SEEN A LOTTA STRANGE WORLDS WITH THE AVENGERS AND CAP. COSMIC %&$#. BUT IN THIS NEIGHBORHOOD, RIGHT HERE, RIGHT NOW?
HARLEM FEELS PRETTY ALIEN TO ME.
FEEL ASHAMED TO ADMIT THAT. BUT ALL THE WORK I BEEN DOING WITH CAP, GOIN' AFTER THE RED SKULL. I AIN'T BEEN BACK HERE FOR A WHILE.
THERE'S THE CHURCH THAT DADDY PREACHED IN. THE CHURCH HE GOT KILLED OUTSIDE OF, TRYING TO STOP A FIGHT.
LOOKS LIKE IT'S FALLING APART.
NOT FAR FROM HERE MOMMA WAS MURDERED.
HISTORY LIKE THAT, IT AIN'T A QUESTION OF IF YOU'RE GONNA TURN OUT BAD.
IT'S A MIRACLE IF YOU *DON'T*.
SNAP

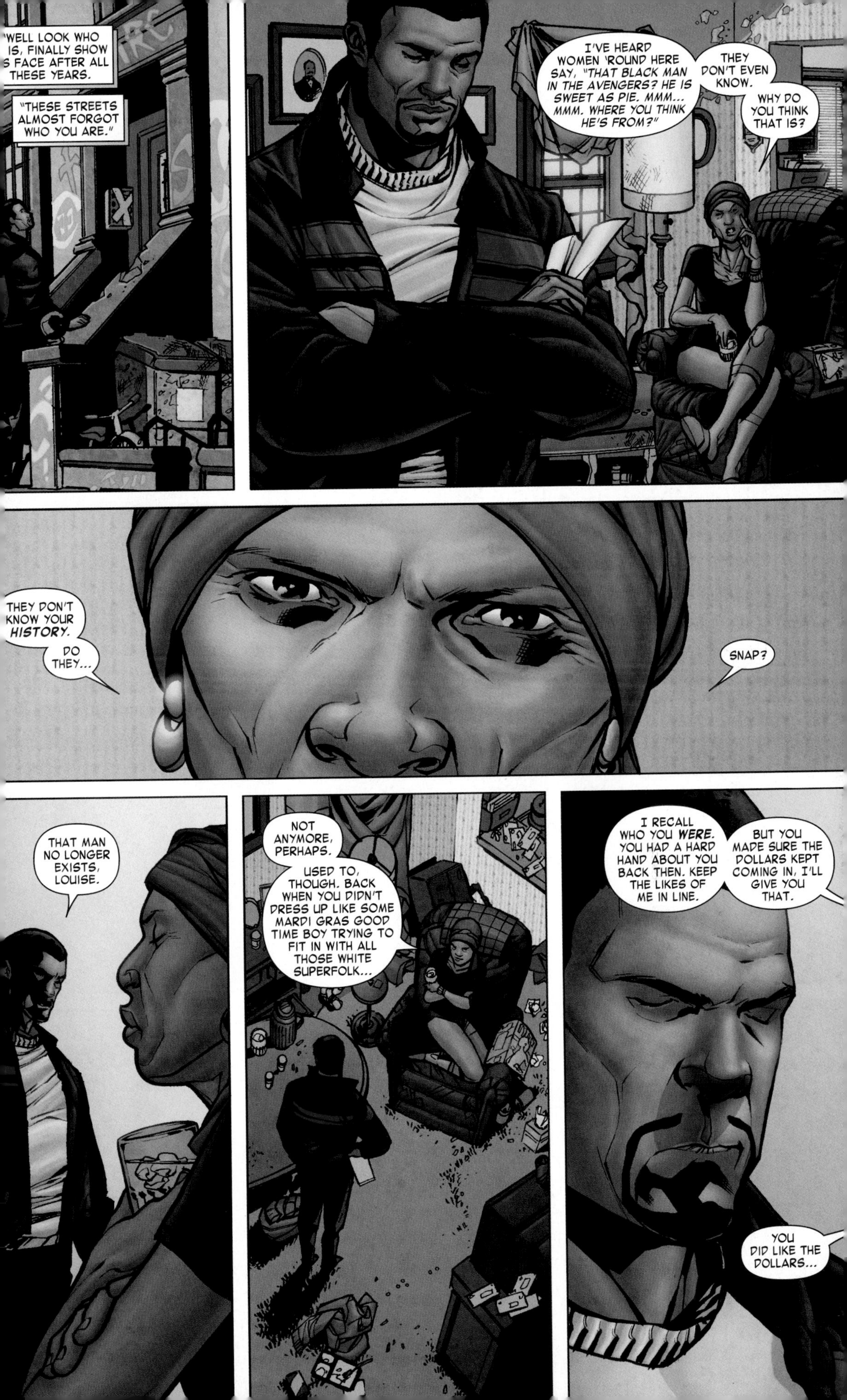
"WELL LOOK WHO IS, FINALLY SHOW S FACE AFTER ALL THESE YEARS.
"THESE STREETS ALMOST FORGOT WHO YOU ARE."
I'VE HEARD WOMEN 'ROUND HERE SAY, "THAT BLACK MAN IN THE AVENGERS? HE IS SWEET AS PIE. MMM... MMM. WHERE YOU THINK HE'S FROM?"
THEY DON'T EVEN KNOW.
WHY DO YOU THINK THAT IS?
THEY DON'T KNOW YOUR *HISTORY*.
DO THEY...
SNAP?
THAT MAN NO LONGER EXISTS, LOUISE.
NOT ANYMORE, PERHAPS.
USED TO, THOUGH. BACK WHEN YOU DIDN'T DRESS UP LIKE SOME MARDI GRAS GOOD TIME BOY TRYING TO FIT IN WITH ALL THOSE WHITE SUPERFOLK...
I RECALL WHO YOU *WERE*. YOU HAD A HARD HAND ABOUT YOU BACK THEN. KEEP THE LIKES OF ME IN LINE.
BUT YOU MADE SURE THE DOLLARS KEPT COMING IN, I'LL GIVE YOU THAT.
YOU DID LIKE THE DOLLARS...

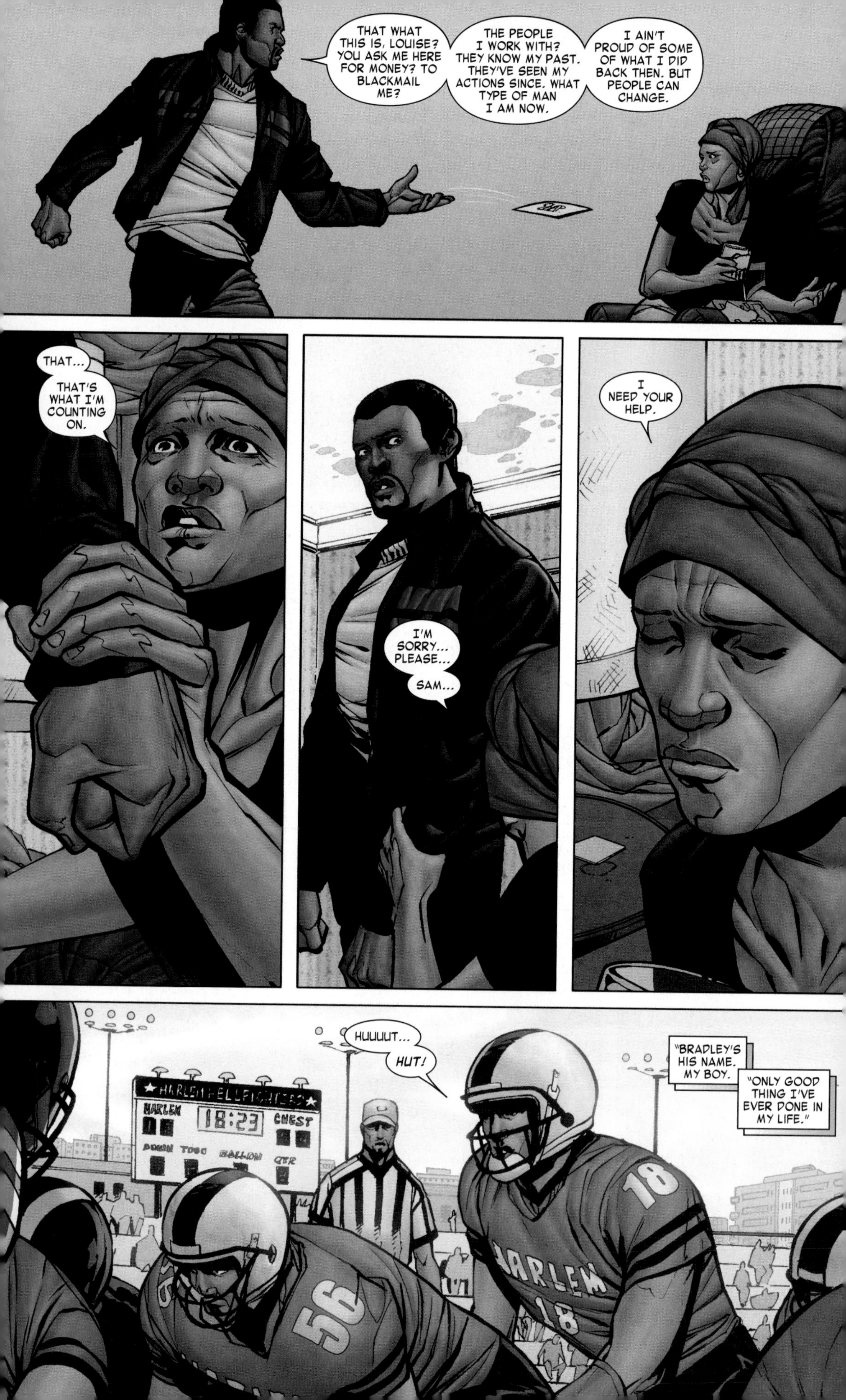
THAT WHAT THIS IS, LOUISE? YOU ASK ME HERE FOR MONEY? TO BLACKMAIL ME?
THE PEOPLE I WORK WITH? THEY KNOW MY PAST. THEY'VE SEEN MY ACTIONS SINCE. WHAT TYPE OF MAN I AM NOW.
I AIN'T PROUD OF SOME OF WHAT I DID BACK THEN. BUT PEOPLE CAN CHANGE.
THAT...
THAT'S WHAT I'M COUNTING ON.
I'M SORRY... PLEASE...
SAM...
I NEED YOUR HELP.
HARLEM HELLFIGHTERS
HARLEM
18:23
HUUUUT...
HUT!
"BRADLEY'S HIS NAME. MY BOY.
"ONLY GOOD THING I'VE EVER DONE IN MY LIFE."
HARLEM
18
56

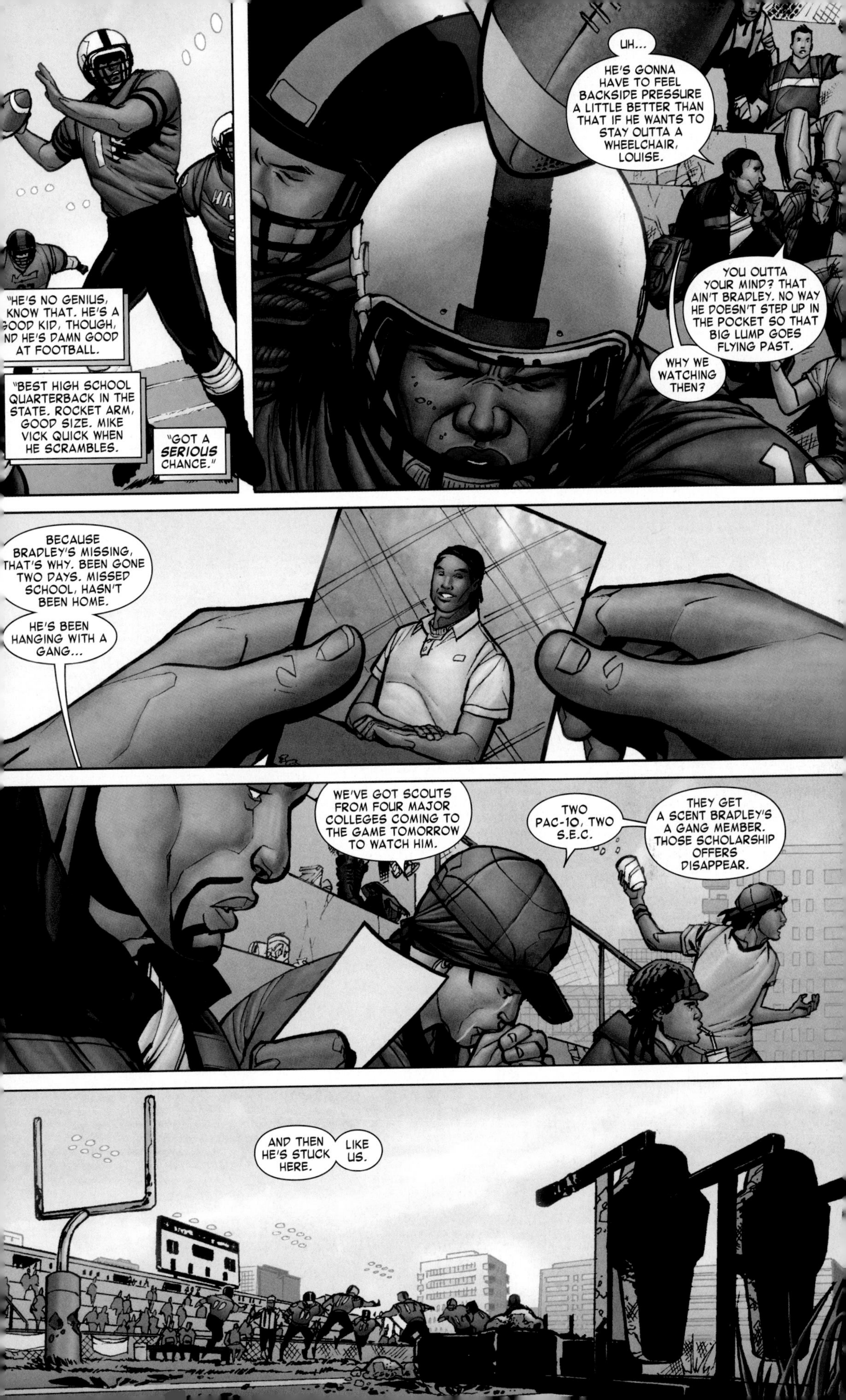
"HE'S NO GENIUS, KNOW THAT. HE'S A GOOD KID, THOUGH, AND HE'S DAMN GOOD AT FOOTBALL.
"BEST HIGH SCHOOL QUARTERBACK IN THE STATE. ROCKET ARM, GOOD SIZE. MIKE VICK QUICK WHEN HE SCRAMBLES.
"GOT A SERIOUS CHANCE."
UH...
HE'S GONNA HAVE TO FEEL BACKSIDE PRESSURE A LITTLE BETTER THAN THAT IF HE WANTS TO STAY OUTTA A WHEELCHAIR, LOUISE.
YOU OUTTA YOUR MIND? THAT AIN'T BRADLEY. NO WAY HE DOESN'T STEP UP IN THE POCKET SO THAT BIG LUMP GOES FLYING PAST.
WHY WE WATCHING THEN?
BECAUSE BRADLEY'S MISSING, THAT'S WHY. BEEN GONE TWO DAYS. MISSED SCHOOL, HASN'T BEEN HOME.
HE'S BEEN HANGING WITH A GANG...
WE'VE GOT SCOUTS FROM FOUR MAJOR COLLEGES COMING TO THE GAME TOMORROW TO WATCH HIM.
TWO PAC-10, TWO S.E.C.
THEY GET A SCENT BRADLEY'S A GANG MEMBER. THOSE SCHOLARSHIP OFFERS DISAPPEAR.
AND THEN HE'S STUCK HERE.
LIKE US.

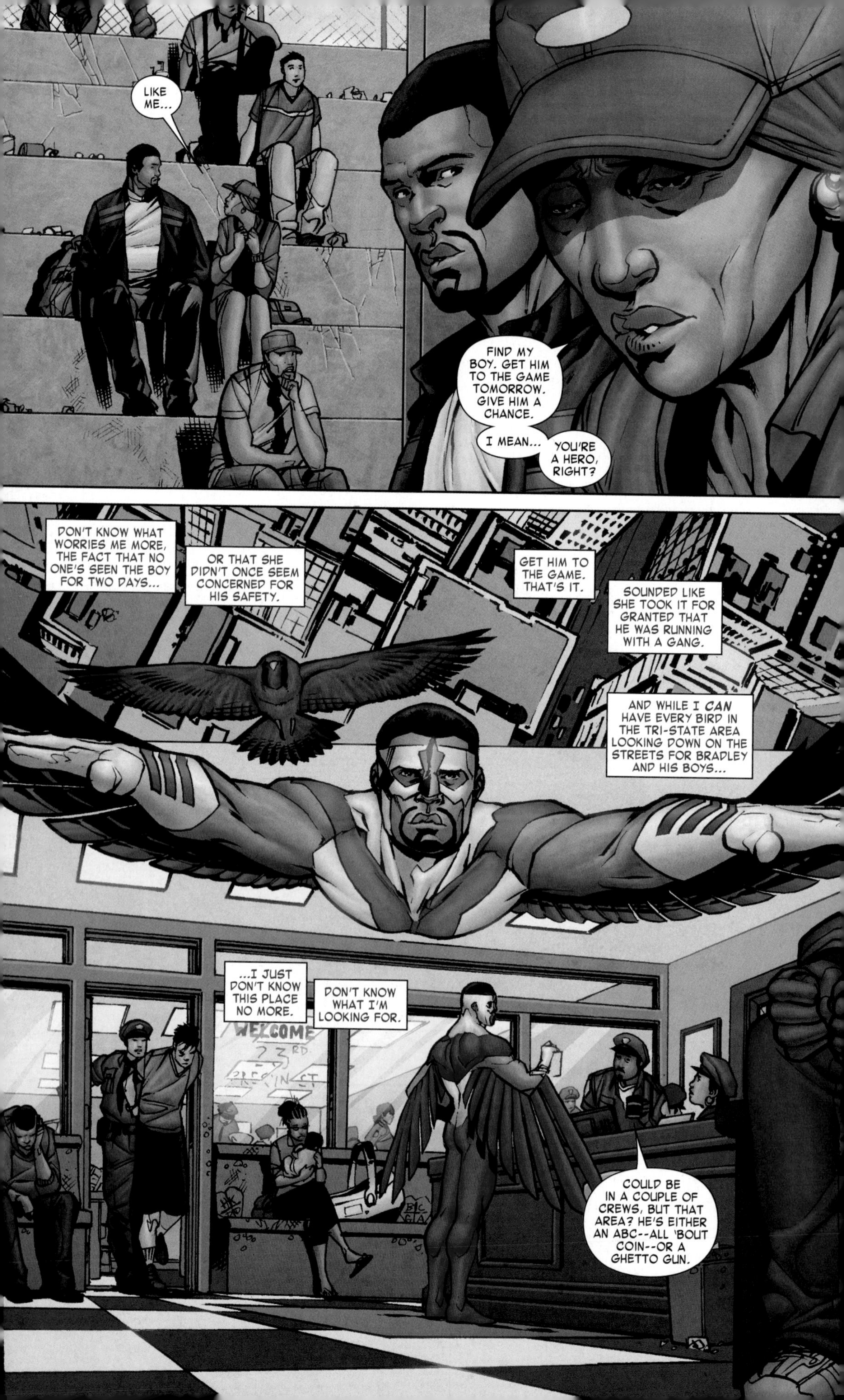
LIKE ME...
FIND MY BOY. GET HIM TO THE GAME TOMORROW. GIVE HIM A CHANCE.
I MEAN...
YOU'RE A HERO, RIGHT?
DON'T KNOW WHAT WORRIES ME MORE, THE FACT THAT NO ONE'S SEEN THE BOY FOR TWO DAYS...
OR THAT SHE DIDN'T ONCE SEEM CONCERNED FOR HIS SAFETY.
GET HIM TO THE GAME. THAT'S IT.
SOUNDED LIKE SHE TOOK IT FOR GRANTED THAT HE WAS RUNNING WITH A GANG.
AND WHILE I CAN HAVE EVERY BIRD IN THE TRI-STATE AREA LOOKING DOWN ON THE STREETS FOR BRADLEY AND HIS BOYS...
...I JUST DON'T KNOW THIS PLACE NO MORE.
DON'T KNOW WHAT I'M LOOKING FOR.
WELCOME 23RD PRECINCT
COULD BE IN A COUPLE OF CREWS, BUT THAT AREA? HE'S EITHER AN ABC--ALL 'BOUT COIN--OR A GHETTO GUN.

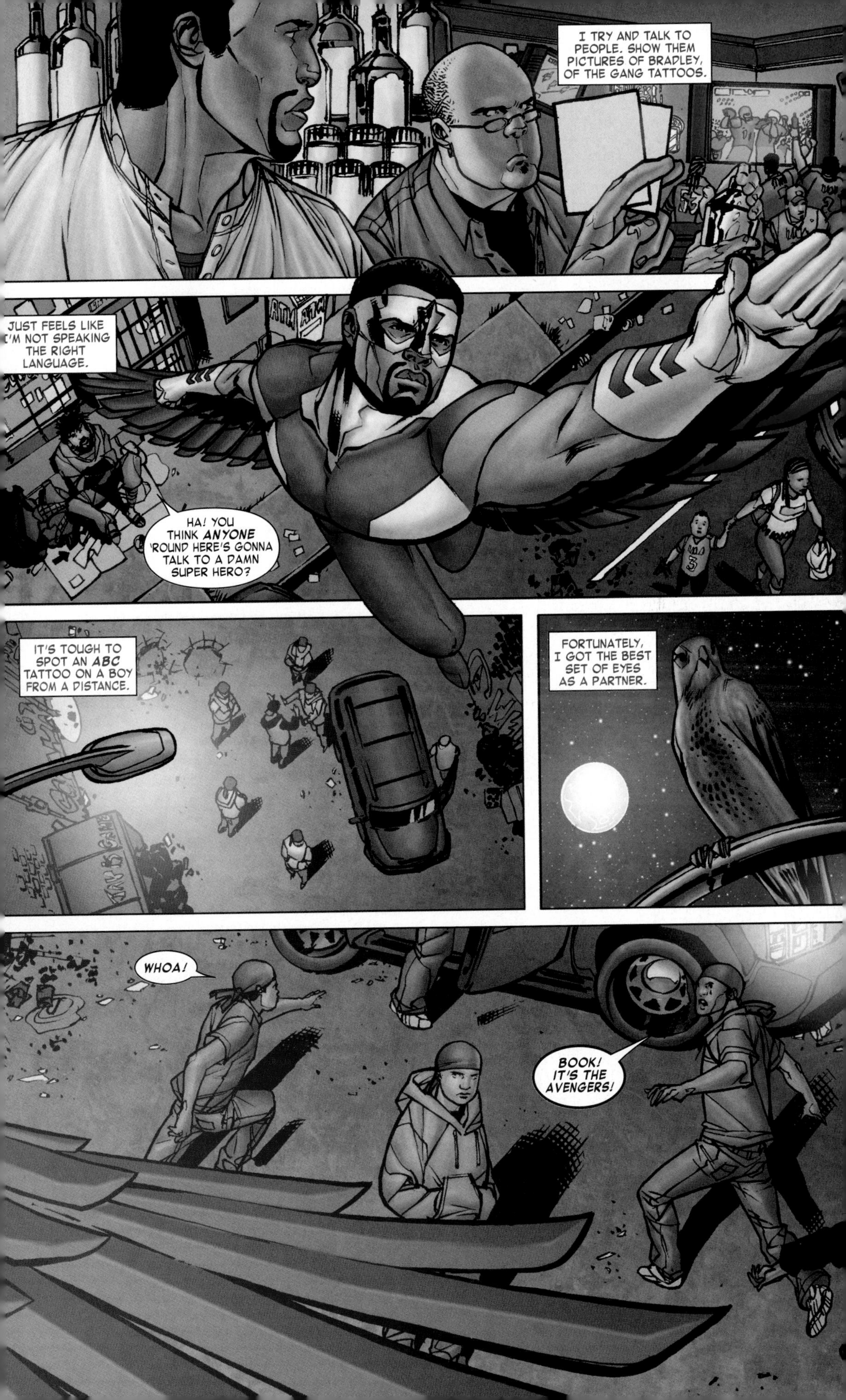
I TRY AND TALK TO PEOPLE. SHOW THEM PICTURES OF BRADLEY, OF THE GANG TATTOOS.
JUST FEELS LIKE I'M NOT SPEAKING THE RIGHT LANGUAGE.
HA! YOU THINK ANYONE 'ROUND HERE'S GONNA TALK TO A DAMN SUPER HERO?
IT'S TOUGH TO SPOT AN ABC TATTOO ON A BOY FROM A DISTANCE.
FORTUNATELY, I GOT THE BEST SET OF EYES AS A PARTNER.
WHOA!
BOOK! IT'S THE AVENGERS!

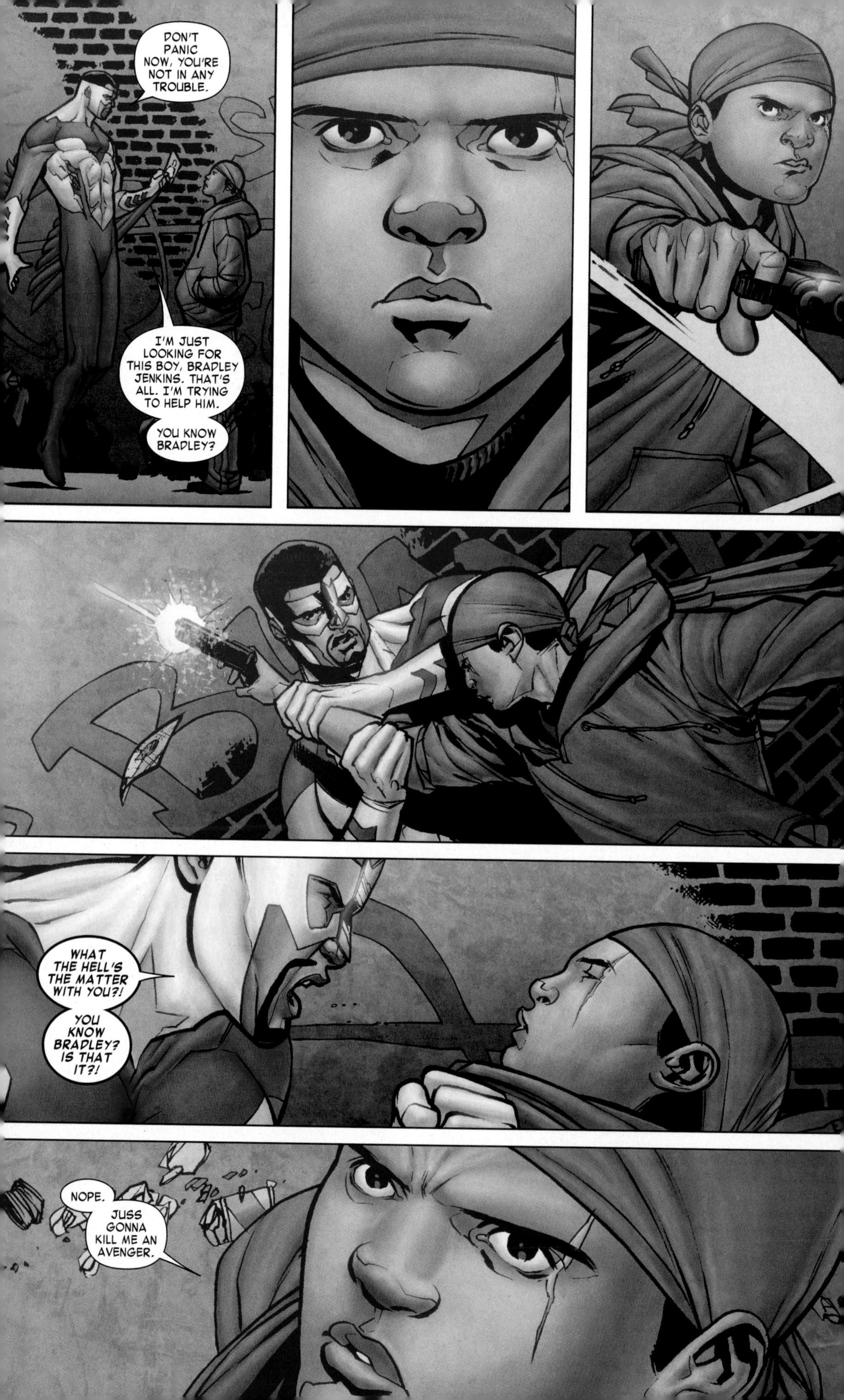
DON'T PANIC NOW, YOU'RE NOT IN ANY TROUBLE.
I'M JUST LOOKING FOR THIS BOY, BRADLEY JENKINS. THAT'S ALL. I'M TRYING TO HELP HIM.
YOU KNOW BRADLEY?
WHAT THE HELL'S THE MATTER WITH YOU?!
YOU KNOW BRADLEY? IS THAT IT?!
NOPE.
JUSS GONNA KILL ME AN AVENGER.

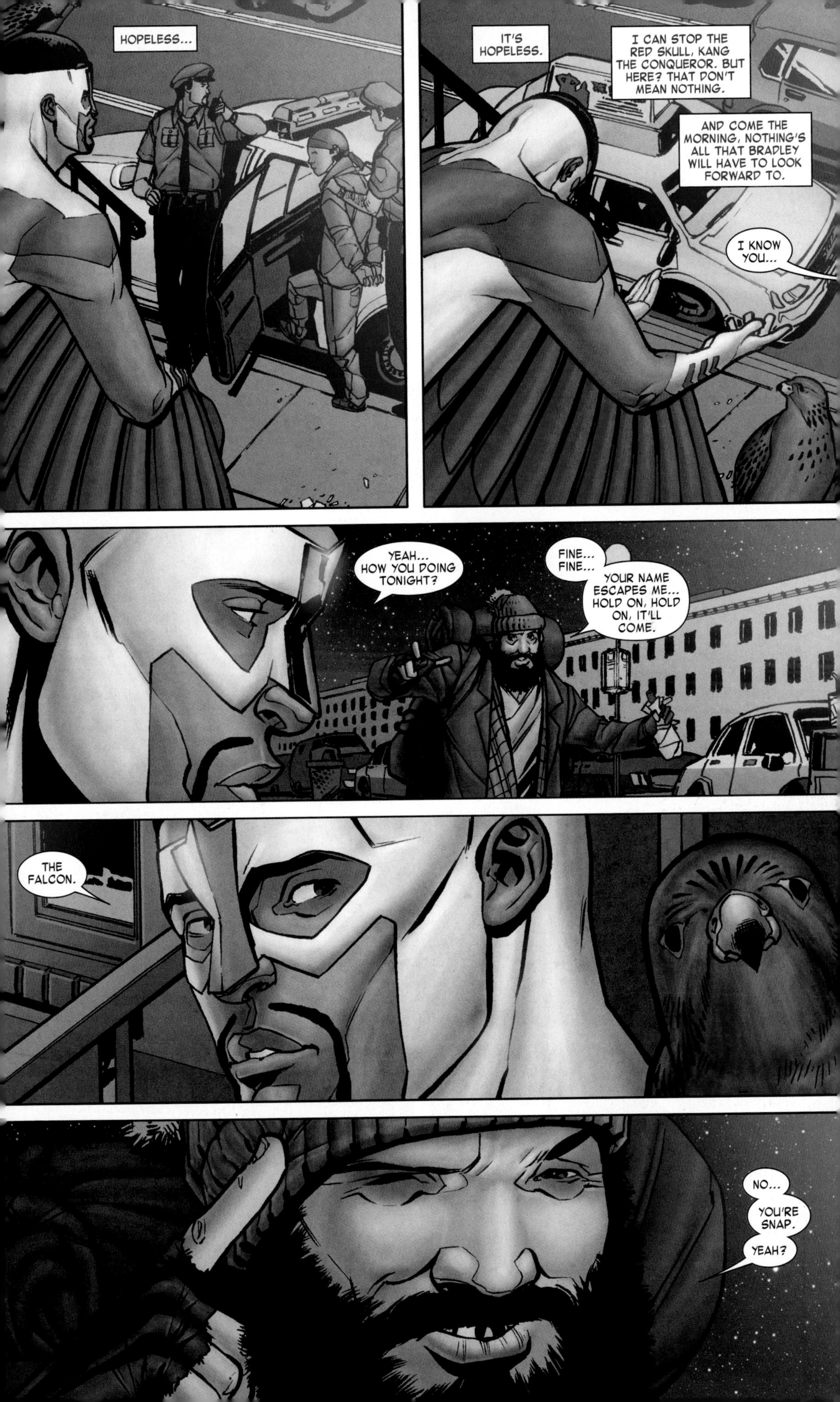
HOPELESS...
IT'S HOPELESS.
I CAN STOP THE RED SKULL, KANG THE CONQUEROR. BUT HERE? THAT DON'T MEAN NOTHING.
AND COME THE MORNING, NOTHING'S ALL THAT BRADLEY WILL HAVE TO LOOK FORWARD TO.
I KNOW YOU...
YEAH... HOW YOU DOING TONIGHT?
FINE... FINE...
YOUR NAME ESCAPES ME... HOLD ON, HOLD ON, IT'LL COME.
THE FALCON.
NO...
YOU'RE SNAP.
YEAH?

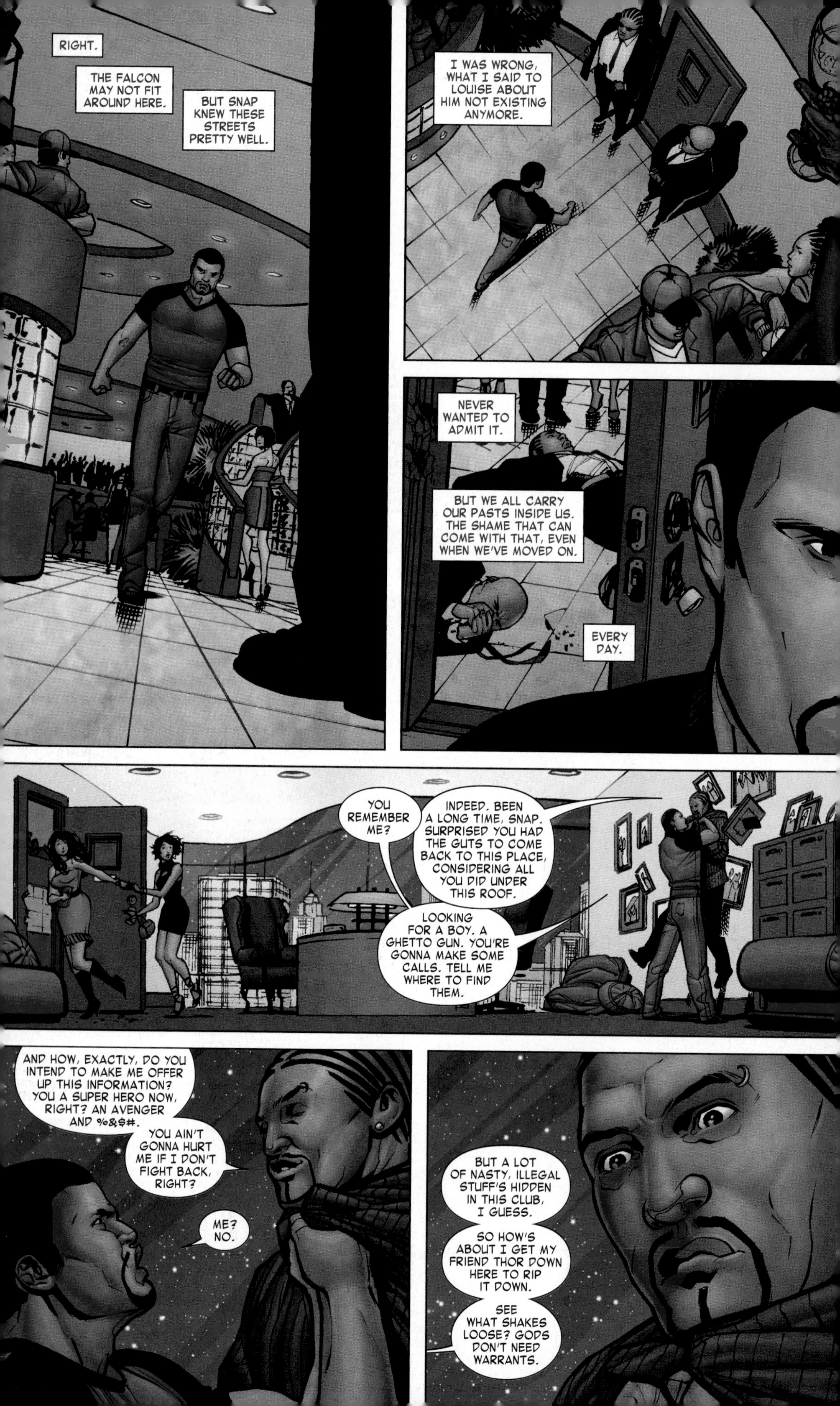
RIGHT.
THE FALCON MAY NOT FIT AROUND HERE.
BUT SNAP KNEW THESE STREETS PRETTY WELL.
I WAS WRONG, WHAT I SAID TO LOUISE ABOUT HIM NOT EXISTING ANYMORE.
NEVER WANTED TO ADMIT IT.
BUT WE ALL CARRY OUR PASTS INSIDE US. THE SHAME THAT CAN COME WITH THAT, EVEN WHEN WE'VE MOVED ON.
EVERY DAY.
YOU REMEMBER ME?
INDEED. BEEN A LONG TIME, SNAP. SURPRISED YOU HAD THE GUTS TO COME BACK TO THIS PLACE, CONSIDERING ALL YOU DID UNDER THIS ROOF.
LOOKING FOR A BOY. A GHETTO GUN. YOU'RE GONNA MAKE SOME CALLS. TELL ME WHERE TO FIND THEM.
AND HOW, EXACTLY, DO YOU INTEND TO MAKE ME OFFER UP THIS INFORMATION? YOU A SUPER HERO NOW, RIGHT? AN AVENGER AND %&$#.
YOU AIN'T GONNA HURT ME IF I DON'T FIGHT BACK, RIGHT?
ME? NO.
BUT A LOT OF NASTY, ILLEGAL STUFF'S HIDDEN IN THIS CLUB, I GUESS.
SO HOW'S ABOUT I GET MY FRIEND THOR DOWN HERE TO RIP IT DOWN.
SEE WHAT SHAKES LOOSE? GODS DON'T NEED WARRANTS.

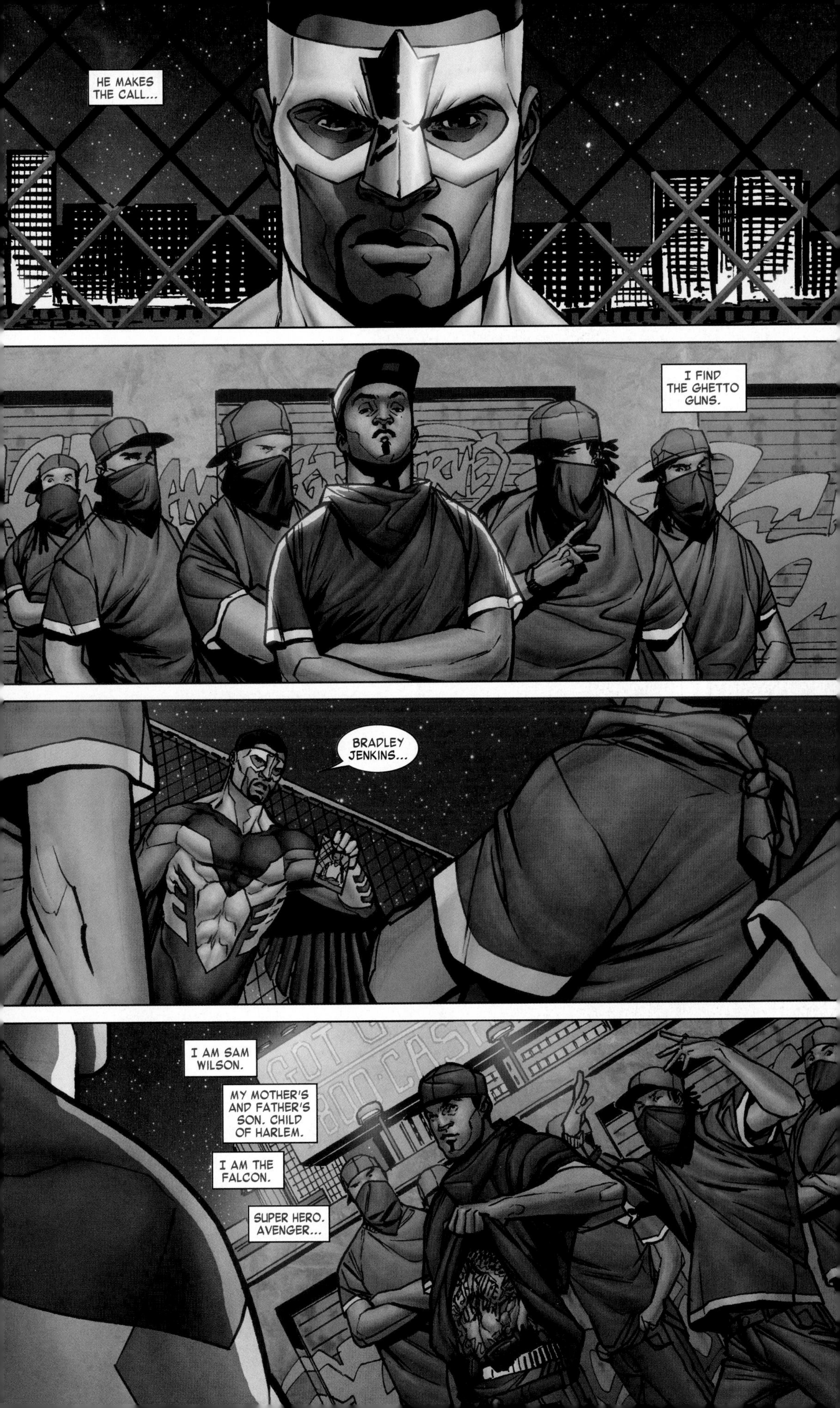
HE MAKES THE CALL...
I FIND THE GHETTO GUNS.
BRADLEY JENKINS...
I AM SAM WILSON.
MY MOTHER'S AND FATHER'S SON. CHILD OF HARLEM.
I AM THE FALCON.
SUPER HERO. AVENGER...

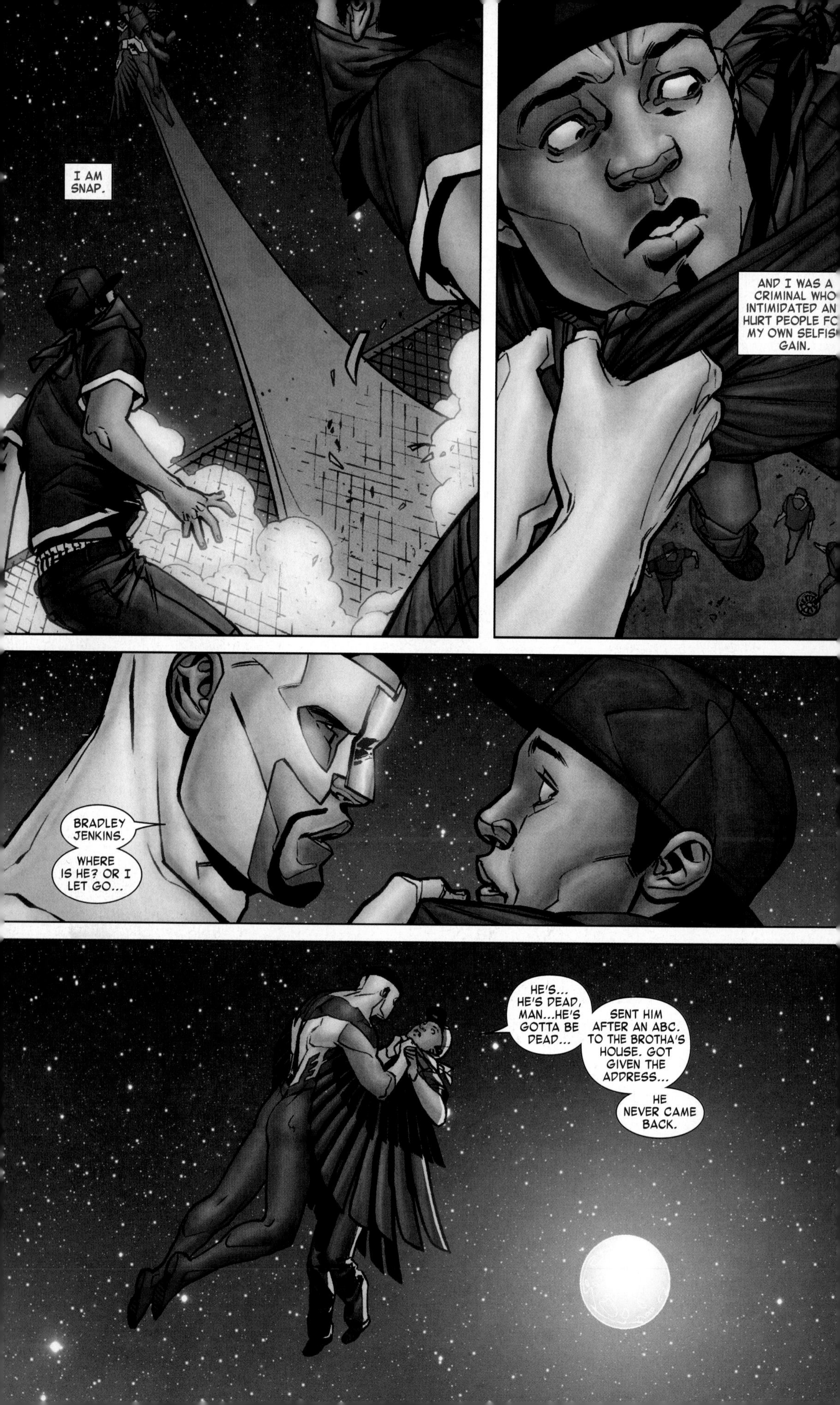
I AM SNAP.
AND I WAS A CRIMINAL WHO INTIMIDATED AN HURT PEOPLE FC MY OWN SELFIS GAIN.
BRADLEY JENKINS.
WHERE IS HE? OR I LET GO...
HE'S... HE'S DEAD, MAN...HE'S GOTTA BE DEAD...
SENT HIM AFTER AN ABC. TO THE BROTHA'S HOUSE. GOT GIVEN THE ADDRESS...
HE NEVER CAME BACK.

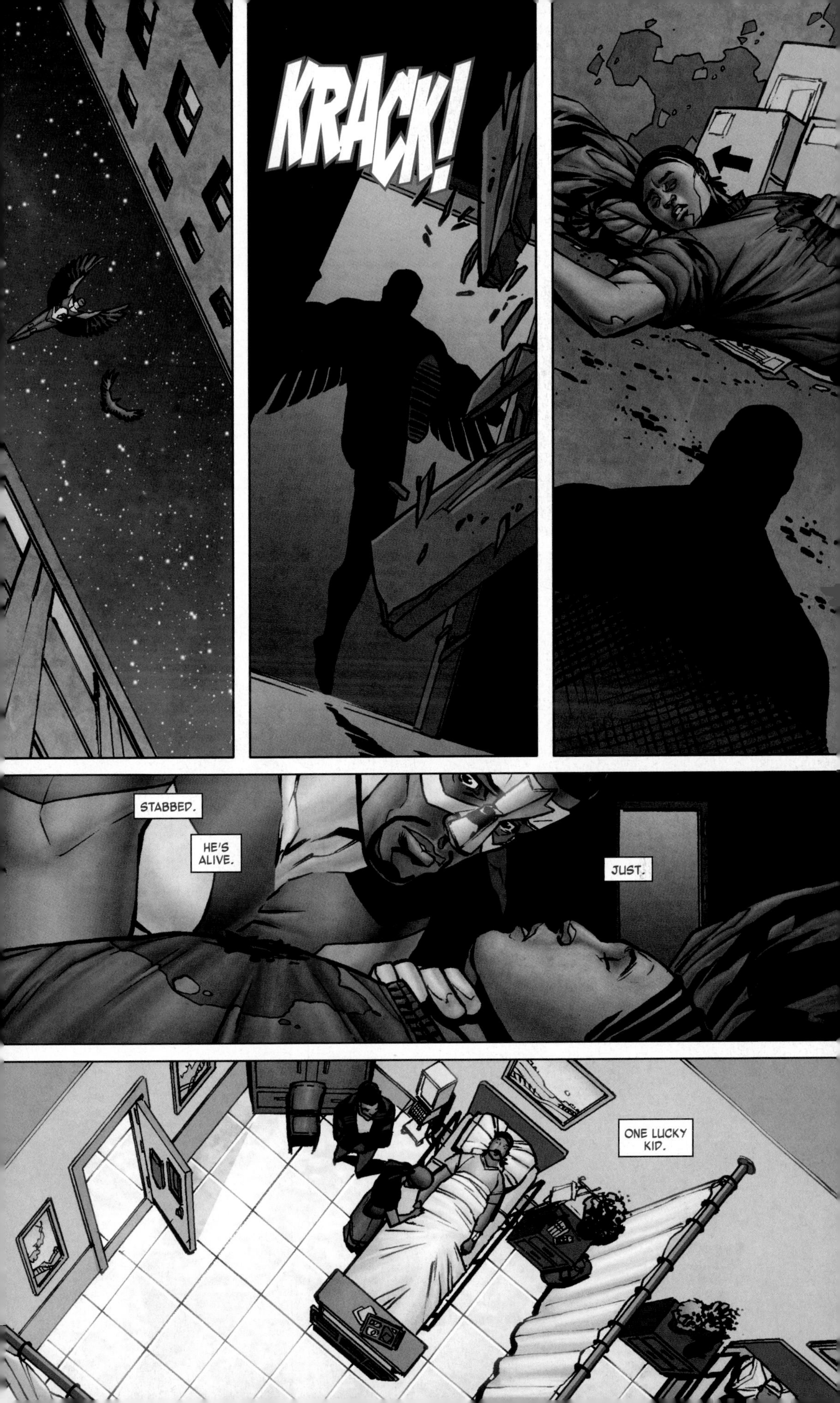
KRACK!
STABBED.
HE'S ALIVE.
JUST.
ONE LUCKY KID.

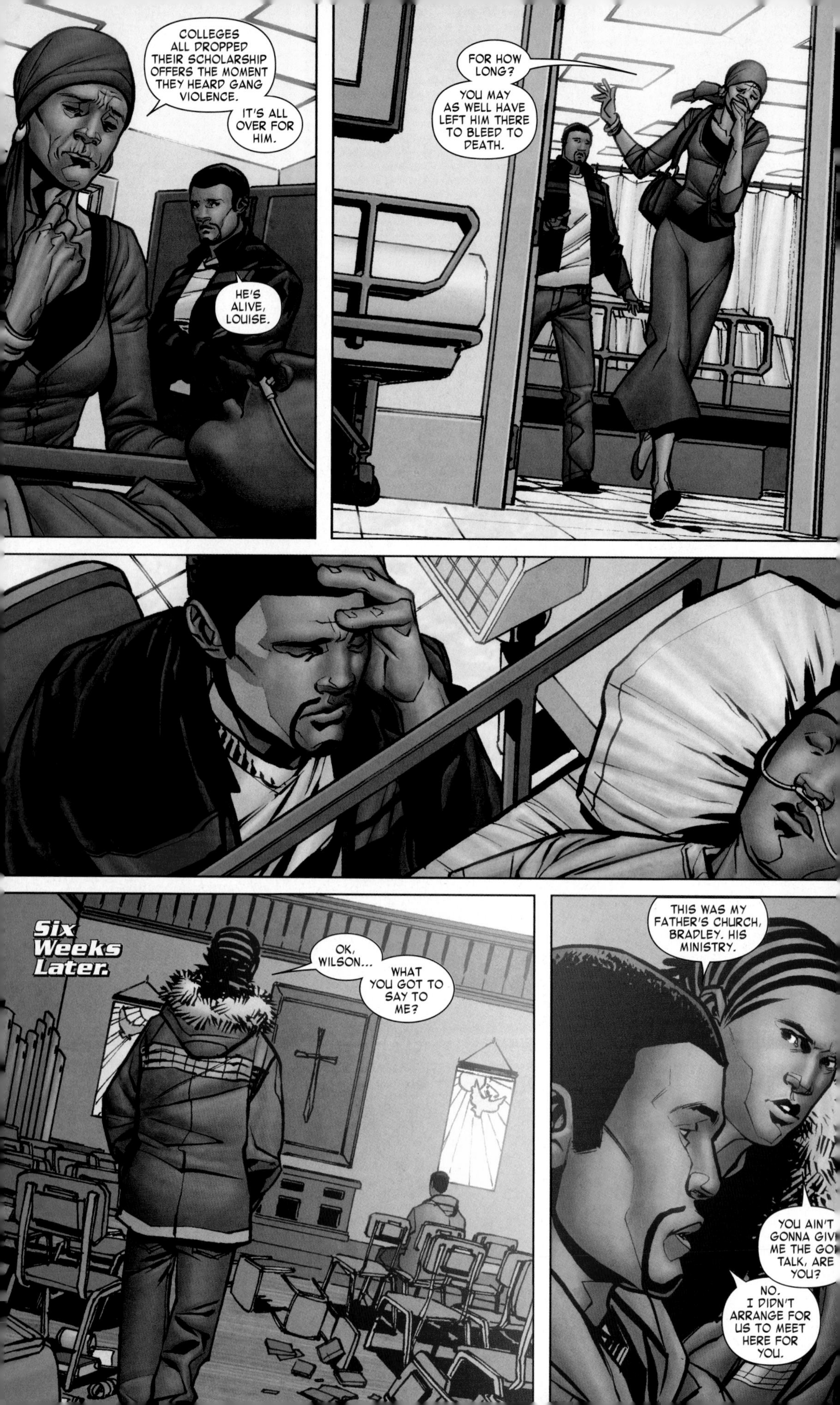
COLLEGES ALL DROPPED THEIR SCHOLARSHIP OFFERS THE MOMENT THEY HEARD GANG VIOLENCE.
IT'S ALL OVER FOR HIM.
HE'S ALIVE, LOUISE.
FOR HOW LONG?
YOU MAY AS WELL HAVE LEFT HIM THERE TO BLEED TO DEATH.
Six Weeks Later.
OK, WILSON...
WHAT YOU GOT TO SAY TO ME?
THIS WAS MY FATHER'S CHURCH, BRADLEY. HIS MINISTRY.
YOU AIN'T GONNA GIV ME THE GO TALK, ARE YOU?
NO. I DIDN'T ARRANGE FOR US TO MEET HERE FOR YOU.

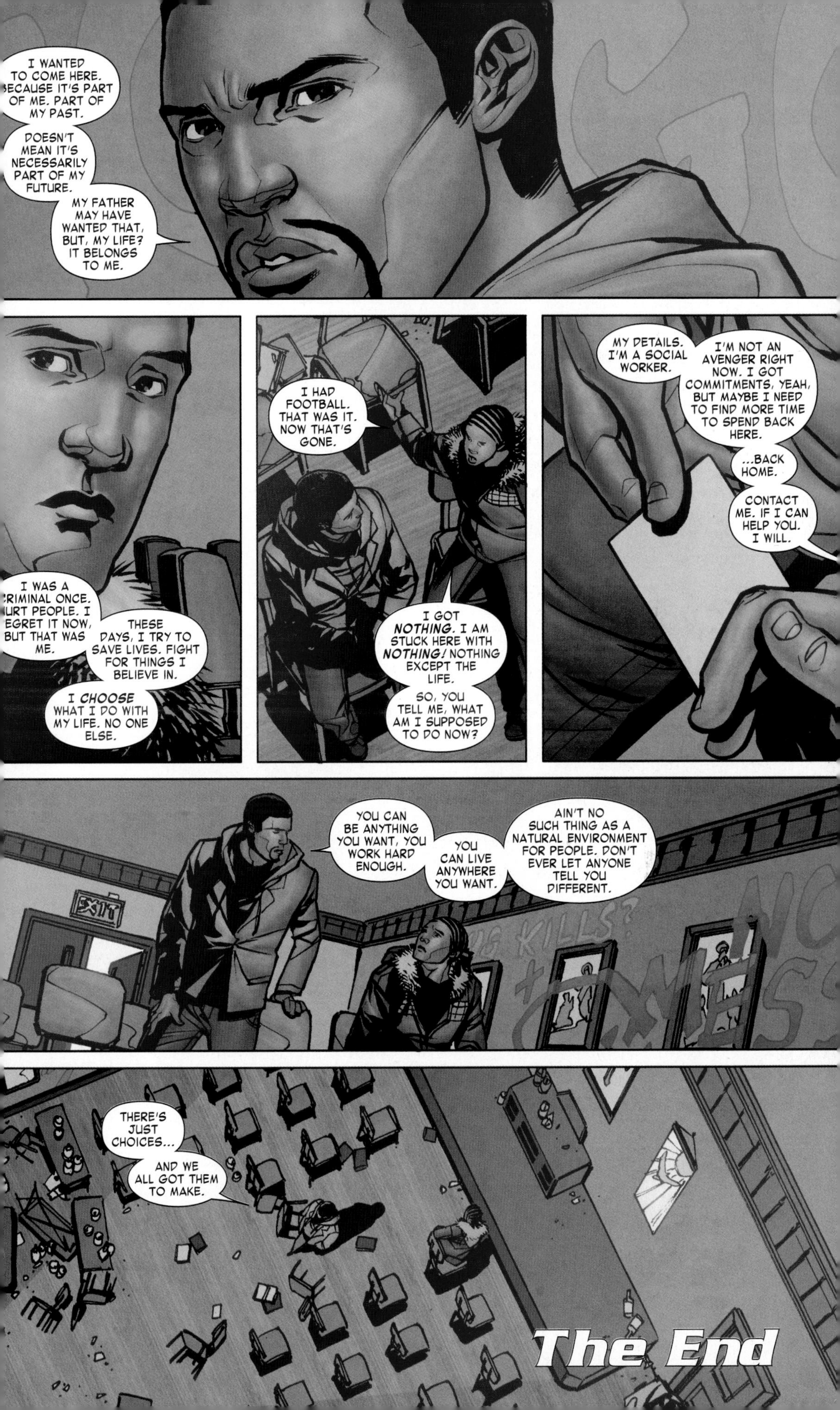

I WANTED TO COME HERE. BECAUSE IT'S PART OF ME. PART OF MY PAST.
DOESN'T MEAN IT'S NECESSARILY PART OF MY FUTURE.
MY FATHER MAY HAVE WANTED THAT, BUT, MY LIFE? IT BELONGS TO ME.
I WAS A CRIMINAL ONCE. HURT PEOPLE. I REGRET IT NOW, BUT THAT WAS ME.
THESE DAYS, I TRY TO SAVE LIVES. FIGHT FOR THINGS I BELIEVE IN.
I *CHOOSE* WHAT I DO WITH MY LIFE. NO ONE ELSE.
I HAD FOOTBALL. THAT WAS IT. NOW THAT'S GONE.
I GOT ***NOTHING.*** I AM STUCK HERE WITH ***NOTHING!*** NOTHING EXCEPT THE LIFE.
SO, YOU TELL ME, WHAT AM I SUPPOSED TO DO NOW?
MY DETAILS. I'M A SOCIAL WORKER.
I'M NOT AN AVENGER RIGHT NOW. I GOT COMMITMENTS, YEAH, BUT MAYBE I NEED TO FIND MORE TIME TO SPEND BACK HERE.
...BACK HOME.
CONTACT ME. IF I CAN HELP YOU. I WILL.
YOU CAN BE ANYTHING YOU WANT, YOU WORK HARD ENOUGH.
YOU CAN LIVE ANYWHERE YOU WANT.
AIN'T NO SUCH THING AS A NATURAL ENVIRONMENT FOR PEOPLE. DON'T EVER LET ANYONE TELL YOU DIFFERENT.
EXIT
THERE'S JUST CHOICES...
AND WE ALL GOT THEM TO MAKE.
The End

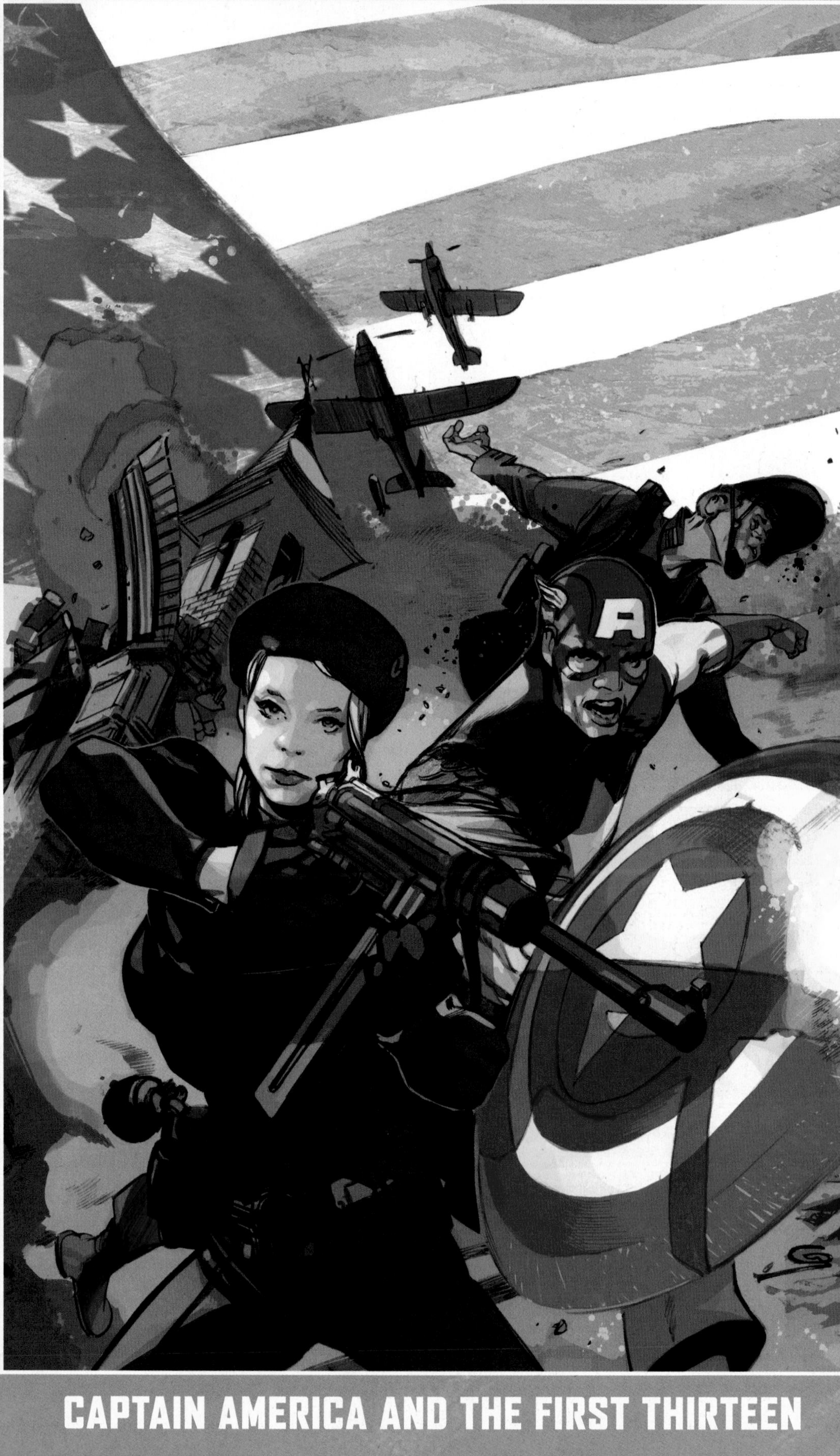

CAPTAIN AMERICA AND THE FIRST THIRTEEN

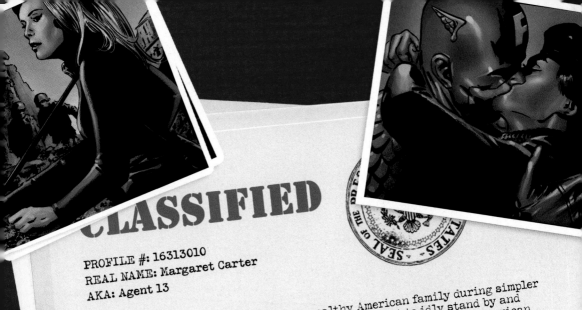

CLASSIFIED

PROFILE #: 16313010
REAL NAME: Margaret Carter
AKA: Agent 13

Margaret "Peggy" Carter was born to a wealthy American family during simpler times. When war broke out in Europe, she was not content to idly stand by and watch as the Nazis invaded the continent. Peggy left her comfortable American life to join the French Resistance and soon became one their bravest and best-trained members.

It was while fighting for their country overseas that she first encountered Captain America. Though their wartime strategies and combat tactics often differed, they were drawn together by a common purpose of service and justice. This bond between the two heroes ultimately blossomed into romance that struggled to endure the war.

Following her service, Peggy became ensconced in the international security agency S.H.I.E.L.D. and furthered her adventures championing for peace and inspiring a new generation of heroes!

"Cherchez La Femme!"

Writer
Kathryn Immonen

Artist
Ramon Perez

Colorist
John Rauch

Letters
Jared K. Fletcher

Cover Artist
Greg Tocchini

Supervising Editor
Tom Brevoort

Editor in Chief
Axel Alonso

Production
Damien Lucchese

Editor
Rachel Pinnelas

Publisher
Dan Buckley

Exec. Producer
Alan Fine

Chief Creative Officer
Joe Quesada

Captain America created by Joe Simon and Jack Kirby

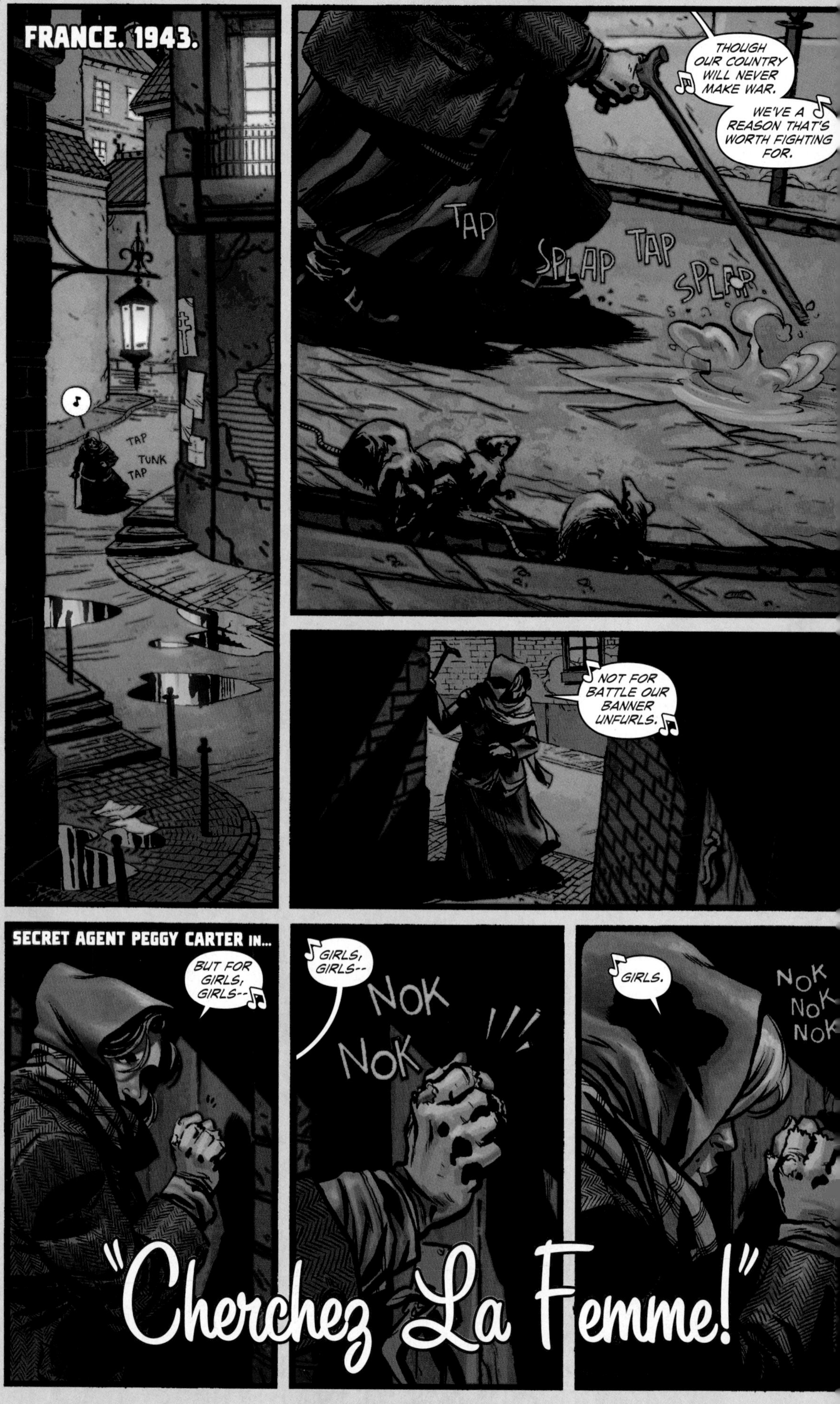

FRANCE. 1943.
TAP
TUNK
TAP
THOUGH OUR COUNTRY WILL NEVER MAKE WAR.
WE'VE A REASON THAT'S WORTH FIGHTING FOR.
TAP
SPLAP
TAP
SPLAP
NOT FOR BATTLE OUR BANNER UNFURLS.
SECRET AGENT PEGGY CARTER IN...
BUT FOR GIRLS, GIRLS--
GIRLS, GIRLS--
NOK
NOK
GIRLS.
NOK
NOK
NOK
"Cherchez La Femme!"

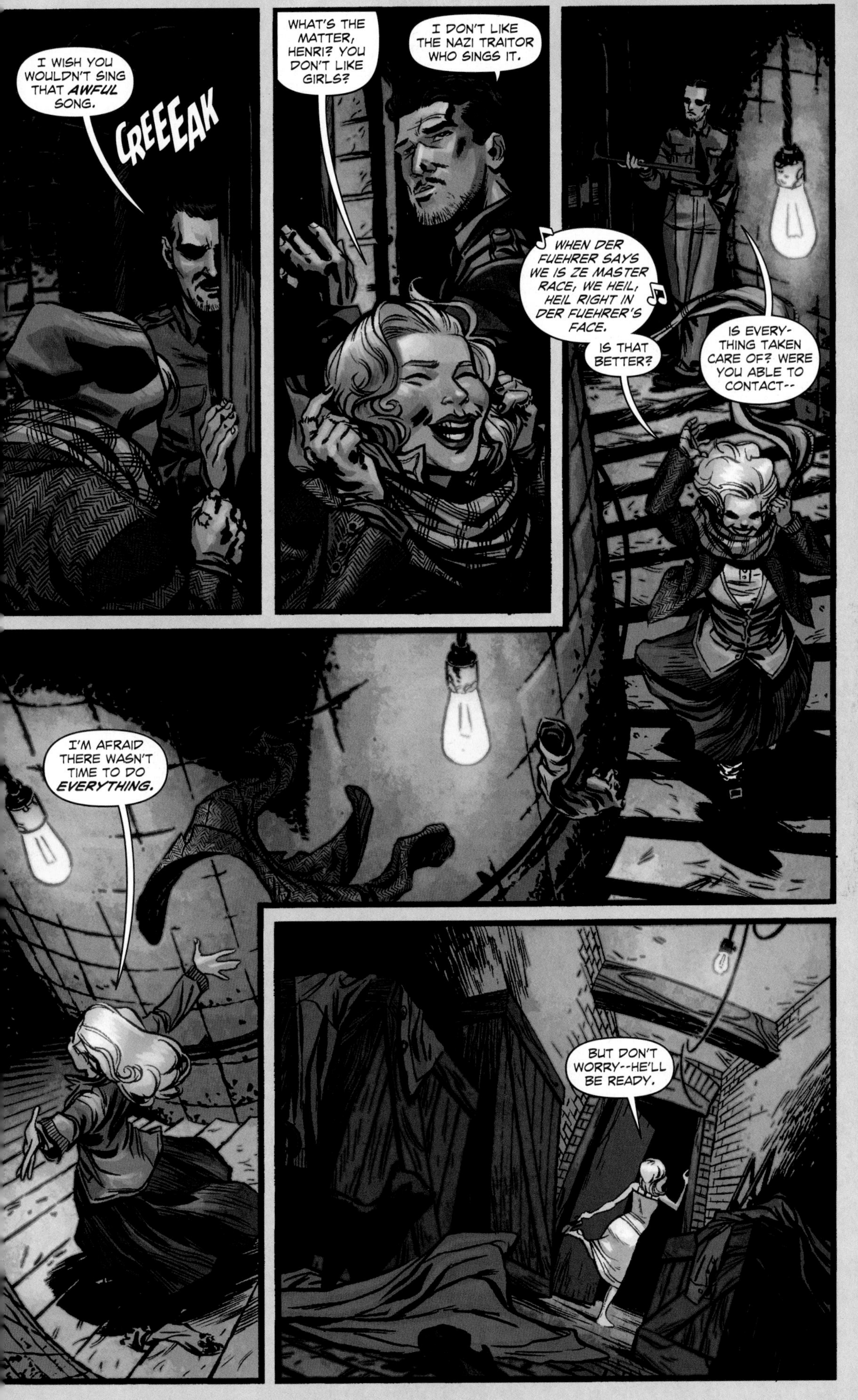
I WISH YOU WOULDN'T SING THAT AWFUL SONG.
CREEEAK
WHAT'S THE MATTER, HENRI? YOU DON'T LIKE GIRLS?
I DON'T LIKE THE NAZI TRAITOR WHO SINGS IT.
WHEN DER FUEHRER SAYS WE IS ZE MASTER RACE; WE HEIL, HEIL RIGHT IN DER FUEHRER'S FACE.
IS THAT BETTER?
IS EVERYTHING TAKEN CARE OF? WERE YOU ABLE TO CONTACT--
I'M AFRAID THERE WASN'T TIME TO DO EVERYTHING.
BUT DON'T WORRY--HE'LL BE READY.

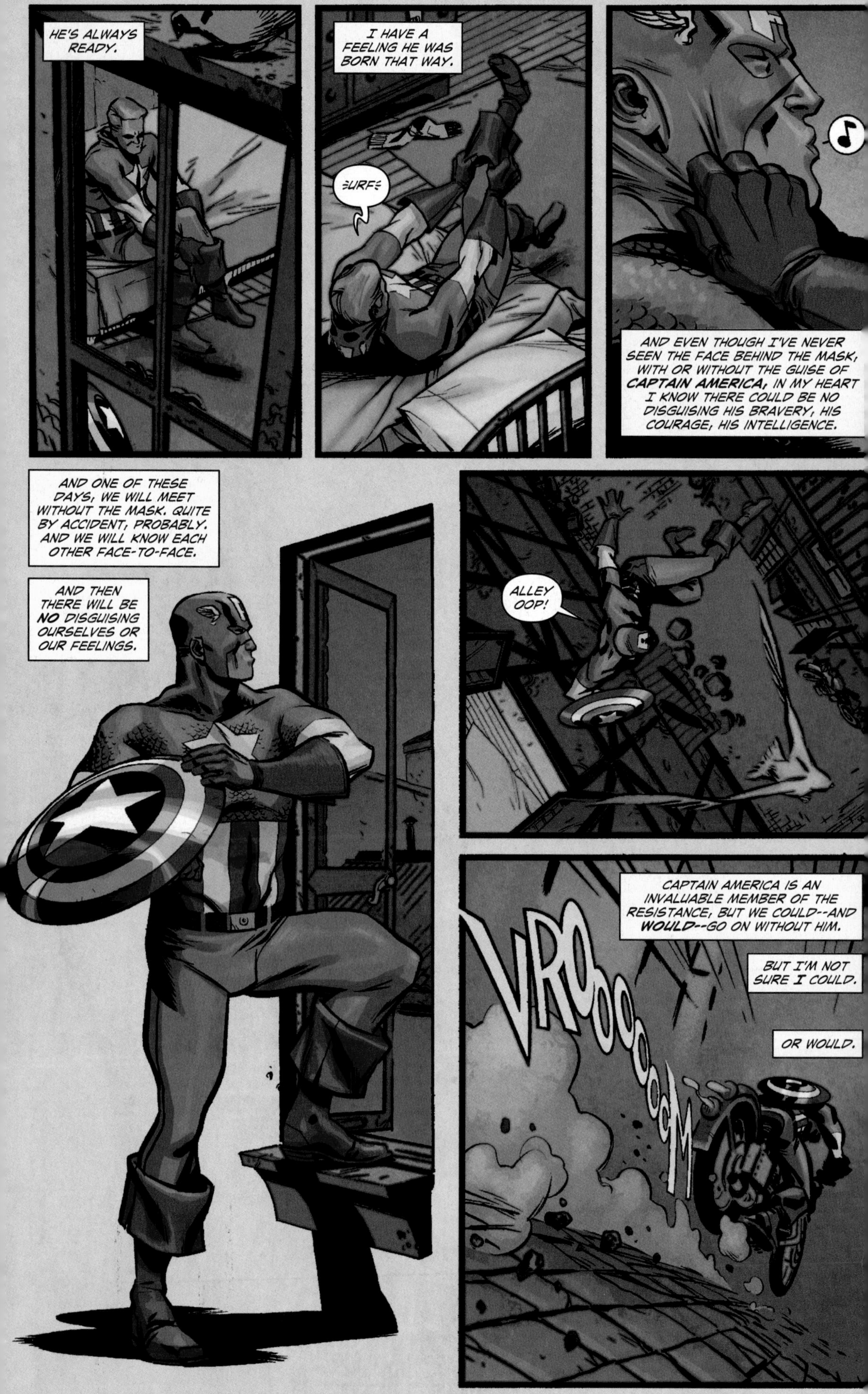
HE'S ALWAYS READY.
I HAVE A FEELING HE WAS BORN THAT WAY.
=URF=
AND EVEN THOUGH I'VE NEVER SEEN THE FACE BEHIND THE MASK, WITH OR WITHOUT THE GUISE OF CAPTAIN AMERICA, IN MY HEART I KNOW THERE COULD BE NO DISGUISING HIS BRAVERY, HIS COURAGE, HIS INTELLIGENCE.
AND ONE OF THESE DAYS, WE WILL MEET WITHOUT THE MASK. QUITE BY ACCIDENT, PROBABLY. AND WE WILL KNOW EACH OTHER FACE-TO-FACE.
AND THEN THERE WILL BE NO DISGUISING OURSELVES OR OUR FEELINGS.
ALLEY OOP!
CAPTAIN AMERICA IS AN INVALUABLE MEMBER OF THE RESISTANCE, BUT WE COULD--AND WOULD--GO ON WITHOUT HIM.
BUT I'M NOT SURE I COULD.
OR WOULD.
VROOOOOOOM

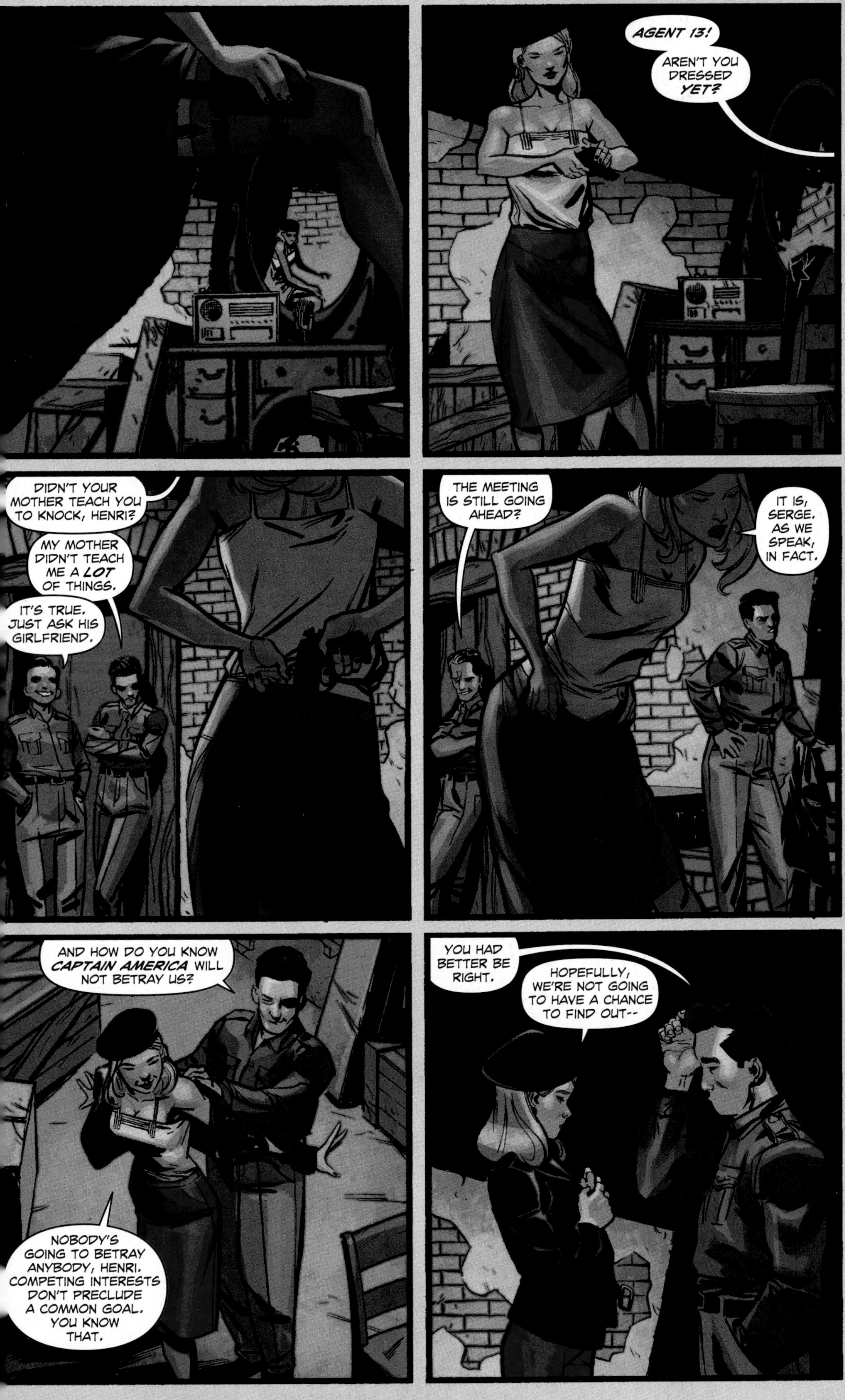
AGENT 13!
AREN'T YOU DRESSED YET?
DIDN'T YOUR MOTHER TEACH YOU TO KNOCK, HENRI?
MY MOTHER DIDN'T TEACH ME A LOT OF THINGS.
IT'S TRUE. JUST ASK HIS GIRLFRIEND.
THE MEETING IS STILL GOING AHEAD?
IT IS, SERGE. AS WE SPEAK, IN FACT.
AND HOW DO YOU KNOW CAPTAIN AMERICA WILL NOT BETRAY US?
NOBODY'S GOING TO BETRAY ANYBODY, HENRI. COMPETING INTERESTS DON'T PRECLUDE A COMMON GOAL. YOU KNOW THAT.
YOU HAD BETTER BE RIGHT.
HOPEFULLY, WE'RE NOT GOING TO HAVE A CHANCE TO FIND OUT--

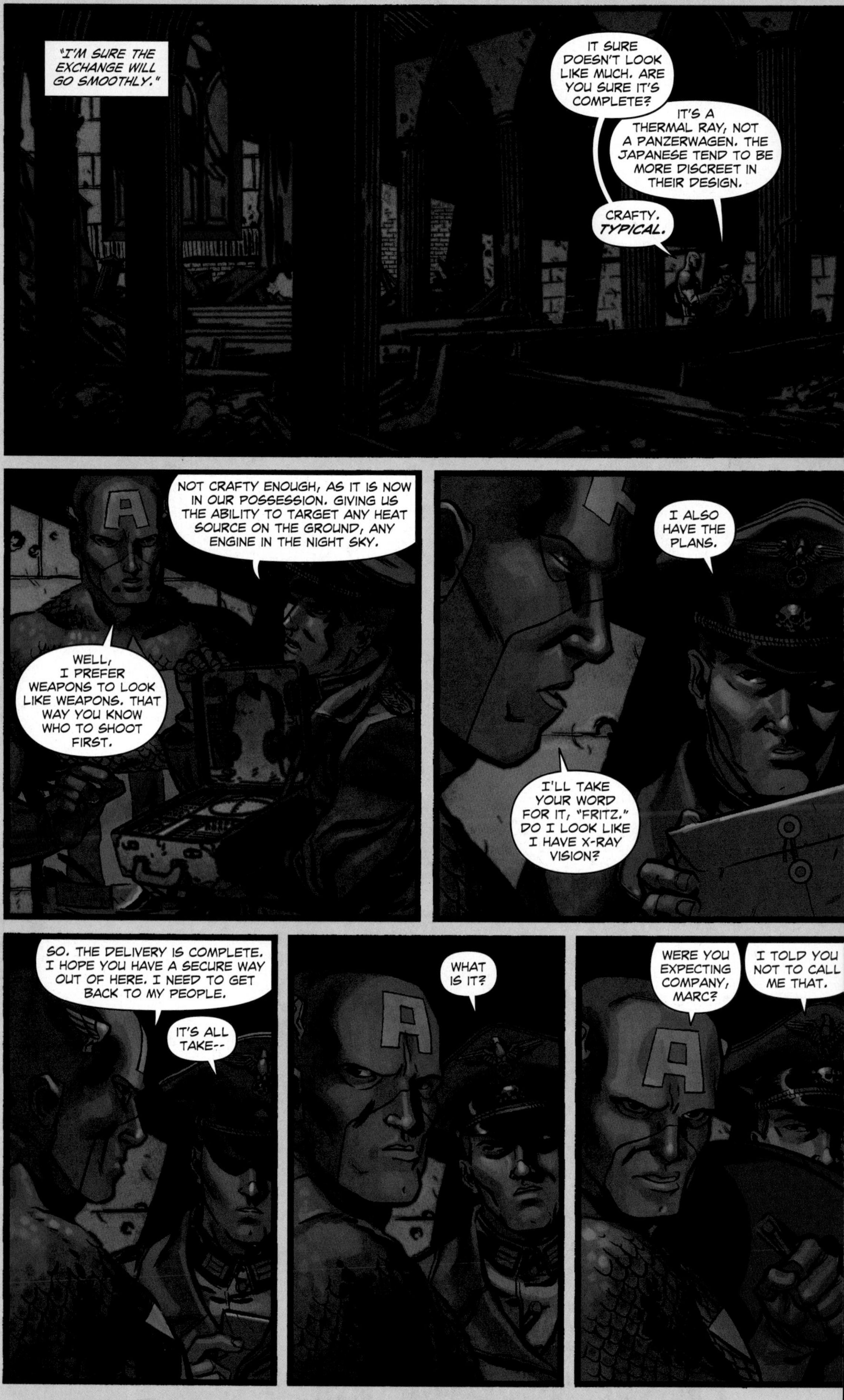
"I'M SURE THE EXCHANGE WILL GO SMOOTHLY."
IT SURE DOESN'T LOOK LIKE MUCH. ARE YOU SURE IT'S COMPLETE?
IT'S A THERMAL RAY, NOT A PANZERWAGEN. THE JAPANESE TEND TO BE MORE DISCREET IN THEIR DESIGN.
CRAFTY. *TYPICAL.*
NOT CRAFTY ENOUGH, AS IT IS NOW IN OUR POSSESSION. GIVING US THE ABILITY TO TARGET ANY HEAT SOURCE ON THE GROUND, ANY ENGINE IN THE NIGHT SKY.
WELL, I PREFER WEAPONS TO LOOK LIKE WEAPONS. THAT WAY YOU KNOW WHO TO SHOOT FIRST.
I ALSO HAVE THE PLANS.
I'LL TAKE YOUR WORD FOR IT, "FRITZ." DO I LOOK LIKE I HAVE X-RAY VISION?
SO. THE DELIVERY IS COMPLETE. I HOPE YOU HAVE A SECURE WAY OUT OF HERE. I NEED TO GET BACK TO MY PEOPLE.
IT'S ALL TAKE--
WHAT IS IT?
WERE YOU EXPECTING COMPANY, MARC?
I TOLD YOU NOT TO CALL ME THAT.

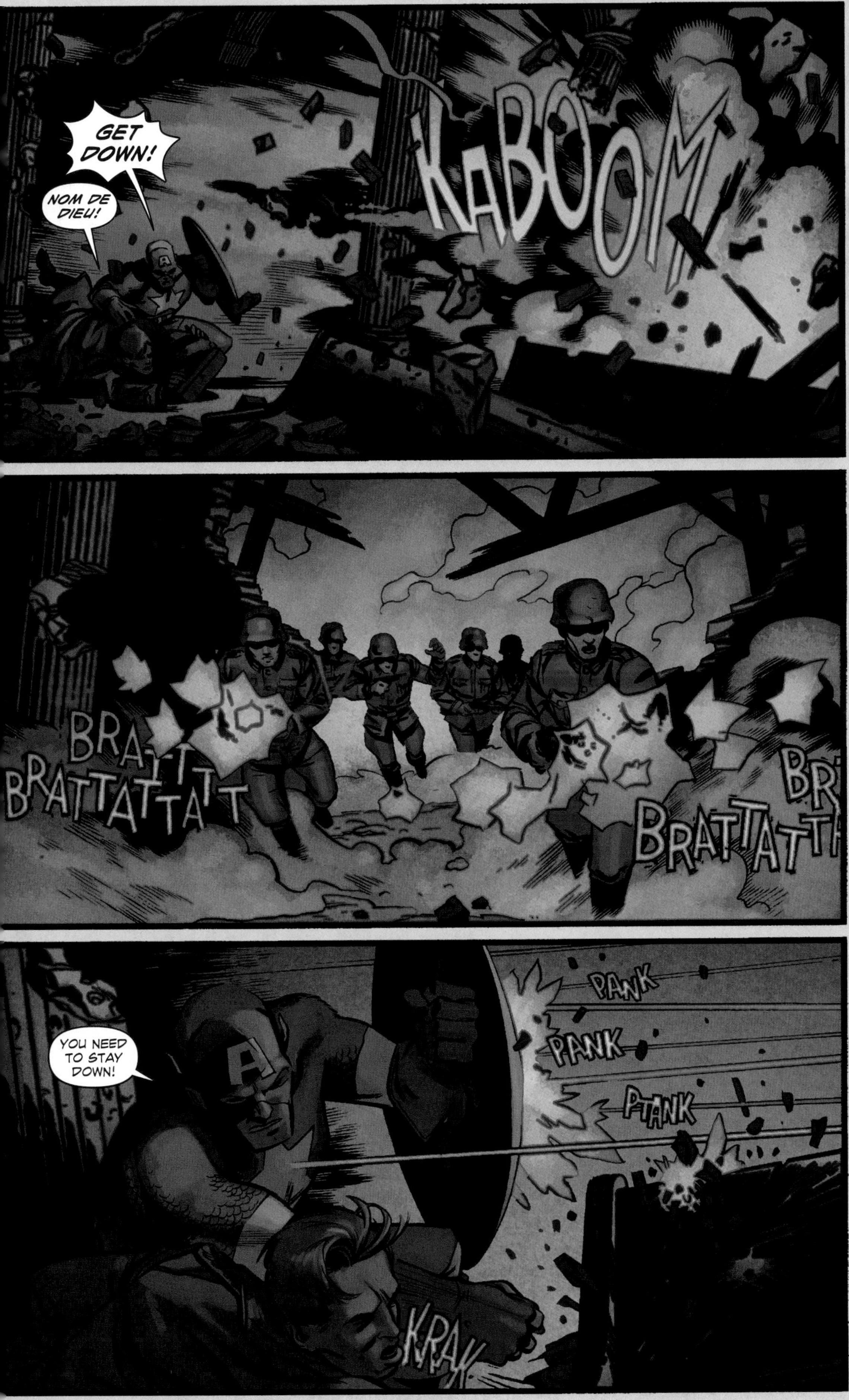
GET DOWN!
NOM DE DIEU!
KABOOM
BRATTATTATT
BRATTATTATT
BR
BRATTATT
YOU NEED TO STAY DOWN!
PANK
PANK
PTANK
KRAK

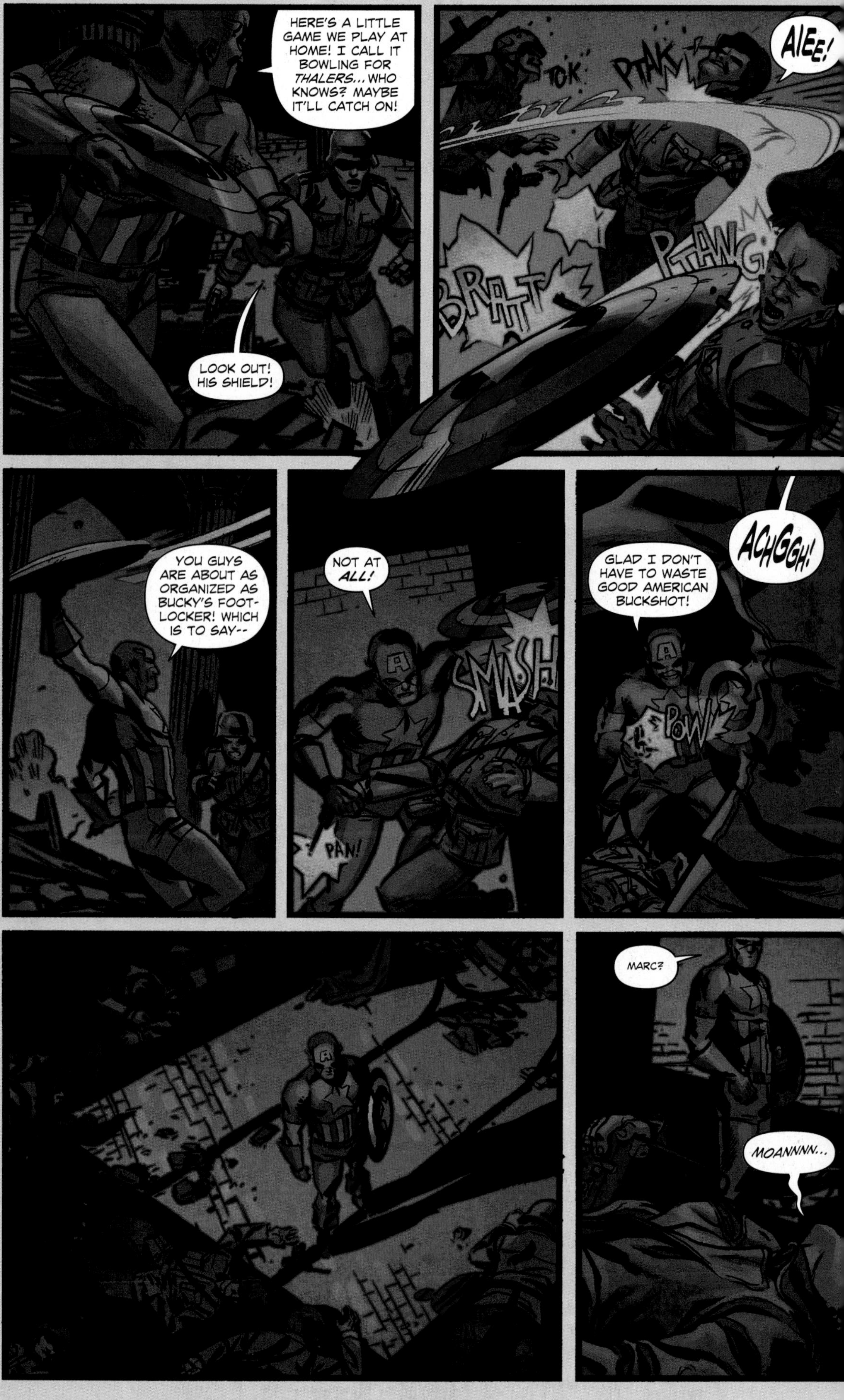
HERE'S A LITTLE GAME WE PLAY AT HOME! I CALL IT BOWLING FOR THALERS... WHO KNOWS? MAYBE IT'LL CATCH ON!
LOOK OUT! HIS SHIELD!
TOK
PTAK
AIEE!
BRATT
PTANG!
YOU GUYS ARE ABOUT AS ORGANIZED AS BUCKY'S FOOT-LOCKER! WHICH IS TO SAY--
NOT AT ALL!
SMASH!
PAN!
GLAD I DON'T HAVE TO WASTE GOOD AMERICAN BUCKSHOT!
ACHGGH!
POW!
MARC?
MOANNNN...

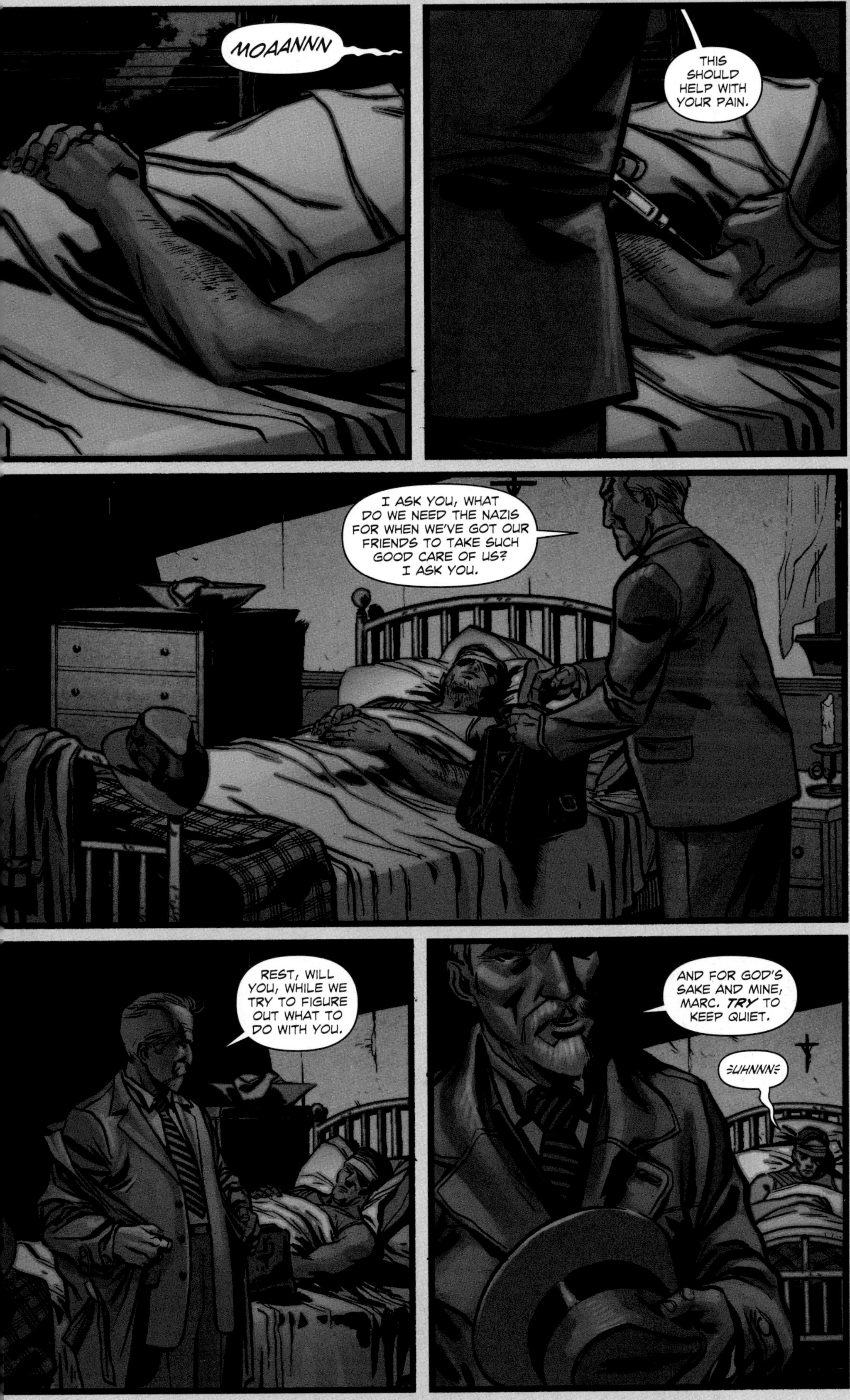
MOAANNN
THIS SHOULD HELP WITH YOUR PAIN.
I ASK YOU, WHAT DO WE NEED THE NAZIS FOR WHEN WE'VE GOT OUR FRIENDS TO TAKE SUCH GOOD CARE OF US? I ASK YOU.
REST, WILL YOU, WHILE WE TRY TO FIGURE OUT WHAT TO DO WITH YOU.
AND FOR GOD'S SAKE AND MINE, MARC. TRY TO KEEP QUIET.
UHNNN

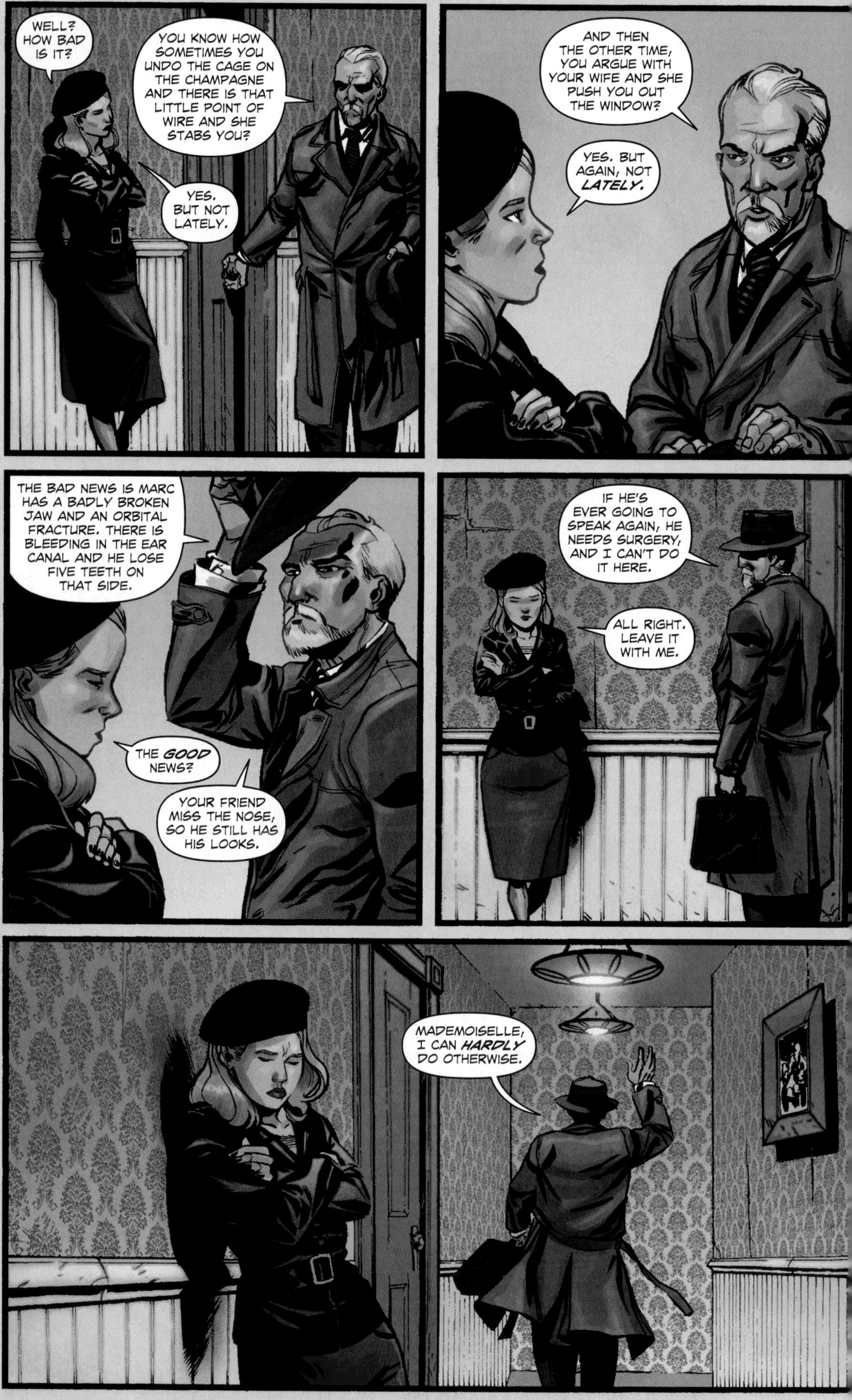
WELL? HOW BAD IS IT?
YOU KNOW HOW SOMETIMES YOU UNDO THE CAGE ON THE CHAMPAGNE AND THERE IS THAT LITTLE POINT OF WIRE AND SHE STABS YOU?
YES. BUT NOT LATELY.
AND THEN THE OTHER TIME, YOU ARGUE WITH YOUR WIFE AND SHE PUSH YOU OUT THE WINDOW?
YES. BUT AGAIN, NOT *LATELY.*
THE BAD NEWS IS MARC HAS A BADLY BROKEN JAW AND AN ORBITAL FRACTURE. THERE IS BLEEDING IN THE EAR CANAL AND HE LOSE FIVE TEETH ON THAT SIDE.
THE *GOOD* NEWS?
YOUR FRIEND MISS THE NOSE, SO HE STILL HAS HIS LOOKS.
IF HE'S EVER GOING TO SPEAK AGAIN, HE NEEDS SURGERY, AND I CAN'T DO IT HERE.
ALL RIGHT. LEAVE IT WITH ME.
MADEMOISELLE, I CAN *HARDLY* DO OTHERWISE.

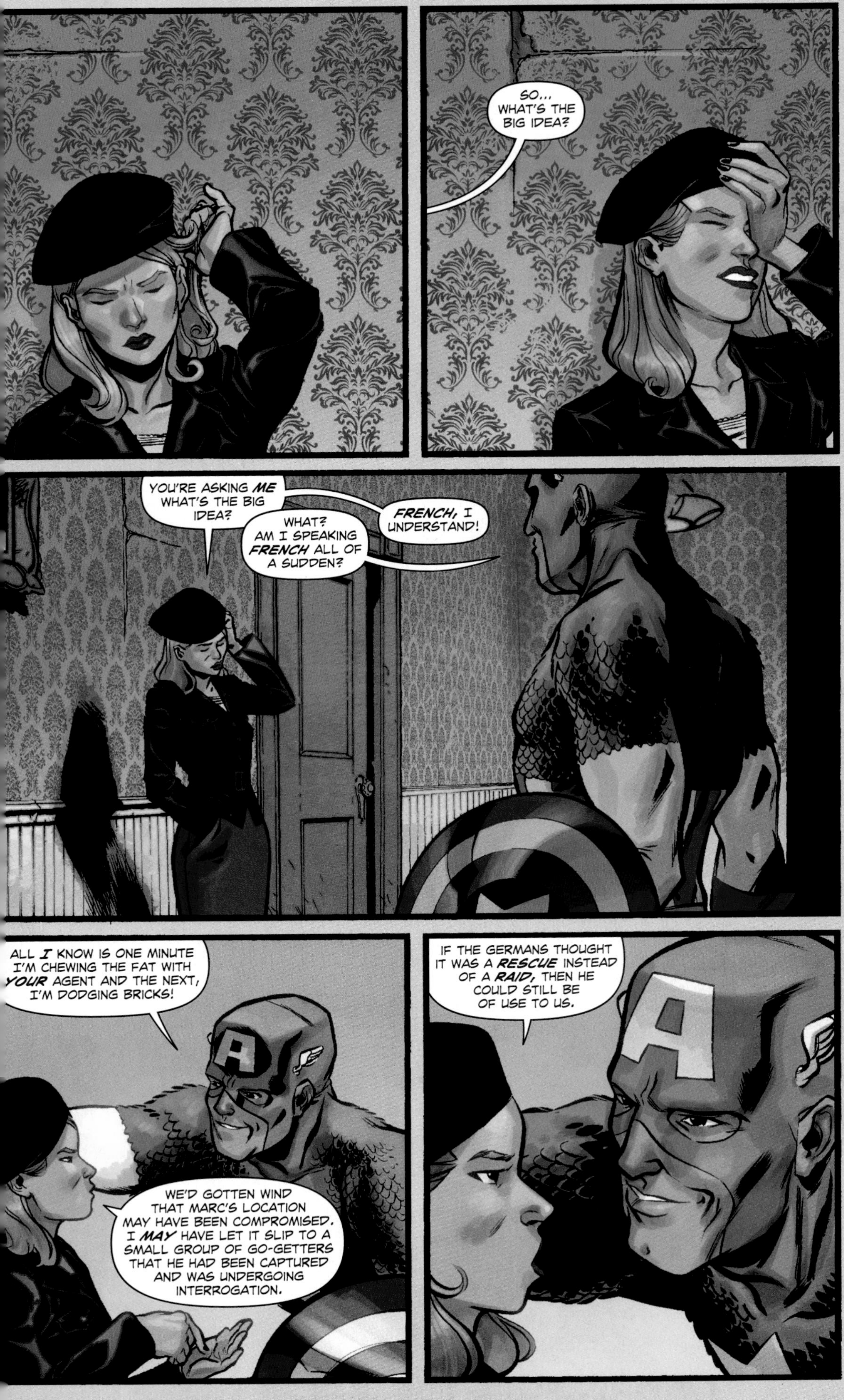
SO... WHAT'S THE BIG IDEA?
YOU'RE ASKING ME WHAT'S THE BIG IDEA?
WHAT? AM I SPEAKING FRENCH ALL OF A SUDDEN?
FRENCH, I UNDERSTAND!
ALL I KNOW IS ONE MINUTE I'M CHEWING THE FAT WITH YOUR AGENT AND THE NEXT, I'M DODGING BRICKS!
WE'D GOTTEN WIND THAT MARC'S LOCATION MAY HAVE BEEN COMPROMISED. I MAY HAVE LET IT SLIP TO A SMALL GROUP OF GO-GETTERS THAT HE HAD BEEN CAPTURED AND WAS UNDERGOING INTERROGATION.
IF THE GERMANS THOUGHT IT WAS A RESCUE INSTEAD OF A RAID, THEN HE COULD STILL BE OF USE TO US.

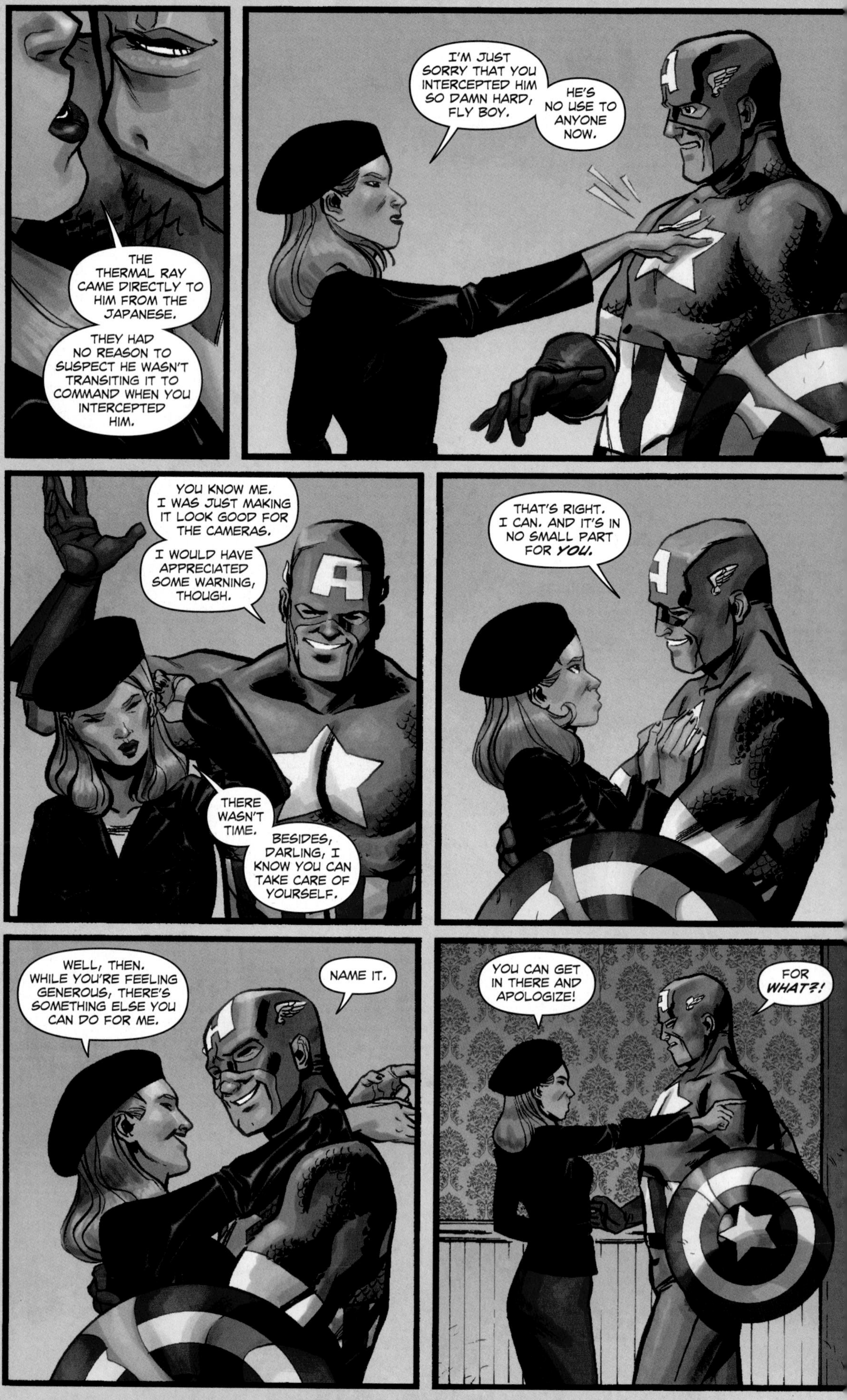
THE THERMAL RAY CAME DIRECTLY TO HIM FROM THE JAPANESE.
THEY HAD NO REASON TO SUSPECT HE WASN'T TRANSITING IT TO COMMAND WHEN YOU INTERCEPTED HIM.
I'M JUST SORRY THAT YOU INTERCEPTED HIM SO DAMN HARD, FLY BOY.
HE'S NO USE TO ANYONE NOW.
YOU KNOW ME. I WAS JUST MAKING IT LOOK GOOD FOR THE CAMERAS.
I WOULD HAVE APPRECIATED SOME WARNING, THOUGH.
THERE WASN'T TIME.
BESIDES, DARLING, I KNOW YOU CAN TAKE CARE OF YOURSELF.
THAT'S RIGHT. I CAN. AND IT'S IN NO SMALL PART FOR *YOU.*
WELL, THEN. WHILE YOU'RE FEELING GENEROUS, THERE'S SOMETHING ELSE YOU CAN DO FOR ME.
NAME IT.
YOU CAN GET IN THERE AND APOLOGIZE!
FOR *WHAT?!*

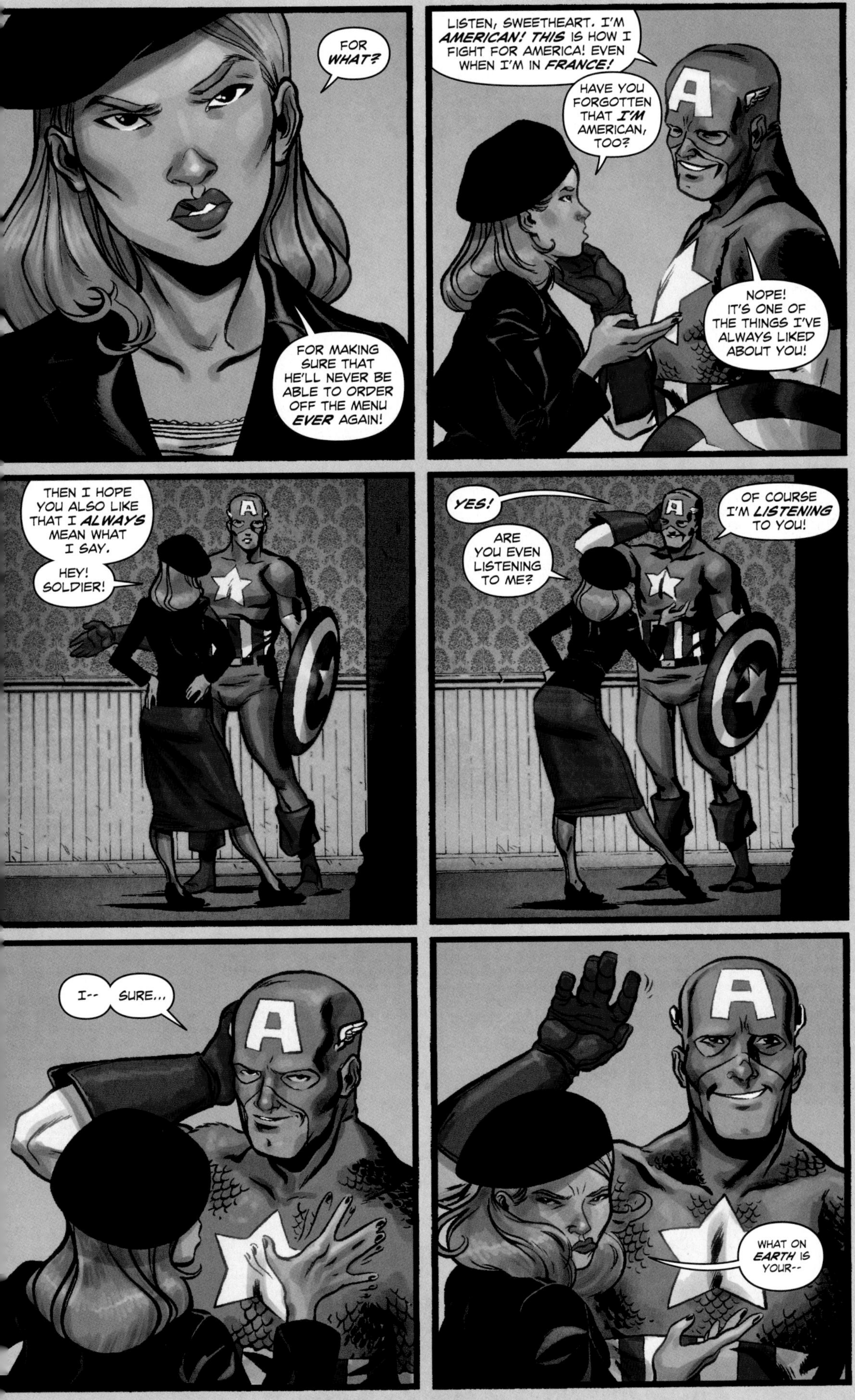
FOR WHAT?
FOR MAKING SURE THAT HE'LL NEVER BE ABLE TO ORDER OFF THE MENU EVER AGAIN!
LISTEN, SWEETHEART. I'M AMERICAN! THIS IS HOW I FIGHT FOR AMERICA! EVEN WHEN I'M IN FRANCE!
HAVE YOU FORGOTTEN THAT I'M AMERICAN, TOO?
NOPE! IT'S ONE OF THE THINGS I'VE ALWAYS LIKED ABOUT YOU!
THEN I HOPE YOU ALSO LIKE THAT I ALWAYS MEAN WHAT I SAY.
HEY! SOLDIER!
YES!
ARE YOU EVEN LISTENING TO ME?
OF COURSE I'M LISTENING TO YOU!
I--
SURE...
WHAT ON EARTH IS YOUR--

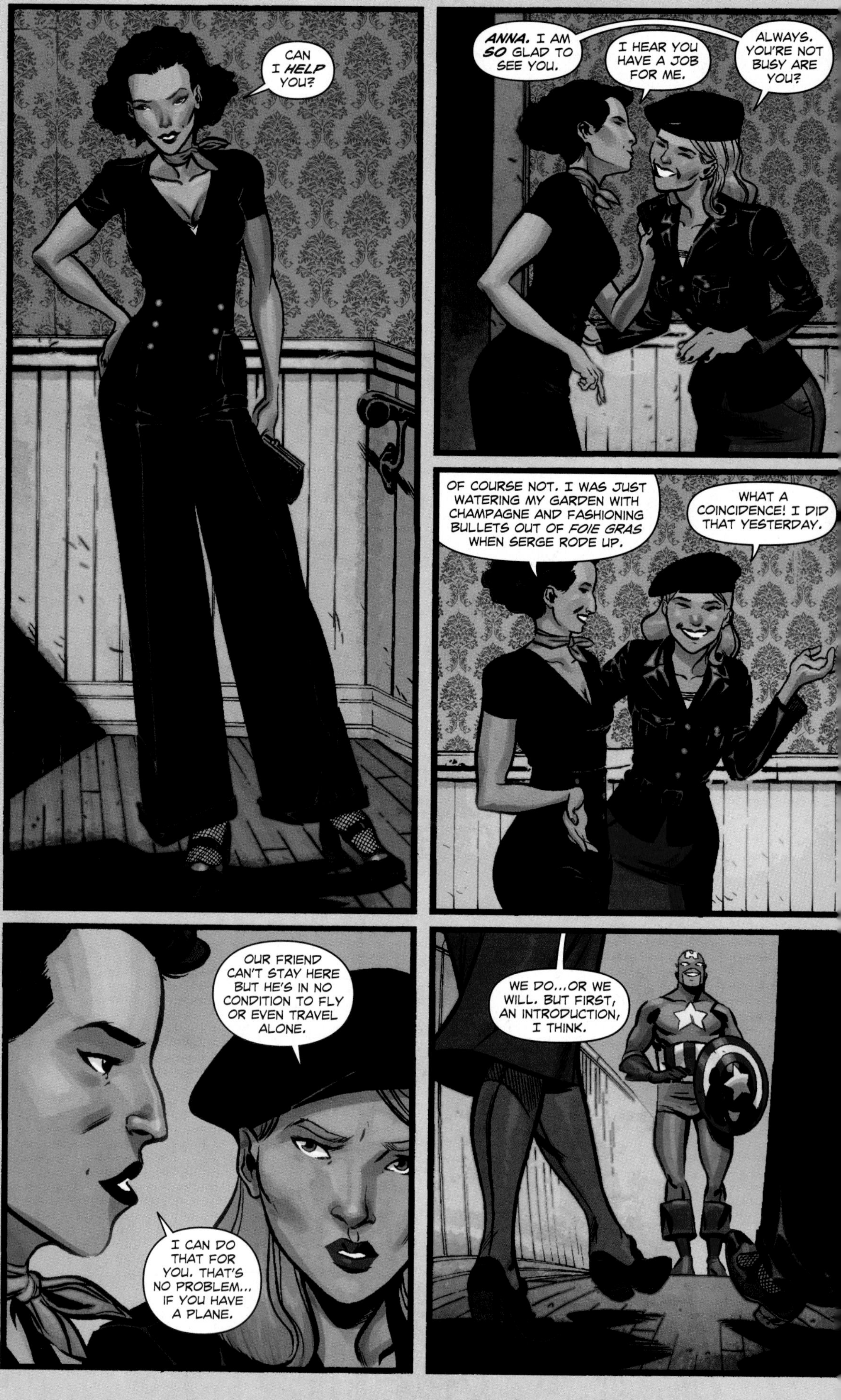
CAN I *HELP* YOU?
ANNA. I AM *SO* GLAD TO SEE YOU.
I HEAR YOU HAVE A JOB FOR ME.
ALWAYS. YOU'RE NOT BUSY ARE YOU?
OF COURSE NOT. I WAS JUST WATERING MY GARDEN WITH CHAMPAGNE AND FASHIONING BULLETS OUT OF *FOIE GRAS* WHEN SERGE RODE UP.
WHAT A COINCIDENCE! I DID THAT YESTERDAY.
OUR FRIEND CAN'T STAY HERE BUT HE'S IN NO CONDITION TO FLY OR EVEN TRAVEL ALONE.
I CAN DO THAT FOR YOU. THAT'S NO PROBLEM... IF YOU HAVE A PLANE.
WE DO...OR WE WILL. BUT FIRST, AN INTRODUCTION, I THINK.

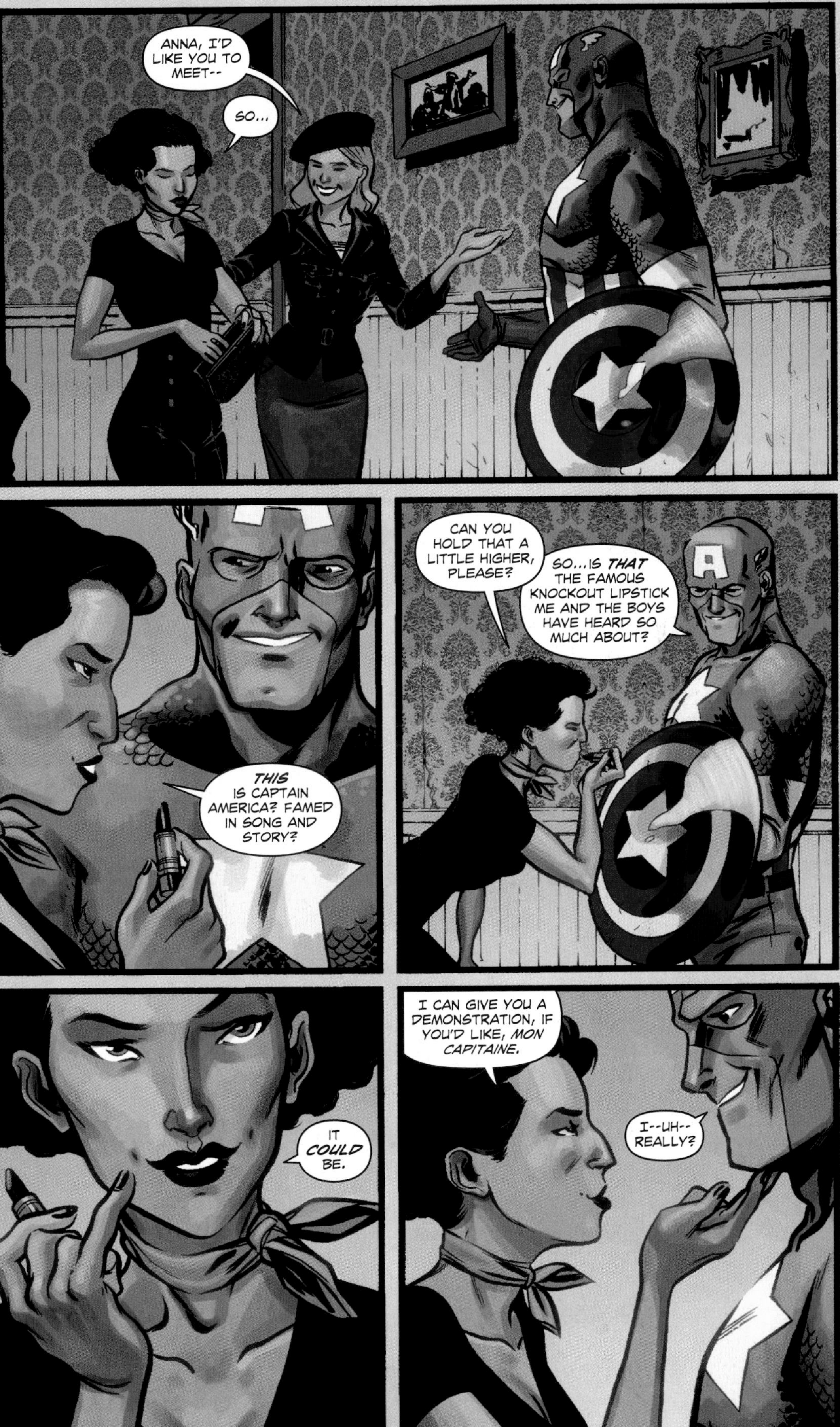
ANNA, I'D LIKE YOU TO MEET--
SO...
THIS IS CAPTAIN AMERICA? FAMED IN SONG AND STORY?
CAN YOU HOLD THAT A LITTLE HIGHER, PLEASE?
SO...IS THAT THE FAMOUS KNOCKOUT LIPSTICK ME AND THE BOYS HAVE HEARD SO MUCH ABOUT?
IT COULD BE.
I CAN GIVE YOU A DEMONSTRATION, IF YOU'D LIKE, MON CAPITAINE.
I--UH-- REALLY?

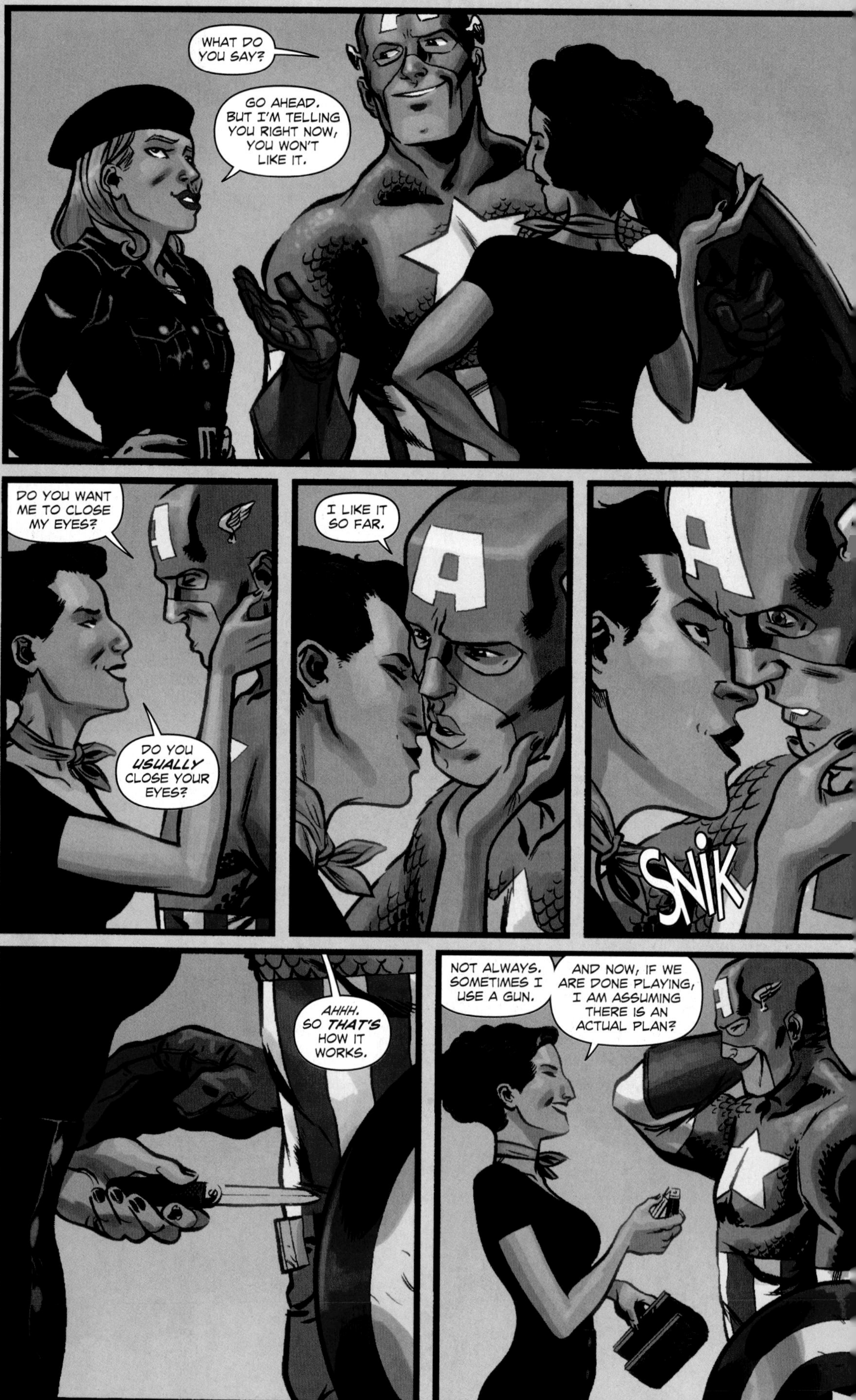
WHAT DO YOU SAY?
GO AHEAD. BUT I'M TELLING YOU RIGHT NOW, YOU WON'T LIKE IT.
DO YOU WANT ME TO CLOSE MY EYES?
DO YOU *USUALLY* CLOSE YOUR EYES?
I LIKE IT SO FAR.
SNIK
AHHH. SO *THAT'S* HOW IT WORKS.
NOT ALWAYS. SOMETIMES I USE A GUN.
AND NOW, IF WE ARE DONE PLAYING, I AM ASSUMING THERE IS AN ACTUAL PLAN?

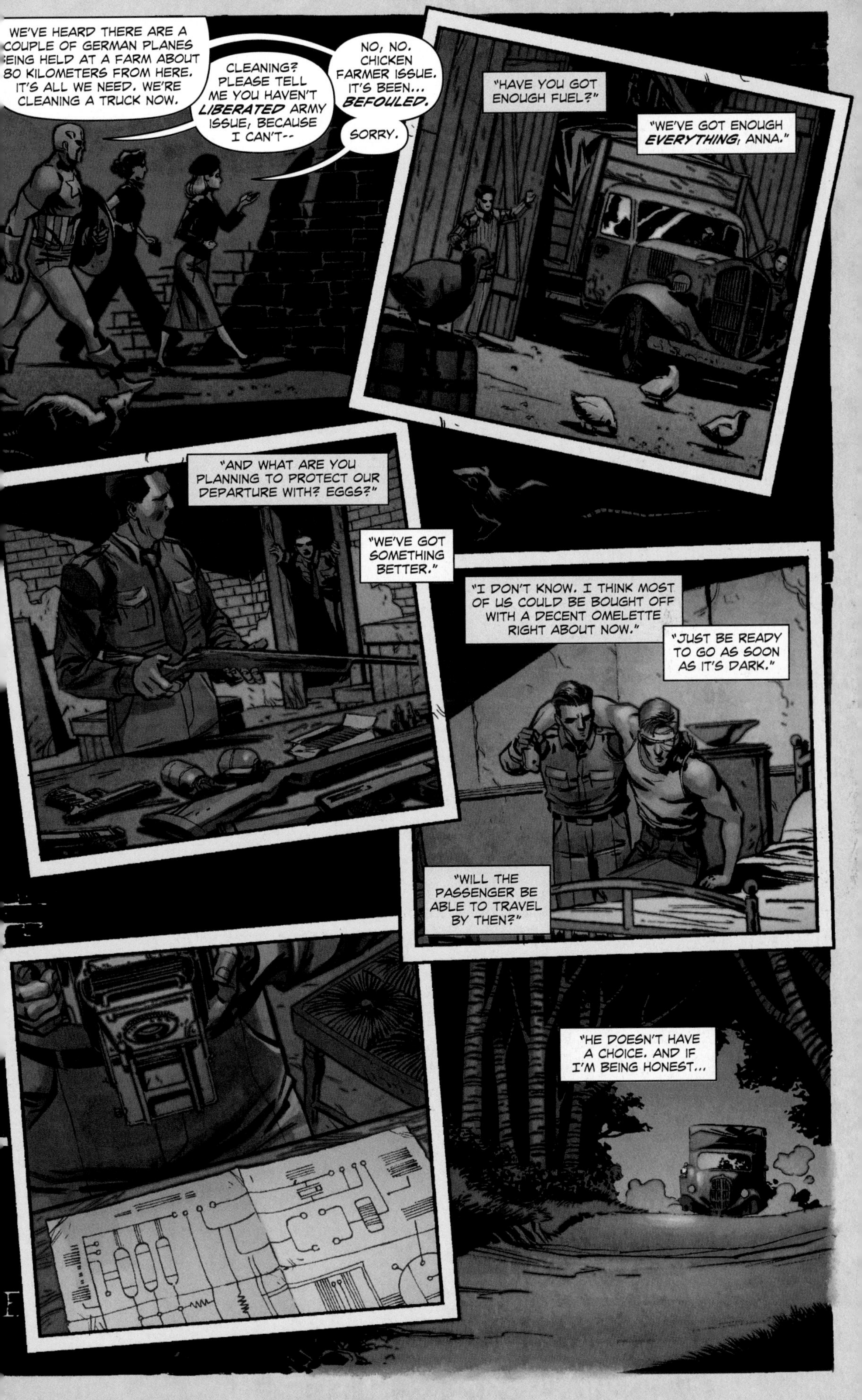
WE'VE HEARD THERE ARE A COUPLE OF GERMAN PLANES BEING HELD AT A FARM ABOUT 80 KILOMETERS FROM HERE. IT'S ALL WE NEED. WE'RE CLEANING A TRUCK NOW.
CLEANING? PLEASE TELL ME YOU HAVEN'T LIBERATED ARMY ISSUE, BECAUSE I CAN'T--
NO, NO. CHICKEN FARMER ISSUE. IT'S BEEN... BEFOULED.
SORRY.
"HAVE YOU GOT ENOUGH FUEL?"
"WE'VE GOT ENOUGH EVERYTHING, ANNA."
"AND WHAT ARE YOU PLANNING TO PROTECT OUR DEPARTURE WITH? EGGS?"
"WE'VE GOT SOMETHING BETTER."
"I DON'T KNOW. I THINK MOST OF US COULD BE BOUGHT OFF WITH A DECENT OMELETTE RIGHT ABOUT NOW."
"JUST BE READY TO GO AS SOON AS IT'S DARK."
"WILL THE PASSENGER BE ABLE TO TRAVEL BY THEN?"
"HE DOESN'T HAVE A CHOICE. AND IF I'M BEING HONEST...

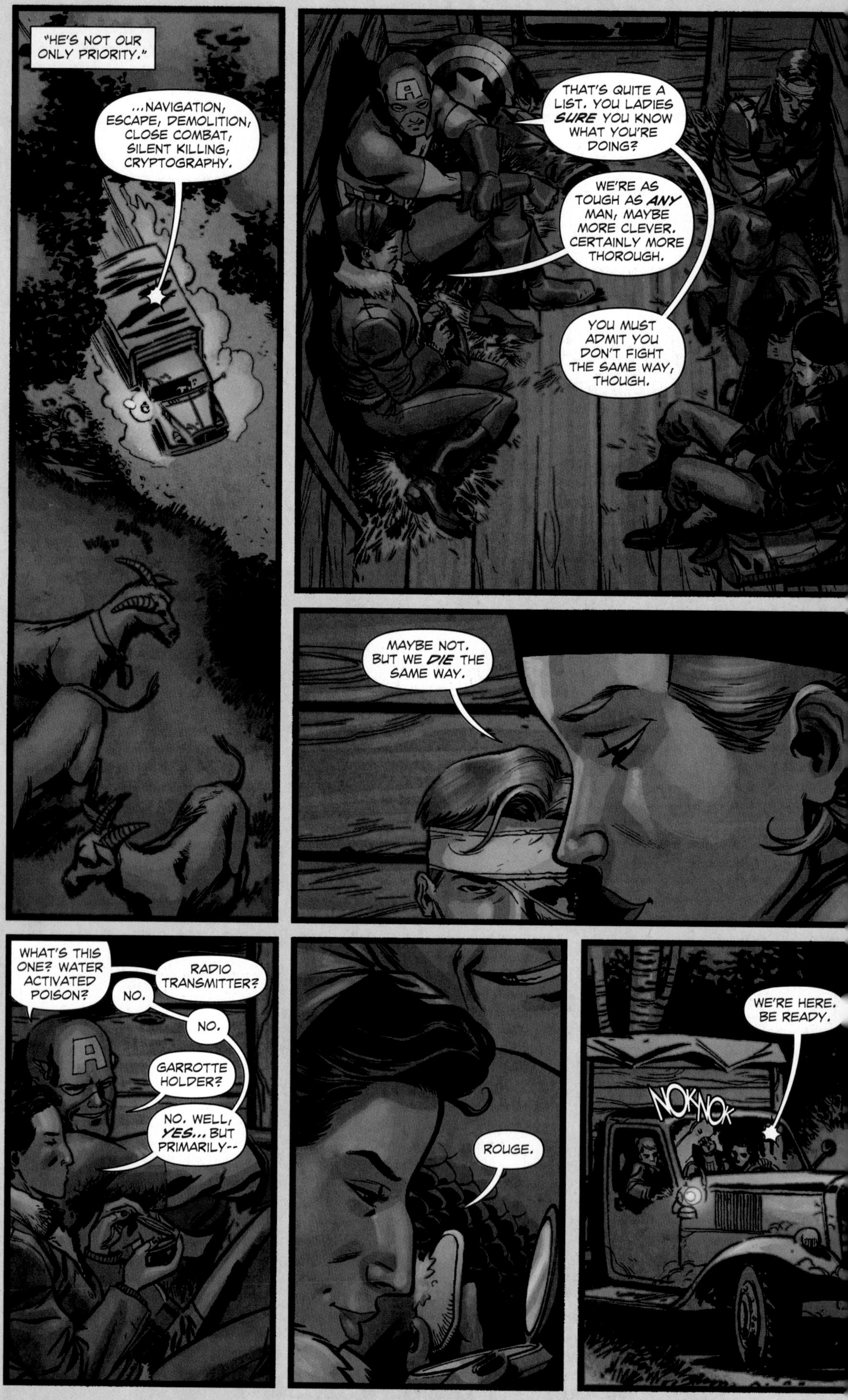
"HE'S NOT OUR ONLY PRIORITY."
...NAVIGATION, ESCAPE, DEMOLITION, CLOSE COMBAT, SILENT KILLING, CRYPTOGRAPHY.
THAT'S QUITE A LIST. YOU LADIES SURE YOU KNOW WHAT YOU'RE DOING?
WE'RE AS TOUGH AS ANY MAN, MAYBE MORE CLEVER. CERTAINLY MORE THOROUGH.
YOU MUST ADMIT YOU DON'T FIGHT THE SAME WAY, THOUGH.
MAYBE NOT. BUT WE DIE THE SAME WAY.
WHAT'S THIS ONE? WATER ACTIVATED POISON?
NO.
RADIO TRANSMITTER?
NO.
GARROTTE HOLDER?
NO. WELL, YES... BUT PRIMARILY--
ROUGE.
NOKNOK
WE'RE HERE. BE READY.

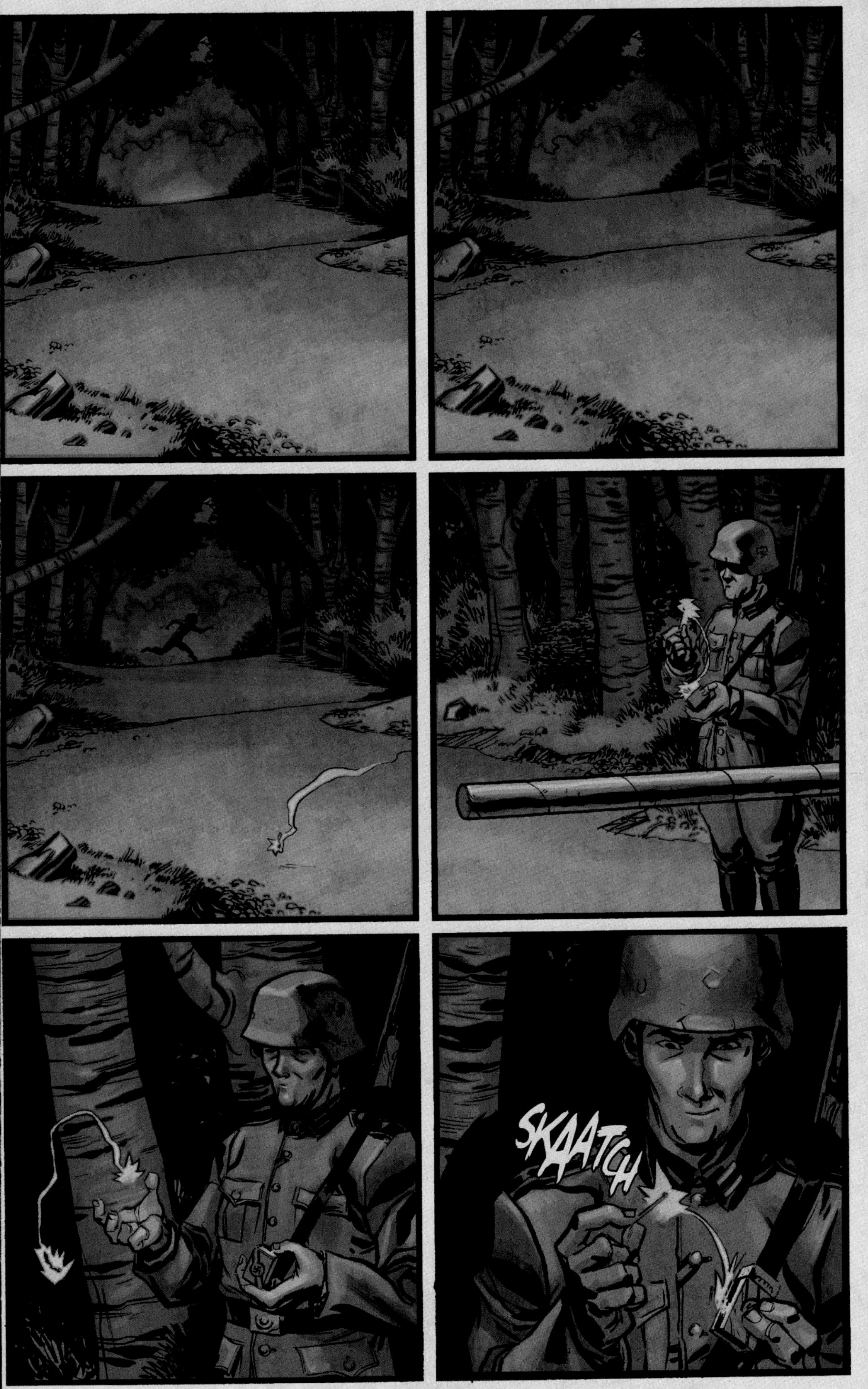
SKAATCH

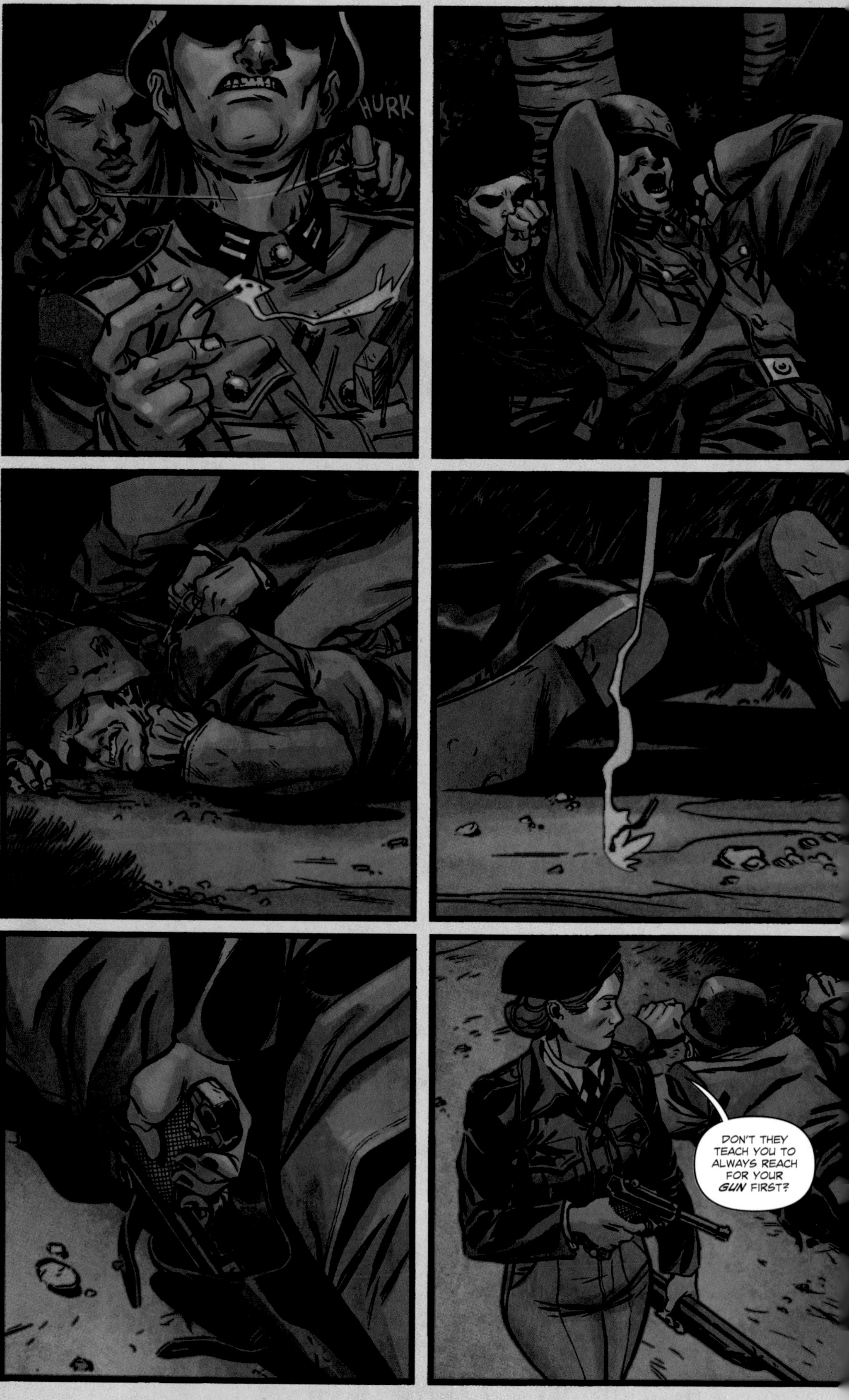
HURK
DON'T THEY TEACH YOU TO ALWAYS REACH FOR YOUR *GUN* FIRST?

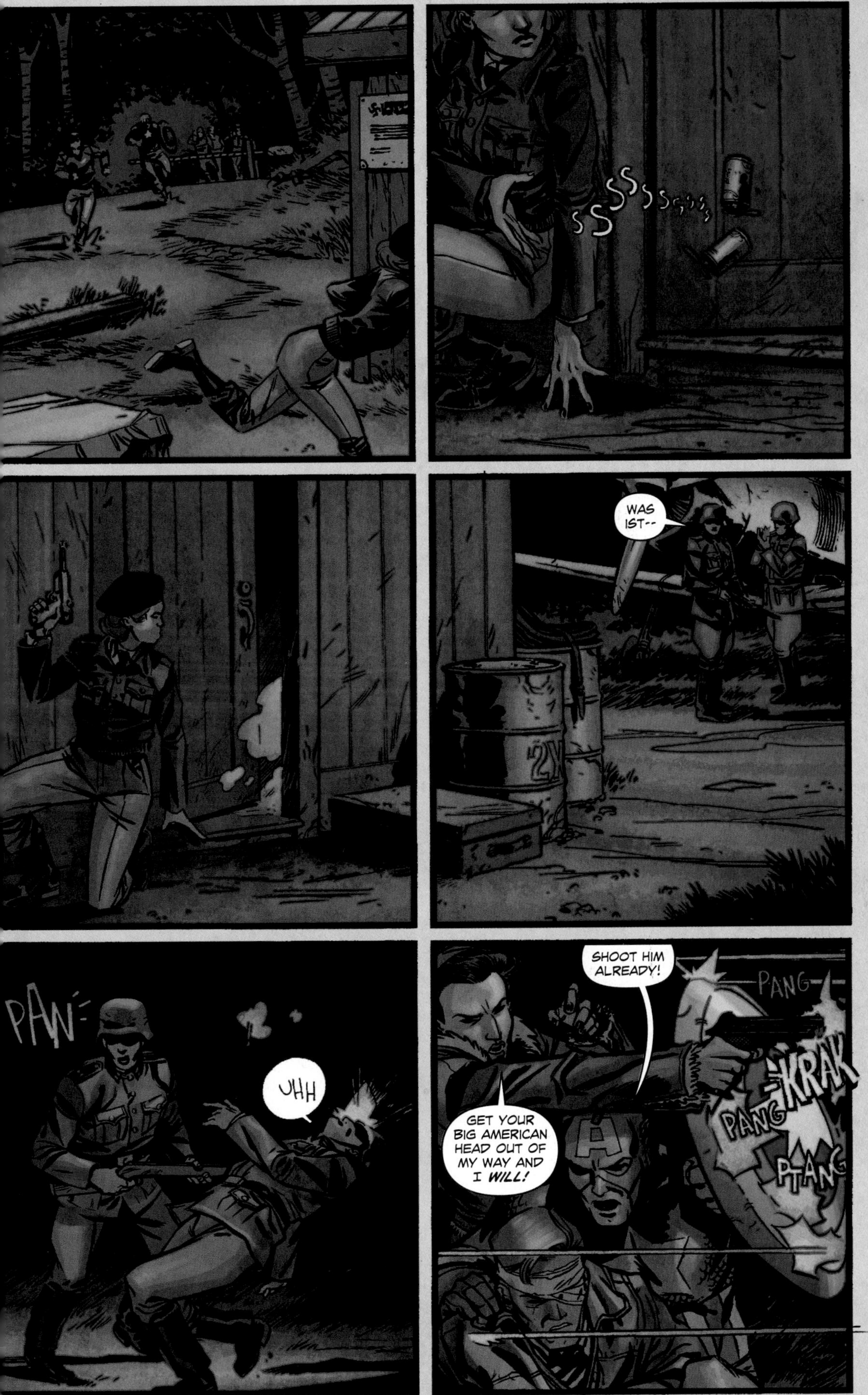
SSSSSSSSS
WAS IST--
PAW
UHH
SHOOT HIM ALREADY!
GET YOUR BIG AMERICAN HEAD OUT OF MY WAY AND I WILL!
PANG
KRAK
PANG
PTANG

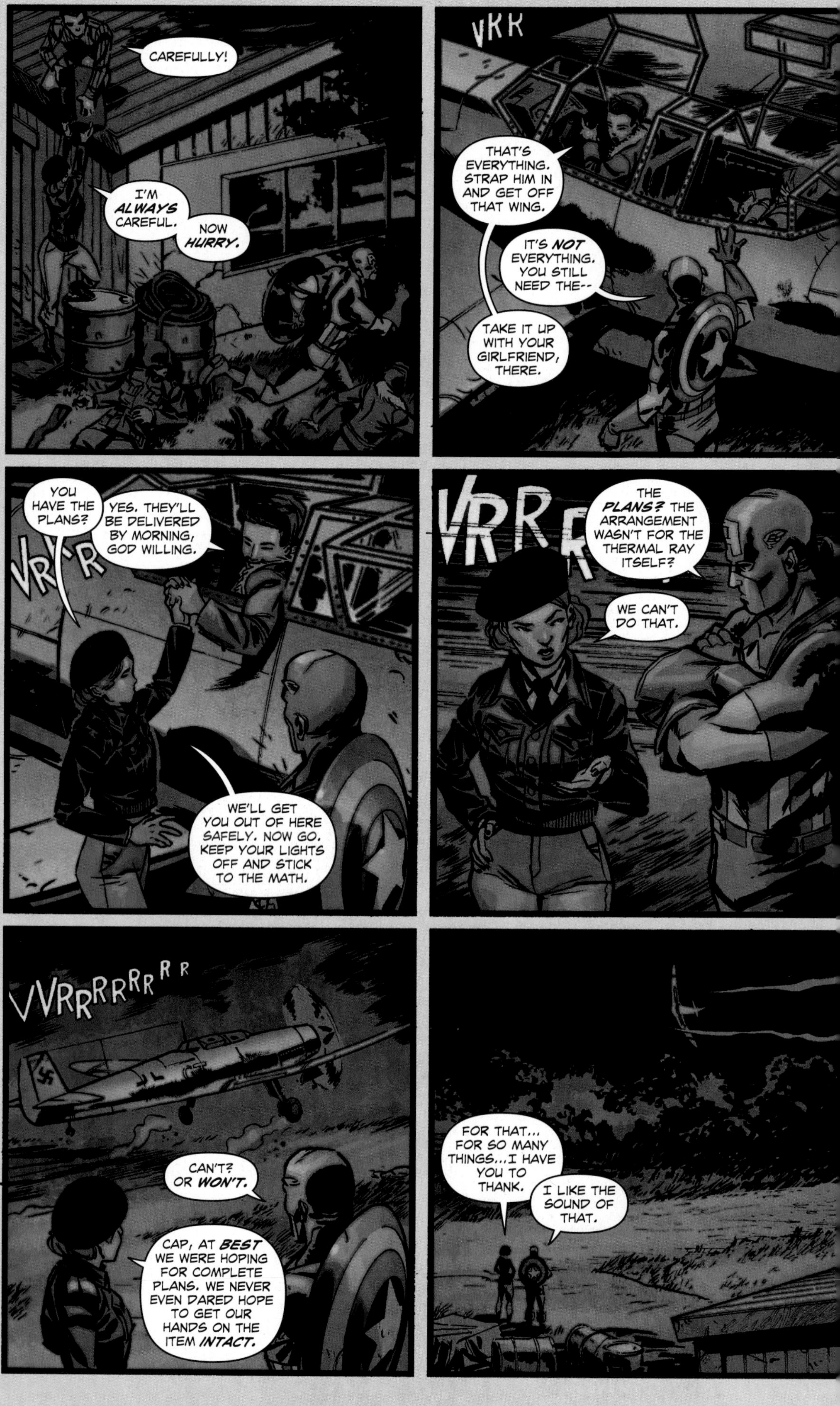

CAREFULLY!
I'M *ALWAYS* CAREFUL.
NOW *HURRY.*
VRR
THAT'S EVERYTHING. STRAP HIM IN AND GET OFF THAT WING.
IT'S *NOT* EVERYTHING. YOU STILL NEED THE--
TAKE IT UP WITH YOUR GIRLFRIEND, THERE.
YOU HAVE THE PLANS?
YES. THEY'LL BE DELIVERED BY MORNING, GOD WILLING.
VRR
WE'LL GET YOU OUT OF HERE SAFELY. NOW GO. KEEP YOUR LIGHTS OFF AND STICK TO THE MATH.
VRRR
THE *PLANS?* THE ARRANGEMENT WASN'T FOR THE THERMAL RAY ITSELF?
WE CAN'T DO THAT.
VVRRRRRRRR
CAN'T? OR *WON'T.*
CAP, AT *BEST* WE WERE HOPING FOR COMPLETE PLANS. WE NEVER EVEN DARED HOPE TO GET OUR HANDS ON THE ITEM *INTACT.*
FOR THAT... FOR SO MANY THINGS...I HAVE YOU TO THANK.
I LIKE THE SOUND OF THAT.

HOW LONG UNTIL THEY'RE OUT OF RANGE, HENRI?

ANOTHER MINUTE. THEY'RE THE ONLY THING IN THE SKY, IF THIS CONTRAPTION IS FUNCTIONING PROPERLY.

I NEVER THOUGHT I'D FIND A REASON TO BE GRATEFUL TO THE JAPANESE.

PEOPLE CAN CHANGE, SERGE.

WE ARE ALL CHANGED.

THEY'RE SAFELY AWAY. LET'S GET OUT OF HERE.

DID YOU CLEAN THE BUILDING?

WHATEVER WE CAN USE IS IN THE TRUCK. WE JUST NEED THE OTHERS. WHERE ARE THEY?

LET'S SEE JUST HOW GOOD THIS THING IS AT DETECTING HEAT, SHALL WE?

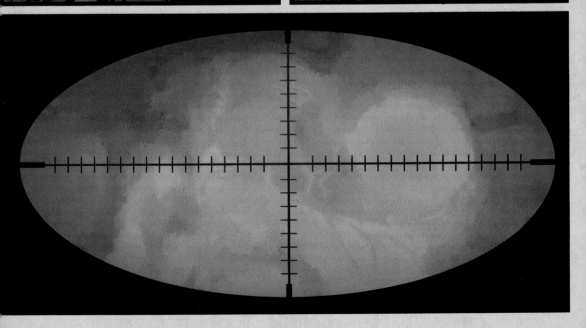

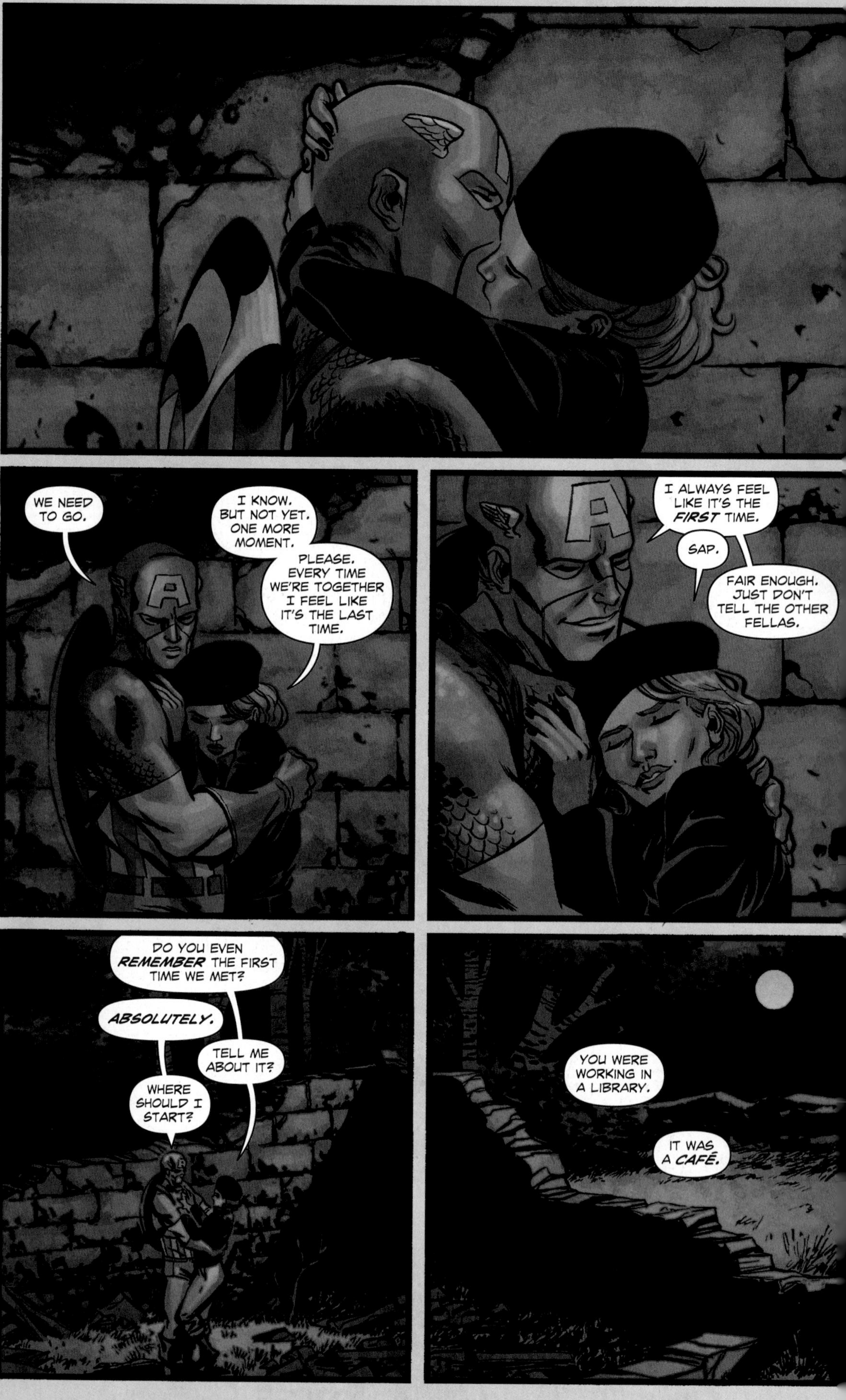
WE NEED TO GO.
I KNOW. BUT NOT YET. ONE MORE MOMENT.
PLEASE. EVERY TIME WE'RE TOGETHER I FEEL LIKE IT'S THE LAST TIME.
I ALWAYS FEEL LIKE IT'S THE *FIRST* TIME.
SAP.
FAIR ENOUGH. JUST DON'T TELL THE OTHER FELLAS.
DO YOU EVEN *REMEMBER* THE FIRST TIME WE MET?
ABSOLUTELY.
TELL ME ABOUT IT?
WHERE SHOULD I START?
YOU WERE WORKING IN A LIBRARY.
IT WAS A *CAFÉ.*

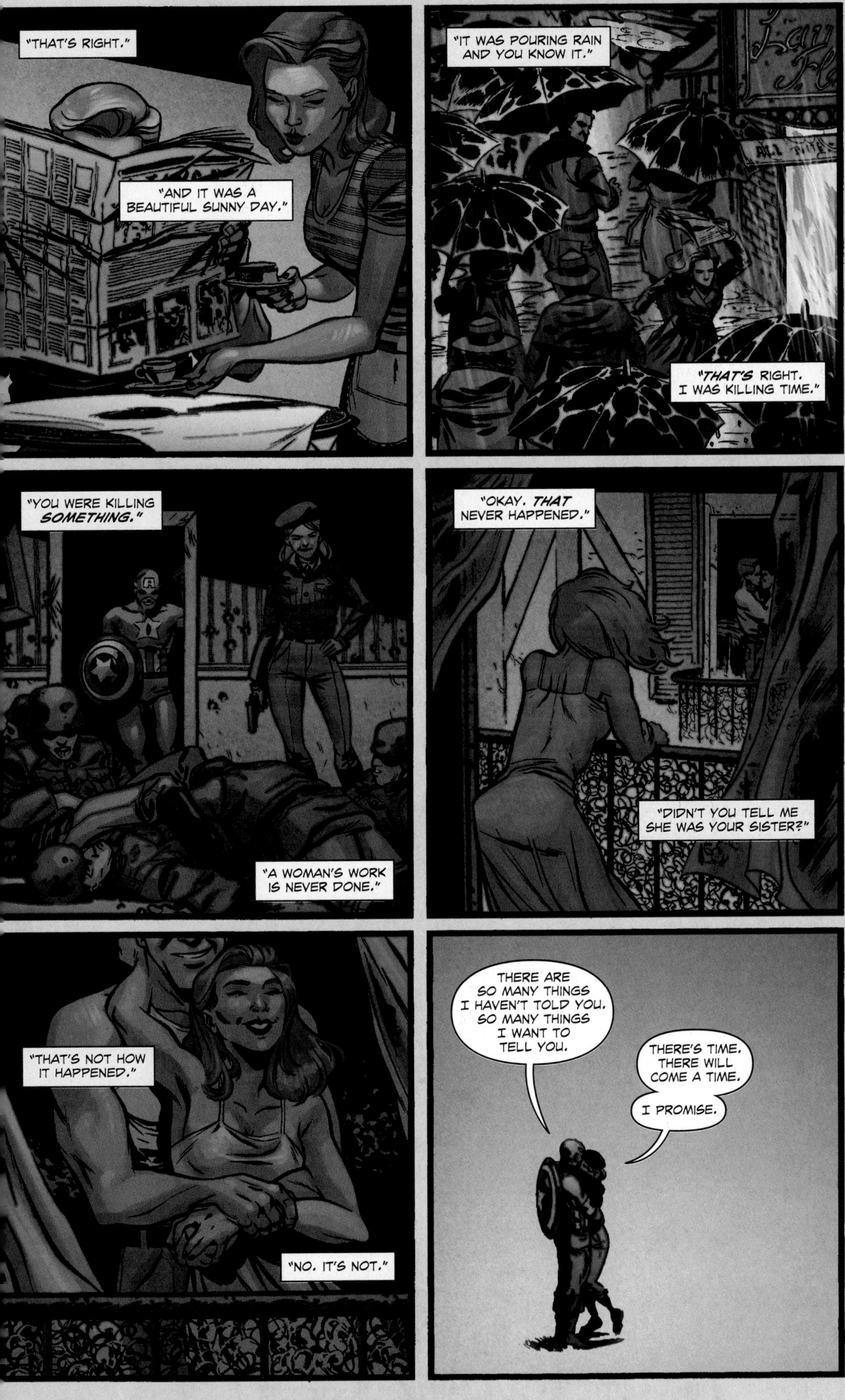
"THAT'S RIGHT."
"AND IT WAS A BEAUTIFUL SUNNY DAY."
"IT WAS POURING RAIN AND YOU KNOW IT."
"*THAT'S* RIGHT. I WAS KILLING TIME."
"YOU WERE KILLING *SOMETHING.*"
"A WOMAN'S WORK IS NEVER DONE."
"OKAY. *THAT* NEVER HAPPENED."
"DIDN'T YOU TELL ME SHE WAS YOUR SISTER?"
"THAT'S NOT HOW IT HAPPENED."
"NO. IT'S NOT."
THERE ARE SO MANY THINGS I HAVEN'T TOLD YOU. SO MANY THINGS I WANT TO TELL YOU.
THERE'S TIME. THERE WILL COME A TIME.
I PROMISE.

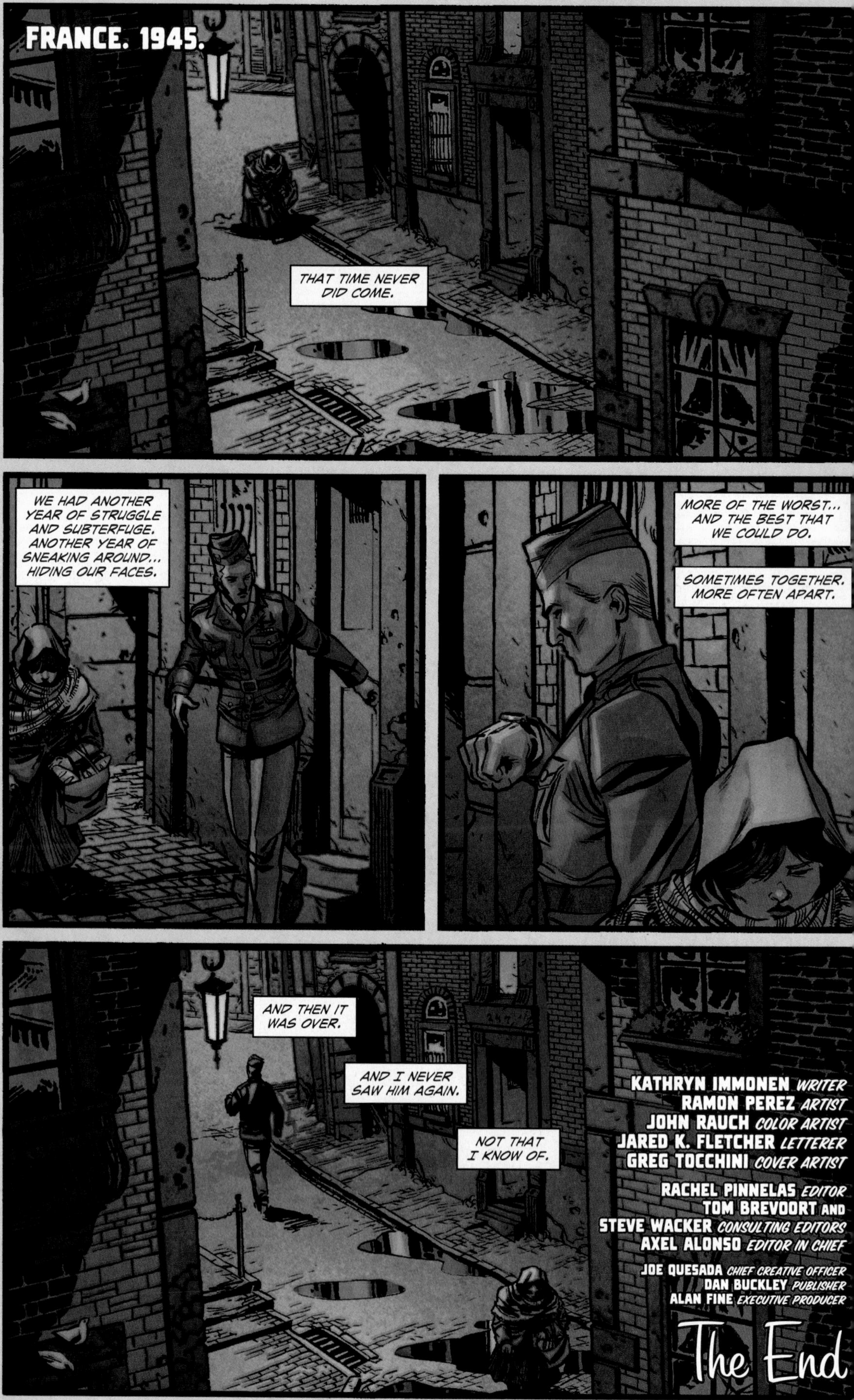
FRANCE. 1945.
THAT TIME NEVER DID COME.
WE HAD ANOTHER YEAR OF STRUGGLE AND SUBTERFUGE. ANOTHER YEAR OF SNEAKING AROUND... HIDING OUR FACES.
MORE OF THE WORST... AND THE BEST THAT WE COULD DO.
SOMETIMES TOGETHER. MORE OFTEN APART.
AND THEN IT WAS OVER.
AND I NEVER SAW HIM AGAIN.
NOT THAT I KNOW OF.
KATHRYN IMMONEN WRITER
RAMON PEREZ ARTIST
JOHN RAUCH COLOR ARTIST
JARED K. FLETCHER LETTERER
GREG TOCCHINI COVER ARTIST
RACHEL PINNELAS EDITOR
TOM BREVOORT AND
STEVE WACKER CONSULTING EDITORS
AXEL ALONSO EDITOR IN CHIEF
JOE QUESADA CHIEF CREATIVE OFFICER
DAN BUCKLEY PUBLISHER
ALAN FINE EXECUTIVE PRODUCER
The End

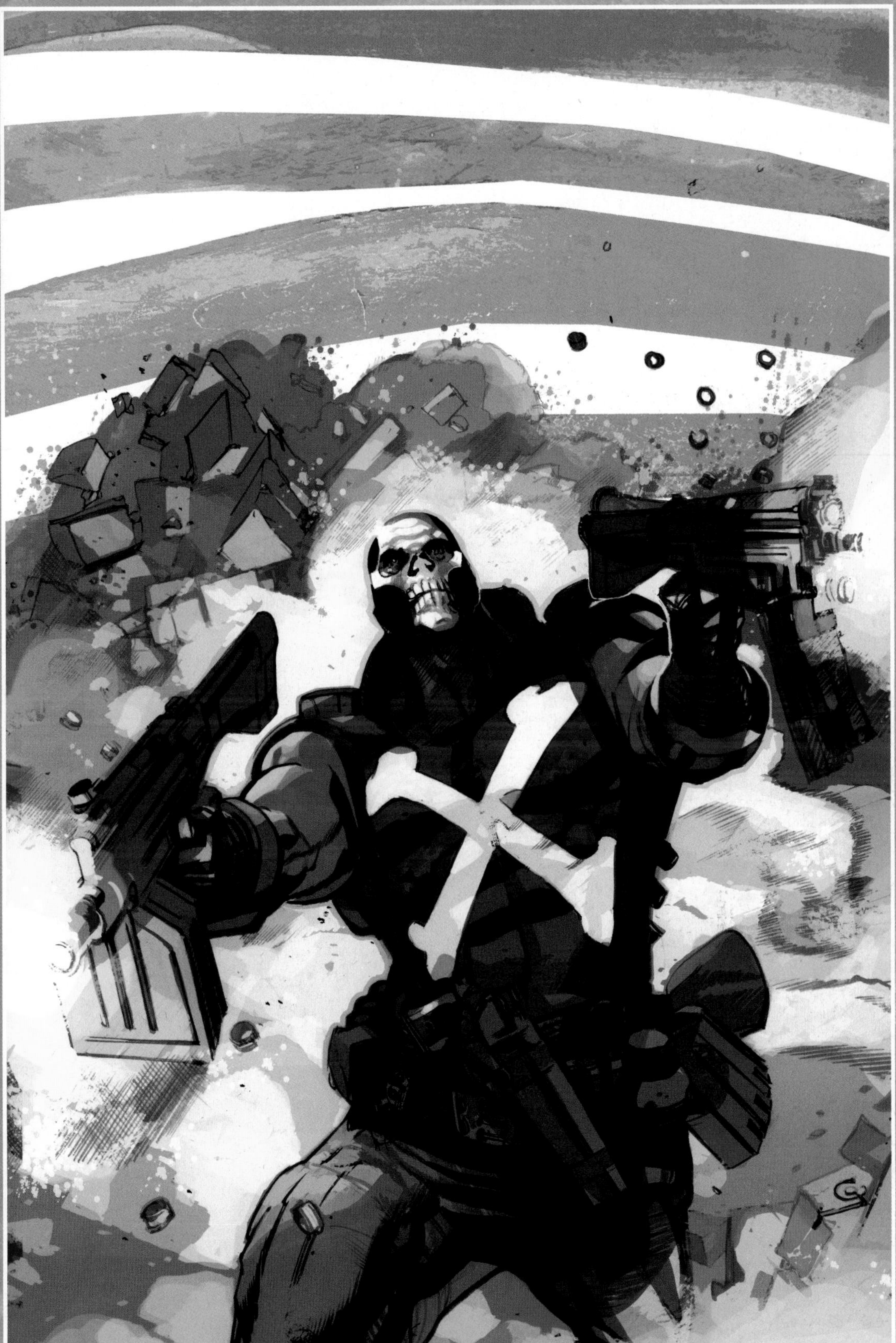

CAPTAIN AMERICA AND CROSSBONES

CLASSIFIED

PROFILE #: 18383722
REAL NAME: Brock Rumlow
AKA: Crossbones

Crossbones was born Brock Rumlow and led the Savage Crims, a gang on New York's Lower East Side. After killing a local boy during a fistfight, Rumlow fled town and joined the super villain Taskmaster's training school for henchmen. Within three years, he became its instructor under the name Bingo Brock. He was later recruited by The Red Skull, Nazi adversary to Steve Rogers, the original Captain America.

Throughout the years, Crossbones worked for numerous villains, often at odds with Rogers. He even seemingly assassinated Rogers at the close of the Super Human Civil War. Recently, Crossbones was imprisoned in The Raft, a superhuman detention center. He was recruited to The Thunderbolts, an initiative geared towards rehabilitating villains by sending them on world-saving missions. Rumlow was in for the action, but wouldn't quell his violent natur

After again attempting to kill Rogers during a recent mission, Crossbones was thrown off the team. He is presently incarcerated, without a chance of parole.

U.S.A. SUPER-HERO

Writer
William
Harms

Artist
Declan
Shalvey

Colorist
Matthew
Wilson

Letterer
Jared K.
Fletcher

Cover Artist
Greg
Tocchini

Associate Editor
Thomas Brennan

Editor
Bill Rosemann

Production
Mayela Gutierrez

Assistant Editor
Rachel Pinnelas

Exec. Producer
Alan Fine

Publisher
Dan Buckley

Editor in Chief
Axel Alonso

Chief Creative Officer
Joe Quesada

Captain America created by Joe Simon and Jack Kirby

To find MARVEL COMICS at a local comic and hobby shop, go to www.comicshoplocator.com or call 1-888-COMICBO

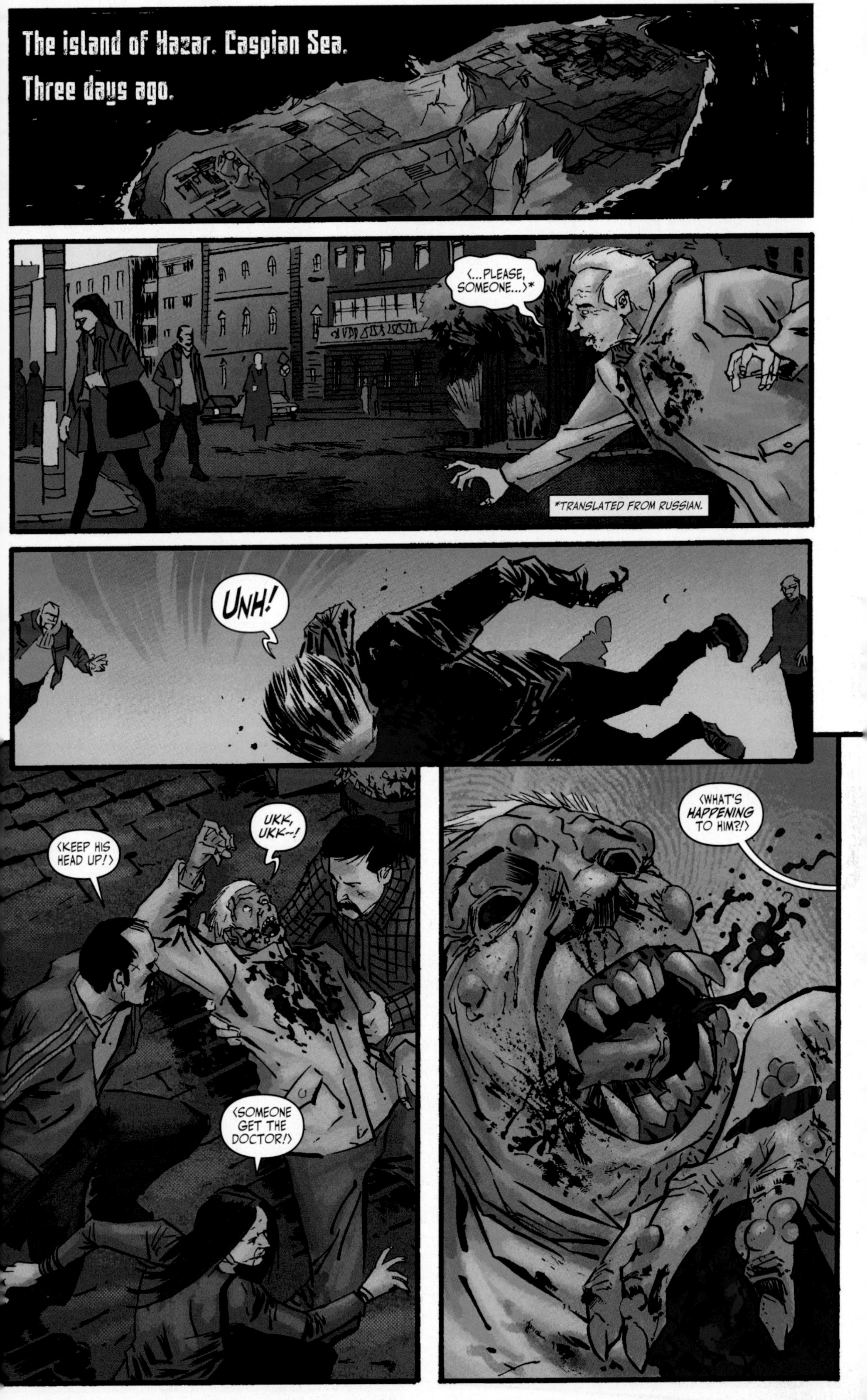
The island of Hazar. Caspian Sea.
Three days ago.
<...PLEASE, SOMEONE...>*
*TRANSLATED FROM RUSSIAN.
UNH!
<KEEP HIS HEAD UP!>
UKK, UKK--!
<SOMEONE GET THE DOCTOR!>
<WHAT'S HAPPENING TO HIM?!>

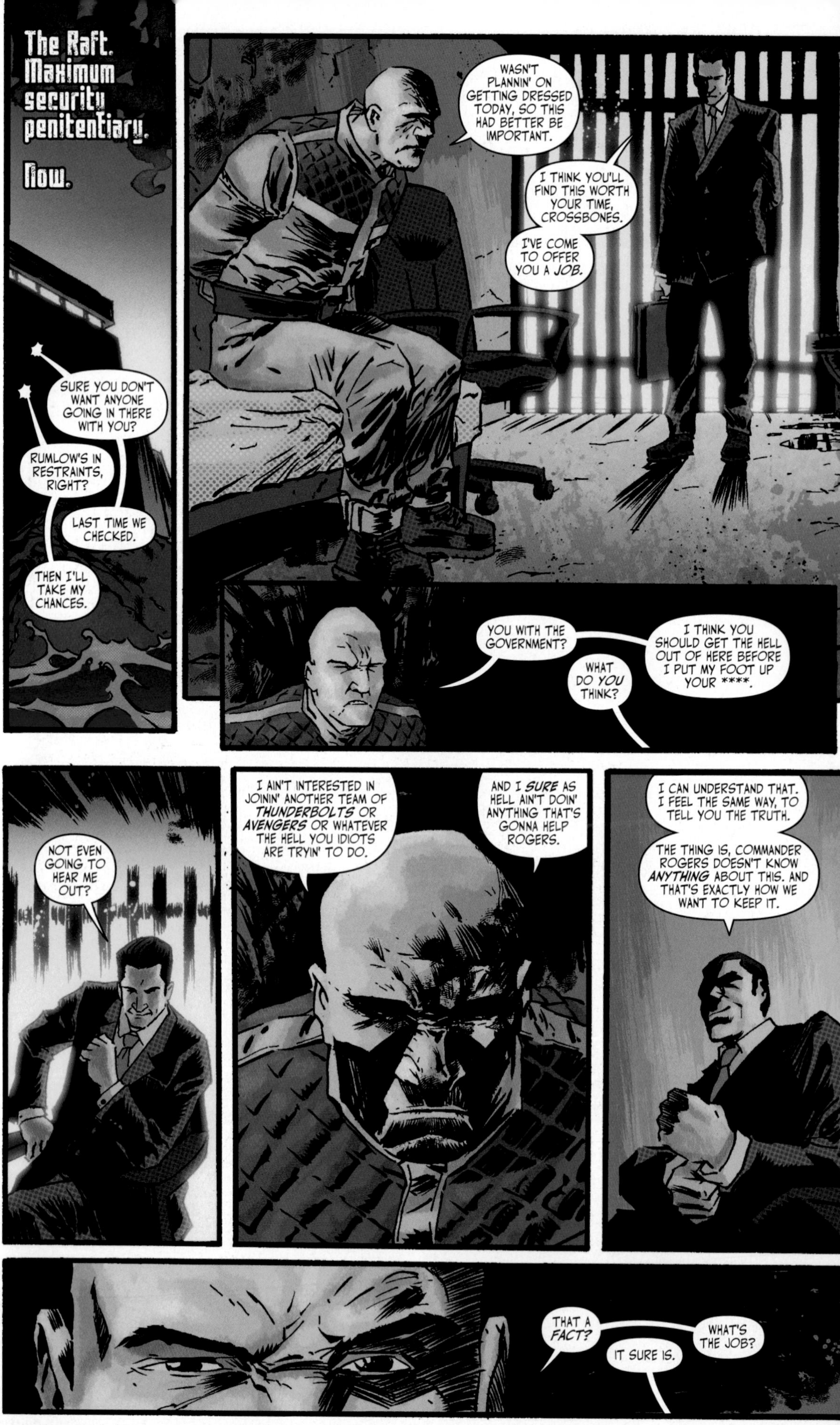
The Raft. Maximum security penitentiary.
Now.
SURE YOU DON'T WANT ANYONE GOING IN THERE WITH YOU?
RUMLOW'S IN RESTRAINTS, RIGHT?
LAST TIME WE CHECKED.
THEN I'LL TAKE MY CHANCES.
WASN'T PLANNIN' ON GETTING DRESSED TODAY, SO THIS HAD BETTER BE IMPORTANT.
I THINK YOU'LL FIND THIS WORTH YOUR TIME, CROSSBONES.
I'VE COME TO OFFER YOU A *JOB*.
YOU WITH THE GOVERNMENT?
WHAT DO *YOU* THINK?
I THINK YOU SHOULD GET THE HELL OUT OF HERE BEFORE I PUT MY FOOT UP YOUR ****.
NOT EVEN GOING TO HEAR ME OUT?
I AIN'T INTERESTED IN JOININ' ANOTHER TEAM OF *THUNDERBOLTS* OR *AVENGERS* OR WHATEVER THE HELL YOU IDIOTS ARE TRYIN' TO DO.
AND I *SURE* AS HELL AIN'T DOIN' ANYTHING THAT'S GONNA HELP ROGERS.
I CAN UNDERSTAND THAT. I FEEL THE SAME WAY, TO TELL YOU THE TRUTH.
THE THING IS, COMMANDER ROGERS DOESN'T KNOW *ANYTHING* ABOUT THIS. AND THAT'S EXACTLY HOW WE WANT TO KEEP IT.
THAT A *FACT?*
IT SURE IS.
WHAT'S THE JOB?

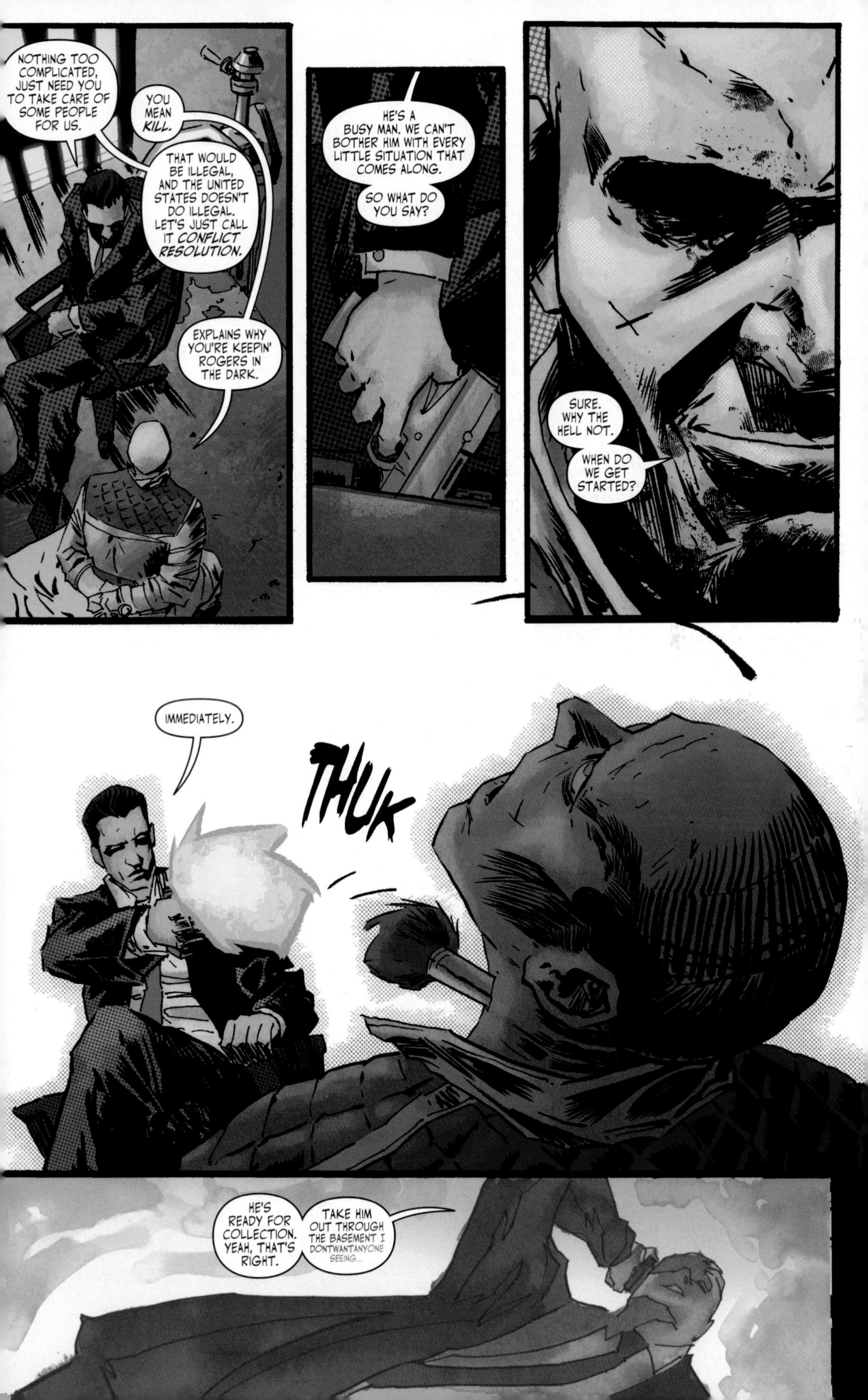
NOTHING TOO COMPLICATED, JUST NEED YOU TO TAKE CARE OF SOME PEOPLE FOR US.
YOU MEAN *KILL*.
THAT WOULD BE ILLEGAL, AND THE UNITED STATES DOESN'T DO ILLEGAL. LET'S JUST CALL IT *CONFLICT RESOLUTION*.
EXPLAINS WHY YOU'RE KEEPIN' ROGERS IN THE DARK.
HE'S A BUSY MAN. WE CAN'T BOTHER HIM WITH EVERY LITTLE SITUATION THAT COMES ALONG.
SO WHAT DO YOU SAY?
SURE. WHY THE HELL NOT.
WHEN DO WE GET STARTED?
IMMEDIATELY.
THUK
HE'S READY FOR COLLECTION. YEAH, THAT'S RIGHT.
TAKE HIM OUT THROUGH THE BASEMENT I DONTWANTANYONE SEEING...

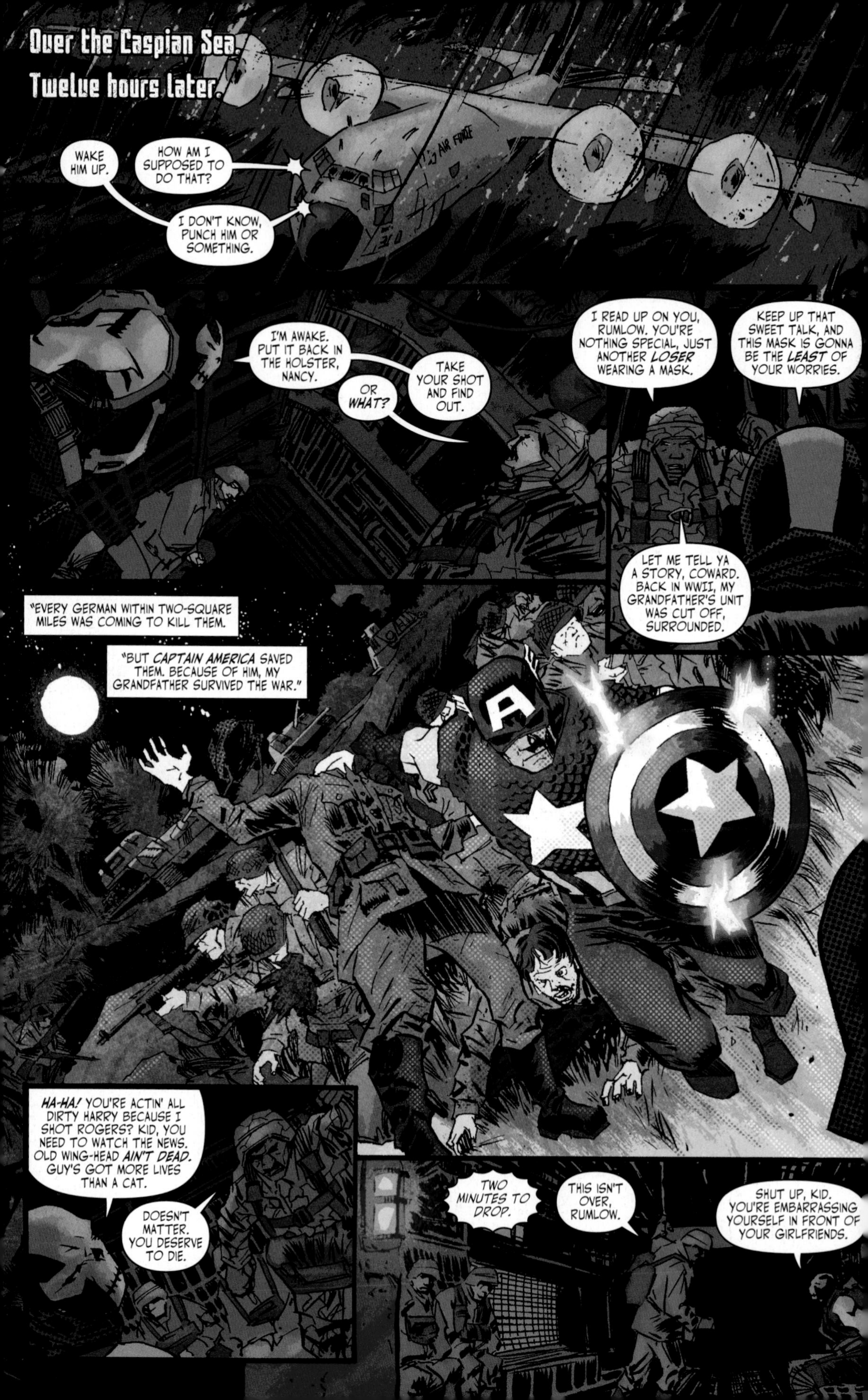
Over the Caspian Sea.
Twelve hours later.
WAKE HIM UP.
HOW AM I SUPPOSED TO DO THAT?
I DON'T KNOW, PUNCH HIM OR SOMETHING.
I'M AWAKE. PUT IT BACK IN THE HOLSTER, NANCY.
OR WHAT?
TAKE YOUR SHOT AND FIND OUT.
I READ UP ON YOU, RUMLOW. YOU'RE NOTHING SPECIAL, JUST ANOTHER LOSER WEARING A MASK.
KEEP UP THAT SWEET TALK, AND THIS MASK IS GONNA BE THE LEAST OF YOUR WORRIES.
LET ME TELL YA A STORY, COWARD. BACK IN WWII, MY GRANDFATHER'S UNIT WAS CUT OFF, SURROUNDED.
"EVERY GERMAN WITHIN TWO-SQUARE MILES WAS COMING TO KILL THEM.
"BUT CAPTAIN AMERICA SAVED THEM. BECAUSE OF HIM, MY GRANDFATHER SURVIVED THE WAR."
HA-HA! YOU'RE ACTIN' ALL DIRTY HARRY BECAUSE I SHOT ROGERS? KID, YOU NEED TO WATCH THE NEWS. OLD WING-HEAD AIN'T DEAD. GUY'S GOT MORE LIVES THAN A CAT.
DOESN'T MATTER. YOU DESERVE TO DIE.
TWO MINUTES TO DROP.
THIS ISN'T OVER, RUMLOW.
SHUT UP, KID. YOU'RE EMBARRASSING YOURSELF IN FRONT OF YOUR GIRLFRIENDS.

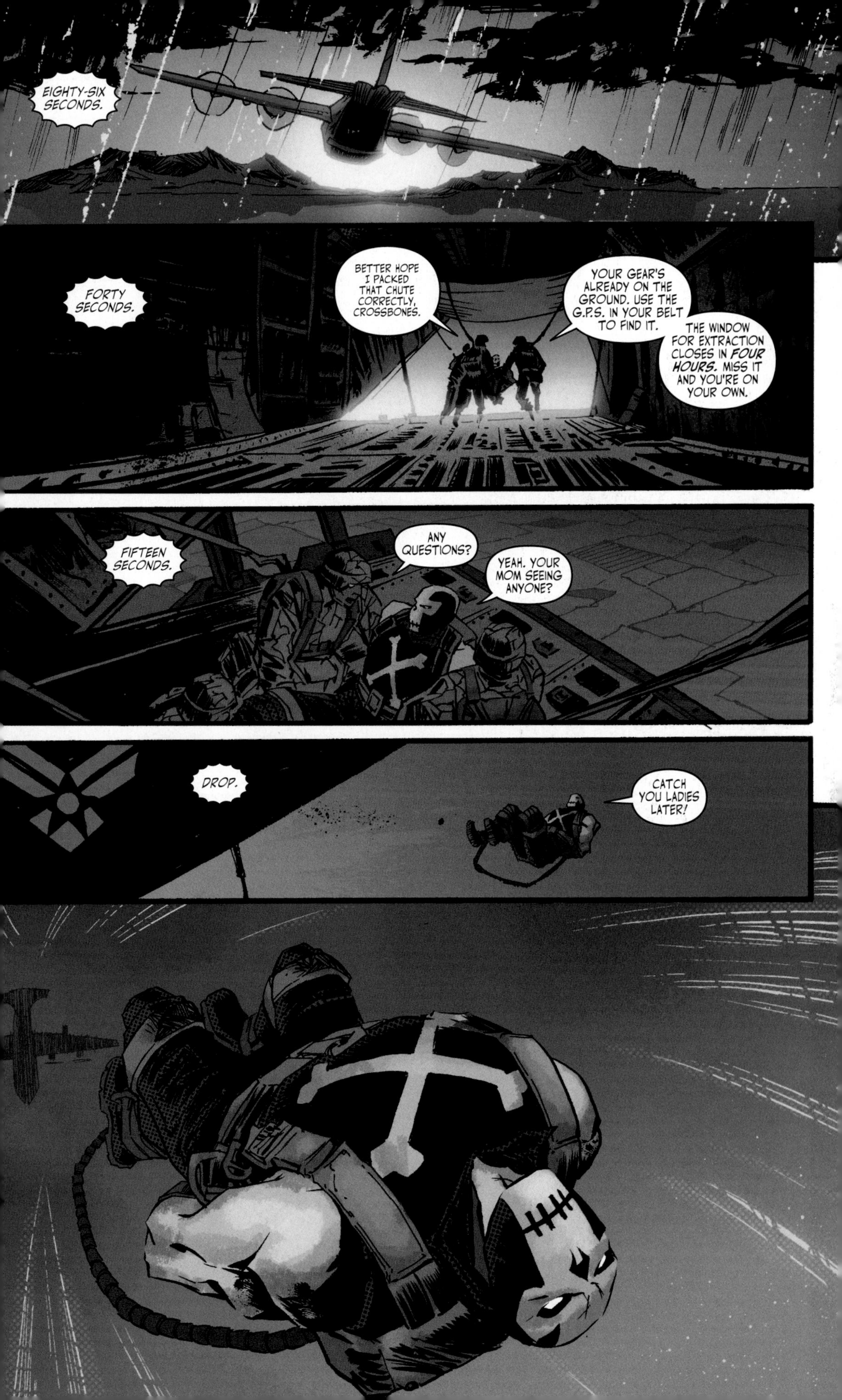

EIGHTY-SIX SECONDS.
FORTY SECONDS.
BETTER HOPE I PACKED THAT CHUTE CORRECTLY, CROSSBONES.
YOUR GEAR'S ALREADY ON THE GROUND. USE THE G.P.S. IN YOUR BELT TO FIND IT.
THE WINDOW FOR EXTRACTION CLOSES IN FOUR HOURS. MISS IT AND YOU'RE ON YOUR OWN.
FIFTEEN SECONDS.
ANY QUESTIONS?
YEAH. YOUR MOM SEEING ANYONE?
DROP.
CATCH YOU LADIES LATER!

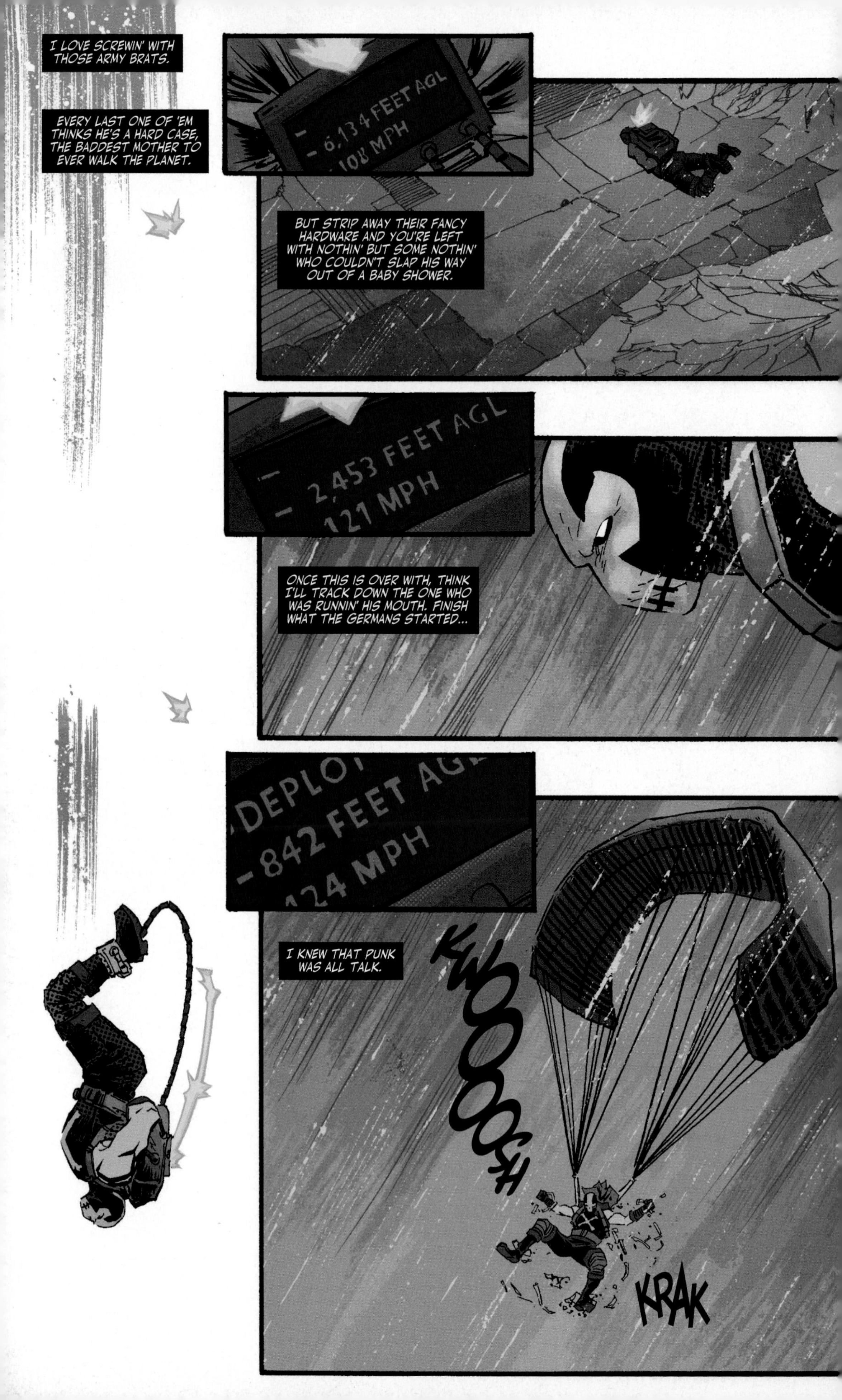
I LOVE SCREWIN' WITH THOSE ARMY BRATS.
EVERY LAST ONE OF 'EM THINKS HE'S A HARD CASE, THE BADDEST MOTHER TO EVER WALK THE PLANET.
- 6,134 FEET AGL
- 108 MPH
BUT STRIP AWAY THEIR FANCY HARDWARE AND YOU'RE LEFT WITH NOTHIN' BUT SOME NOTHIN' WHO COULDN'T SLAP HIS WAY OUT OF A BABY SHOWER.
- 2,453 FEET AGL
- 121 MPH
ONCE THIS IS OVER WITH, THINK I'LL TRACK DOWN THE ONE WHO WAS RUNNIN' HIS MOUTH. FINISH WHAT THE GERMANS STARTED...
- 842 FEET AGL
I KNEW THAT PUNK WAS ALL TALK.
KWOOOOSH
KRAK

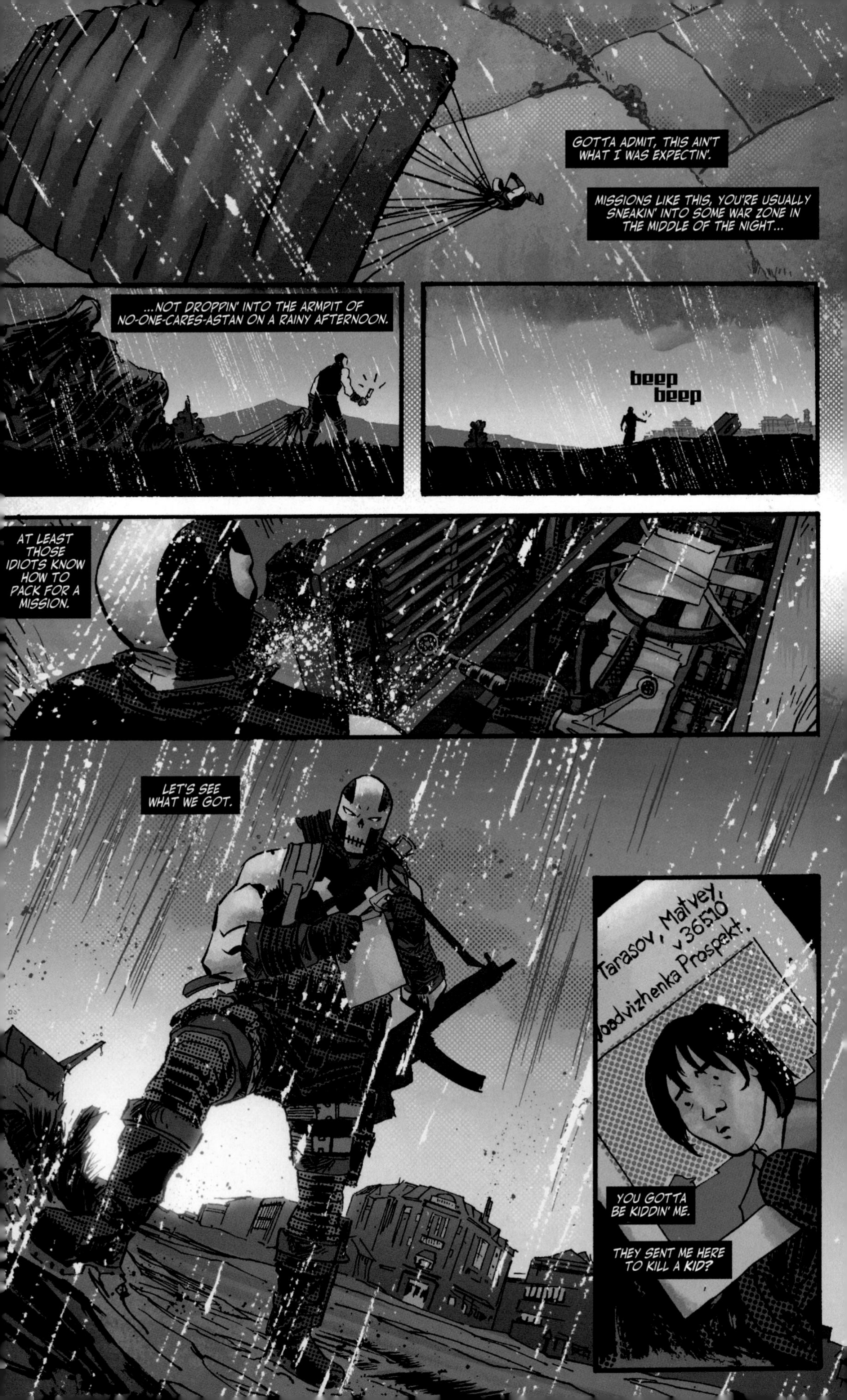
GOTTA ADMIT, THIS AIN'T WHAT I WAS EXPECTIN'.
MISSIONS LIKE THIS, YOU'RE USUALLY SNEAKIN' INTO SOME WAR ZONE IN THE MIDDLE OF THE NIGHT...
...NOT DROPPIN' INTO THE ARMPIT OF NO-ONE-CARES-ASTAN ON A RAINY AFTERNOON.
beep beep
AT LEAST THOSE IDIOTS KNOW HOW TO PACK FOR A MISSION.
LET'S SEE WHAT WE GOT.
Tarasov, Matvey, v 36510 oadvizhenka Prospekt.
YOU GOTTA BE KIDDIN' ME.
THEY SENT ME HERE TO KILL A KID?

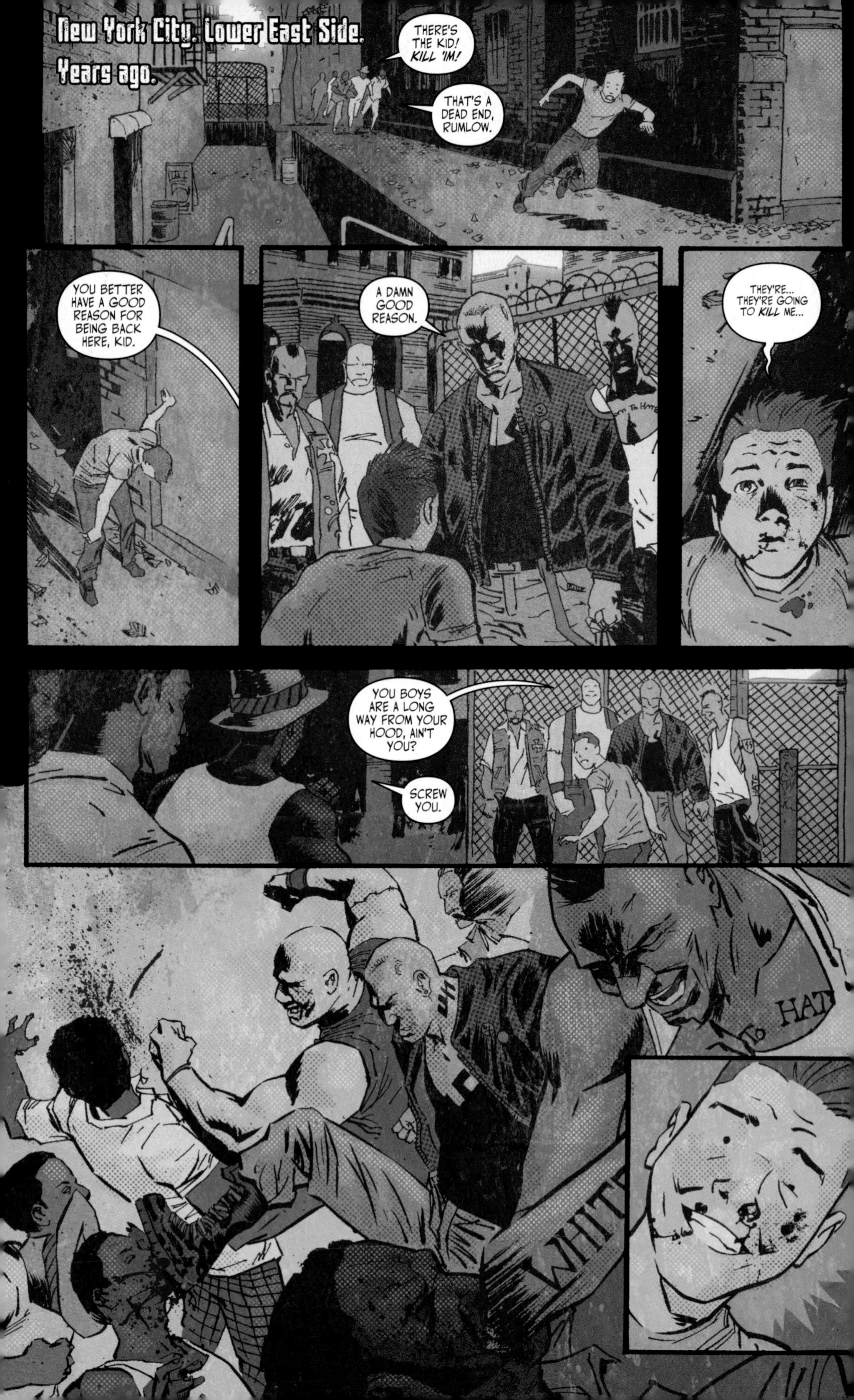
New York City. Lower East Side.
Years ago.
THERE'S THE KID! KILL 'IM!
THAT'S A DEAD END, RUMLOW.
YOU BETTER HAVE A GOOD REASON FOR BEING BACK HERE, KID.
A DAMN GOOD REASON.
THEY'RE... THEY'RE GOING TO KILL ME...
YOU BOYS ARE A LONG WAY FROM YOUR HOOD, AIN'T YOU?
SCREW YOU.

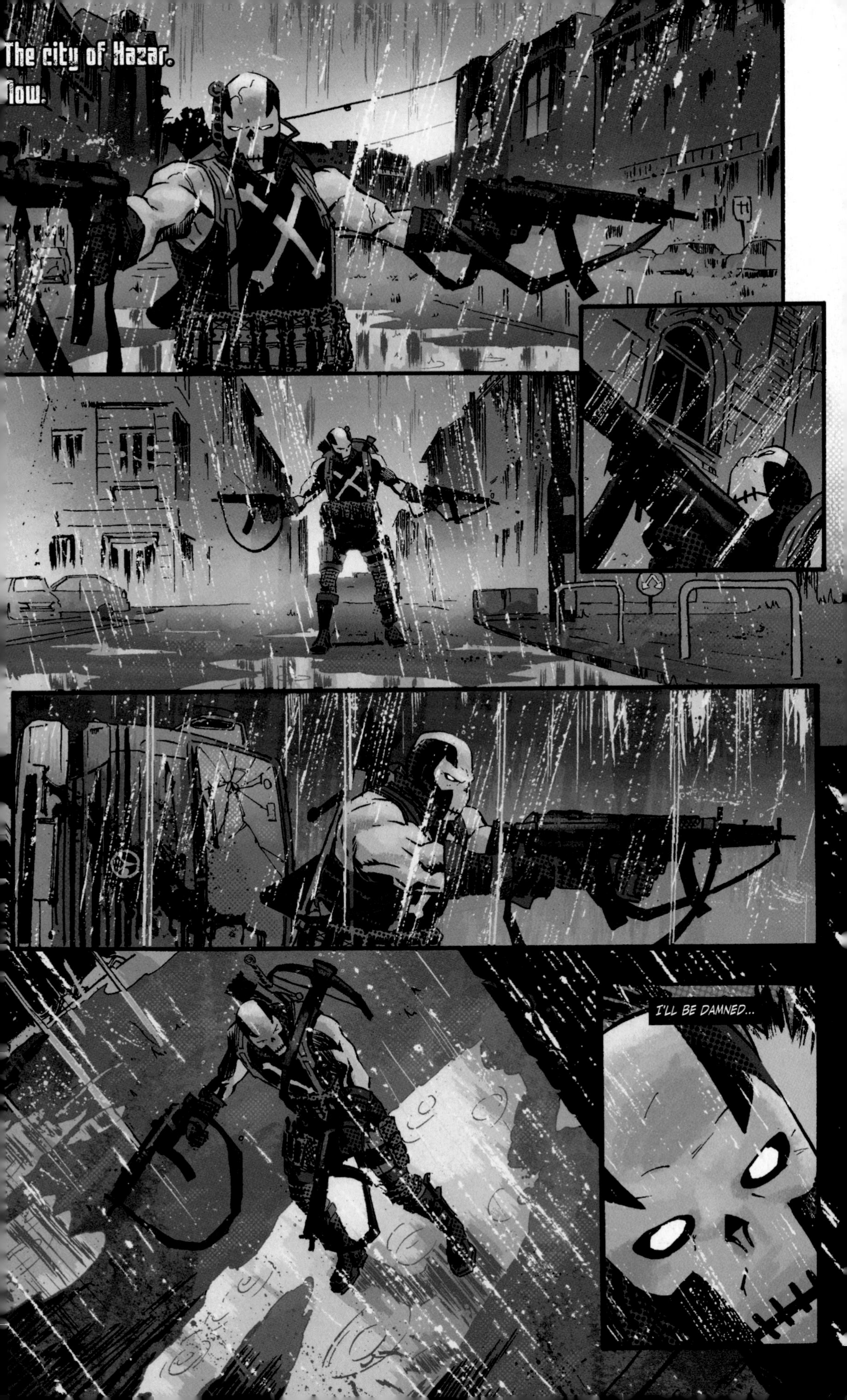
The city of Hazar.
Now.
I'LL BE DAMNED...

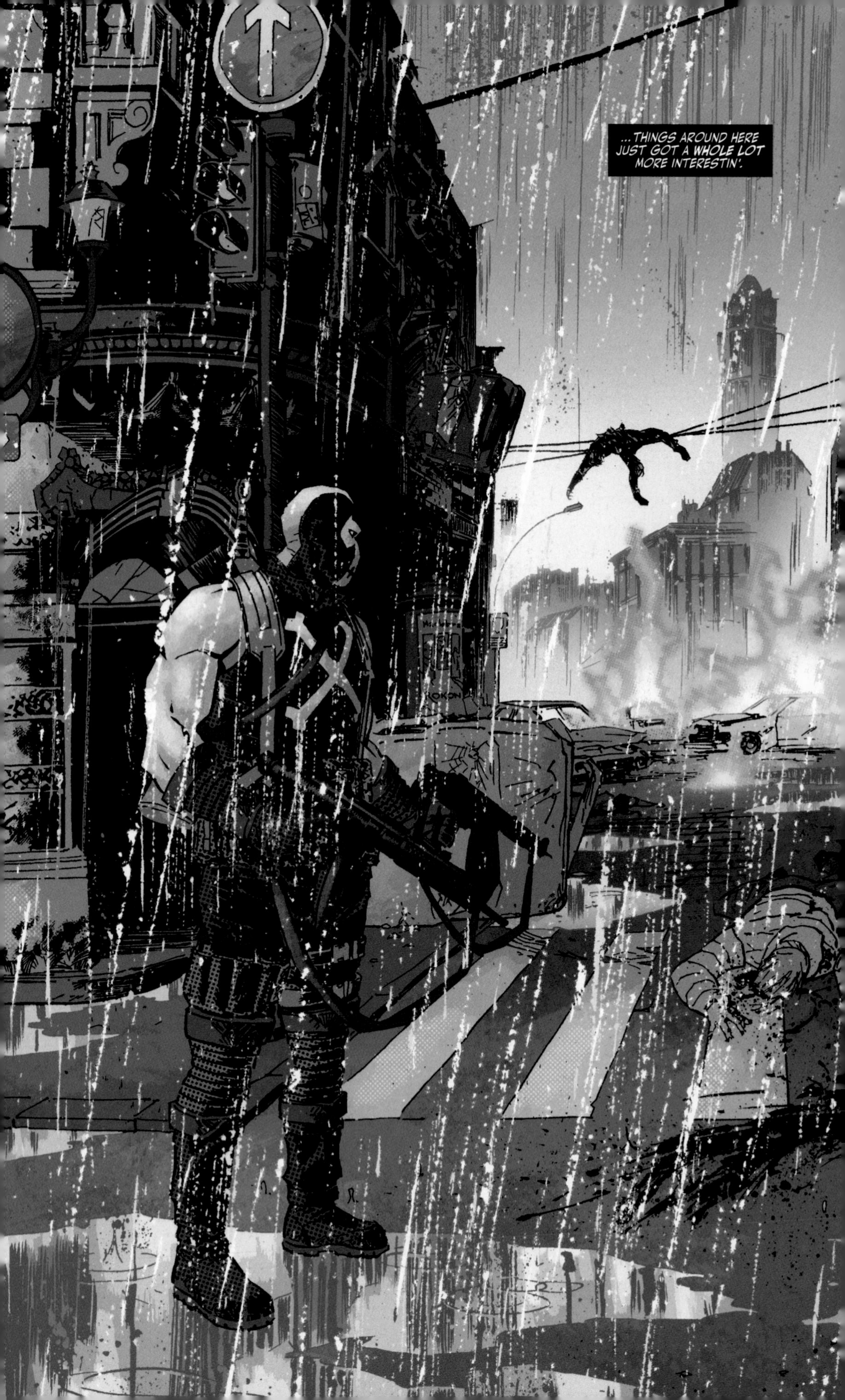
...THINGS AROUND HERE JUST GOT A WHOLE LOT MORE INTERESTIN'.

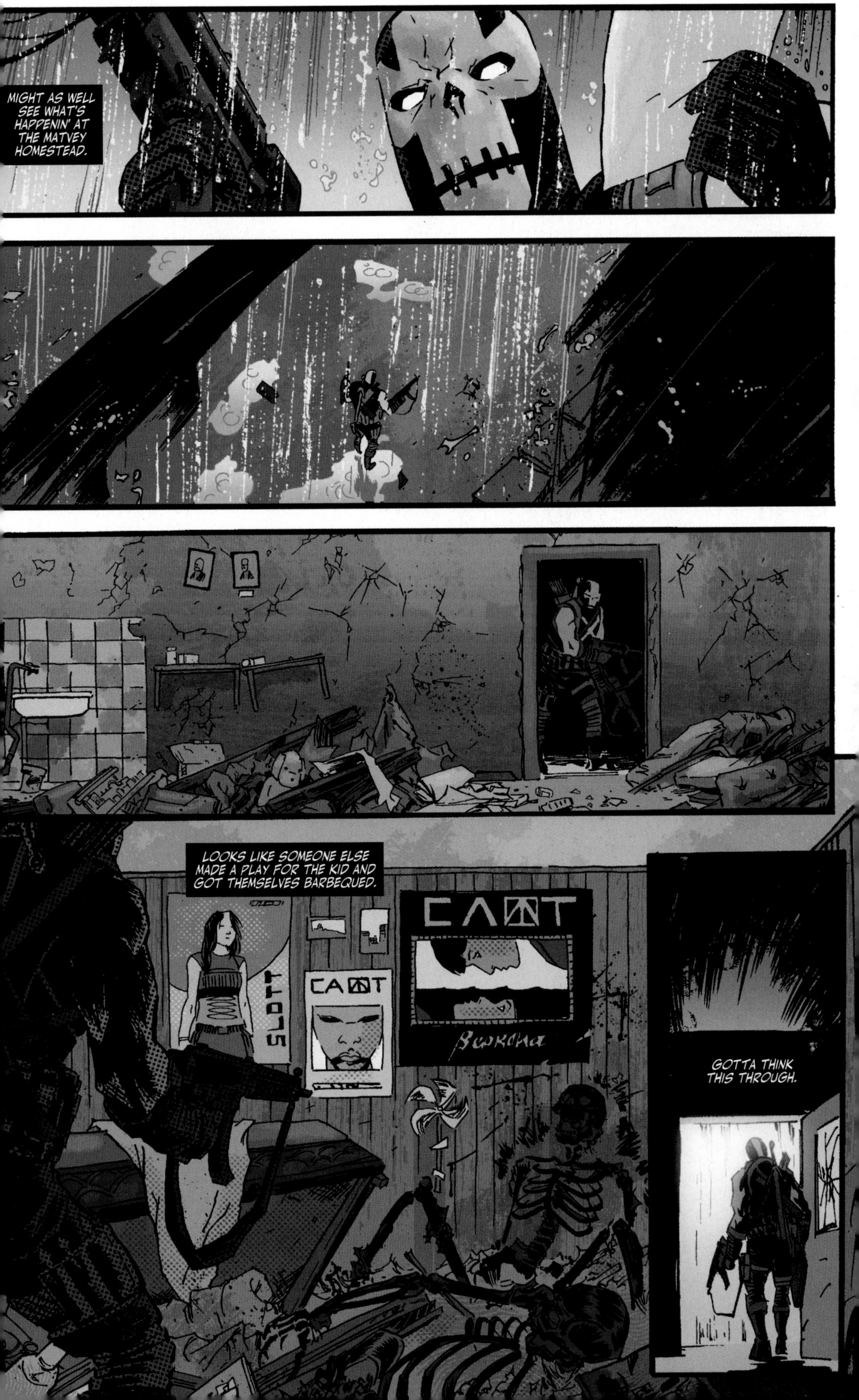
MIGHT AS WELL SEE WHAT'S HAPPENIN' AT THE MATVEY HOMESTEAD.
LOOKS LIKE SOMEONE ELSE MADE A PLAY FOR THE KID AND GOT THEMSELVES BARBEQUED.
GOTTA THINK THIS THROUGH.

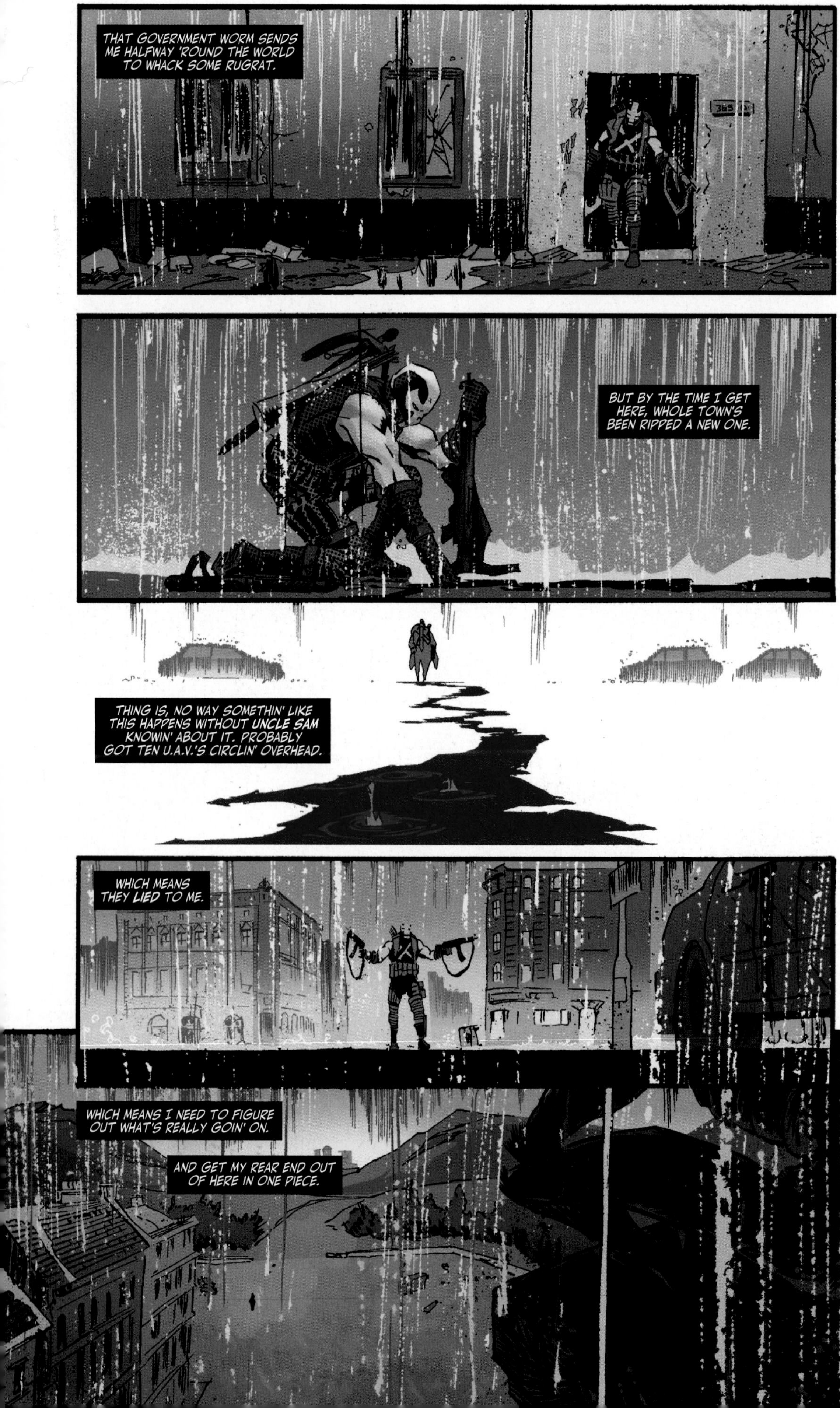
THAT GOVERNMENT WORM SENDS ME HALFWAY 'ROUND THE WORLD TO WHACK SOME RUGRAT.
BUT BY THE TIME I GET HERE, WHOLE TOWN'S BEEN RIPPED A NEW ONE.
THING IS, NO WAY SOMETHIN' LIKE THIS HAPPENS WITHOUT UNCLE SAM KNOWIN' ABOUT IT. PROBABLY GOT TEN U.A.V.'S CIRCLIN' OVERHEAD.
WHICH MEANS THEY LIED TO ME.
WHICH MEANS I NEED TO FIGURE OUT WHAT'S REALLY GOIN' ON.
AND GET MY REAR END OUT OF HERE IN ONE PIECE.

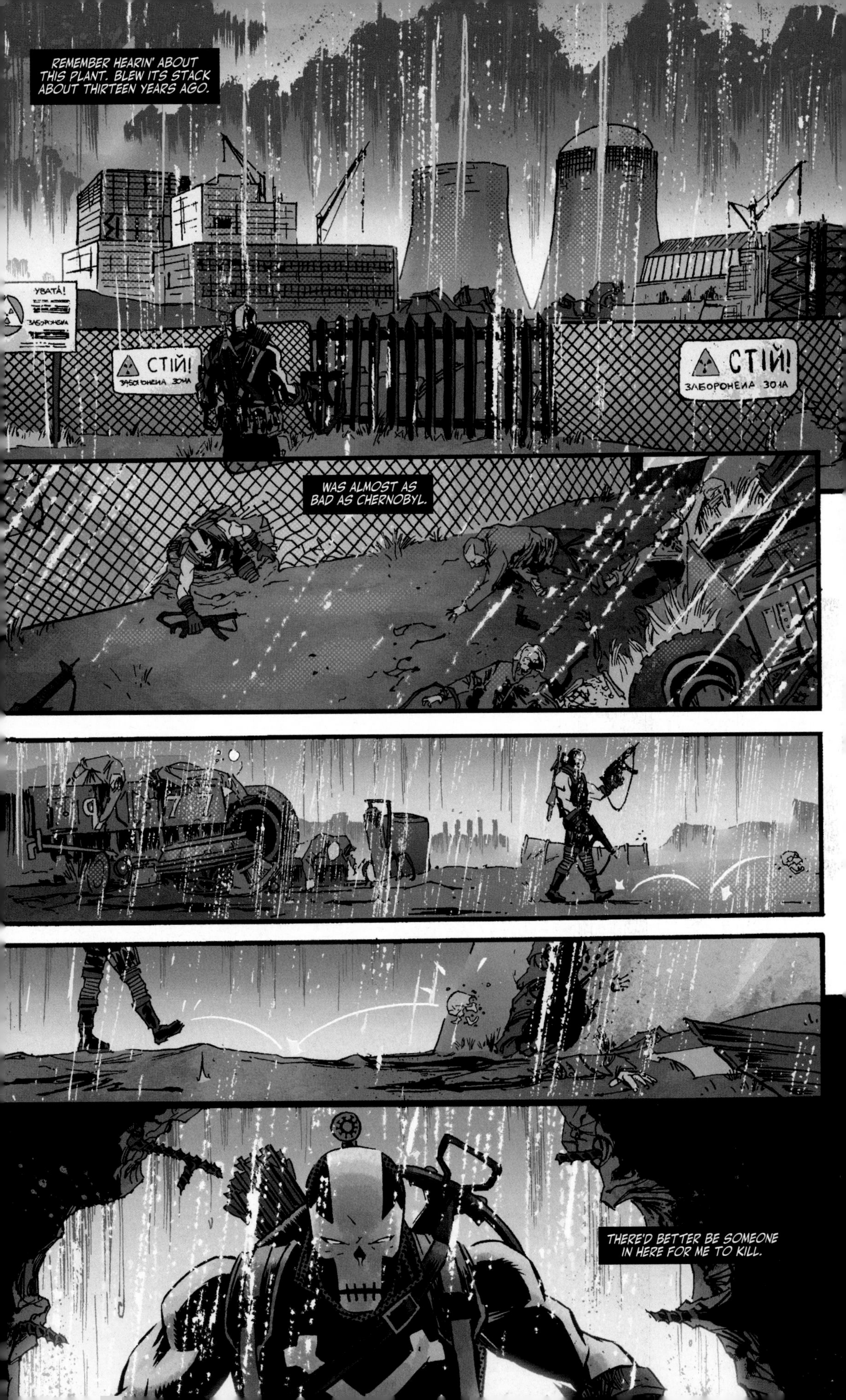
REMEMBER HEARIN' ABOUT THIS PLANT. BLEW ITS STACK ABOUT THIRTEEN YEARS AGO.
СТІЙ!
СТІЙ!
ЗАБОРОНЕНА ЗОНА
WAS ALMOST AS BAD AS CHERNOBYL.
THERE'D BETTER BE SOMEONE IN HERE FOR ME TO KILL.

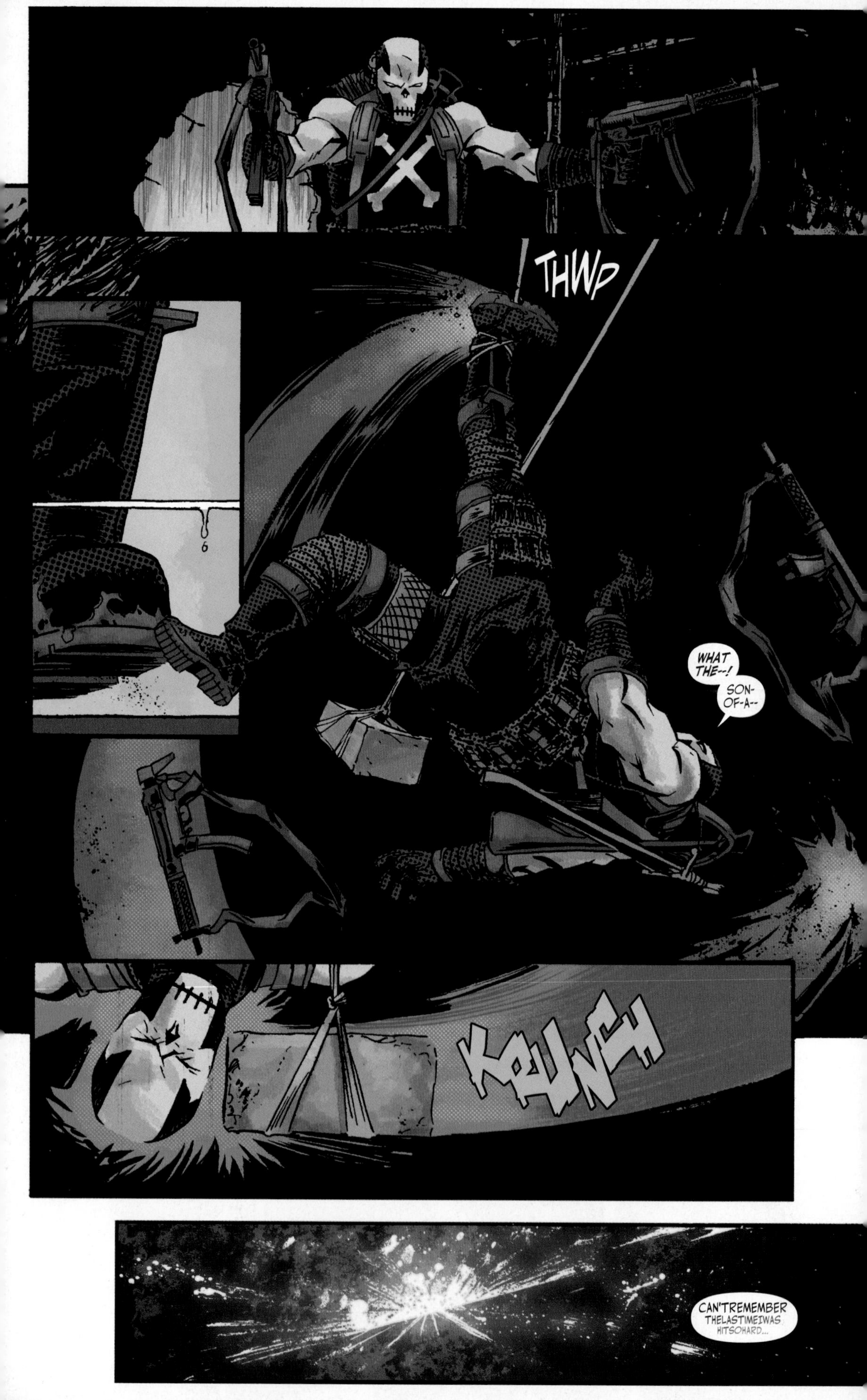
THWP
WHAT THE--! SON-OF-A--
KRUNCH
CAN'TREMEMBER THELASTIMEIWAS HITSOHARD...

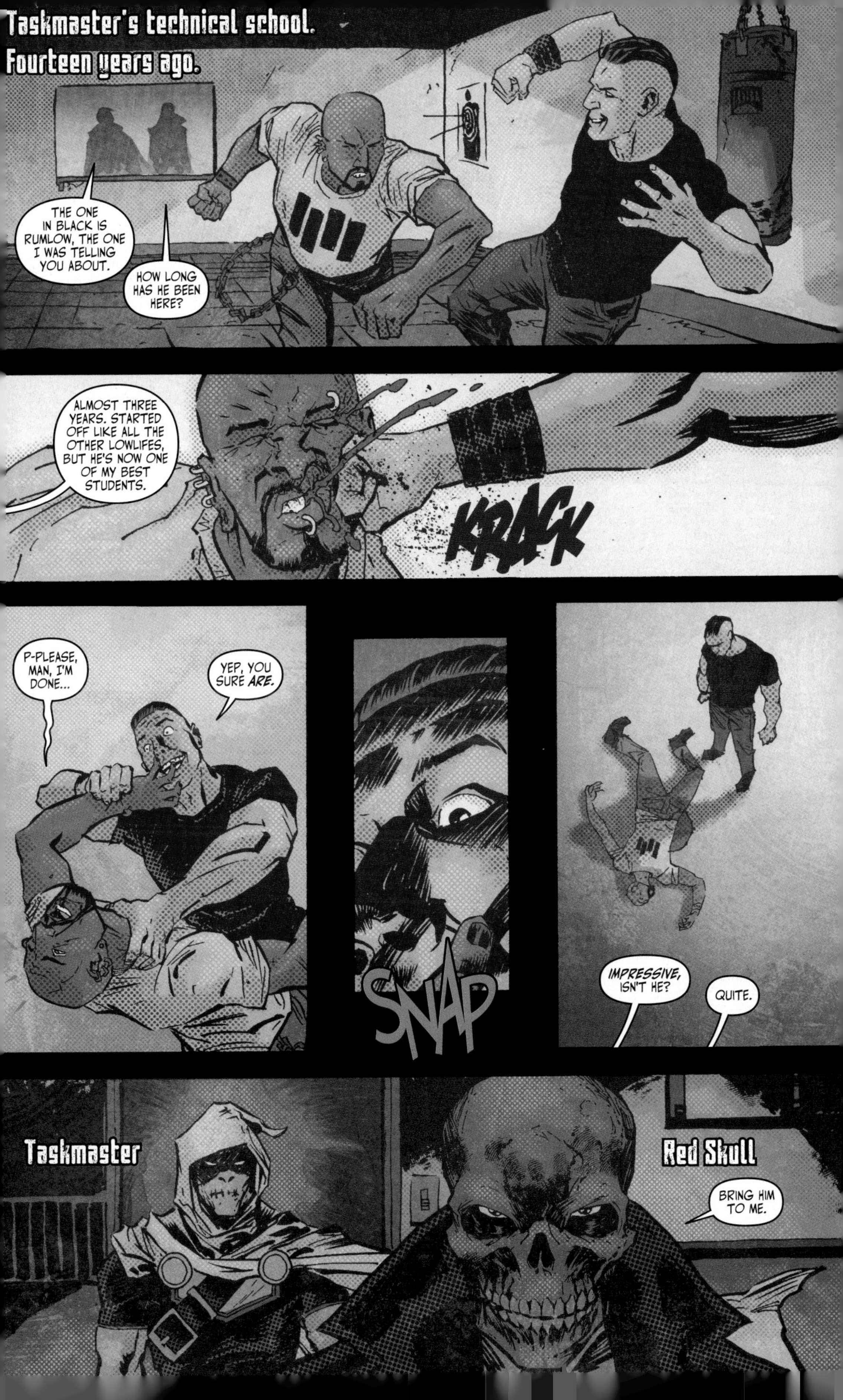

Taskmaster's technical school.
Fourteen years ago.
THE ONE IN BLACK IS RUMLOW, THE ONE I WAS TELLING YOU ABOUT.
HOW LONG HAS HE BEEN HERE?
ALMOST THREE YEARS. STARTED OFF LIKE ALL THE OTHER LOWLIFES, BUT HE'S NOW ONE OF MY BEST STUDENTS.
KRACK
P-PLEASE, MAN, I'M DONE...
YEP, YOU SURE *ARE*.
SNAP
IMPRESSIVE, ISN'T HE?
QUITE.
Taskmaster
Red Skull
BRING HIM TO ME.

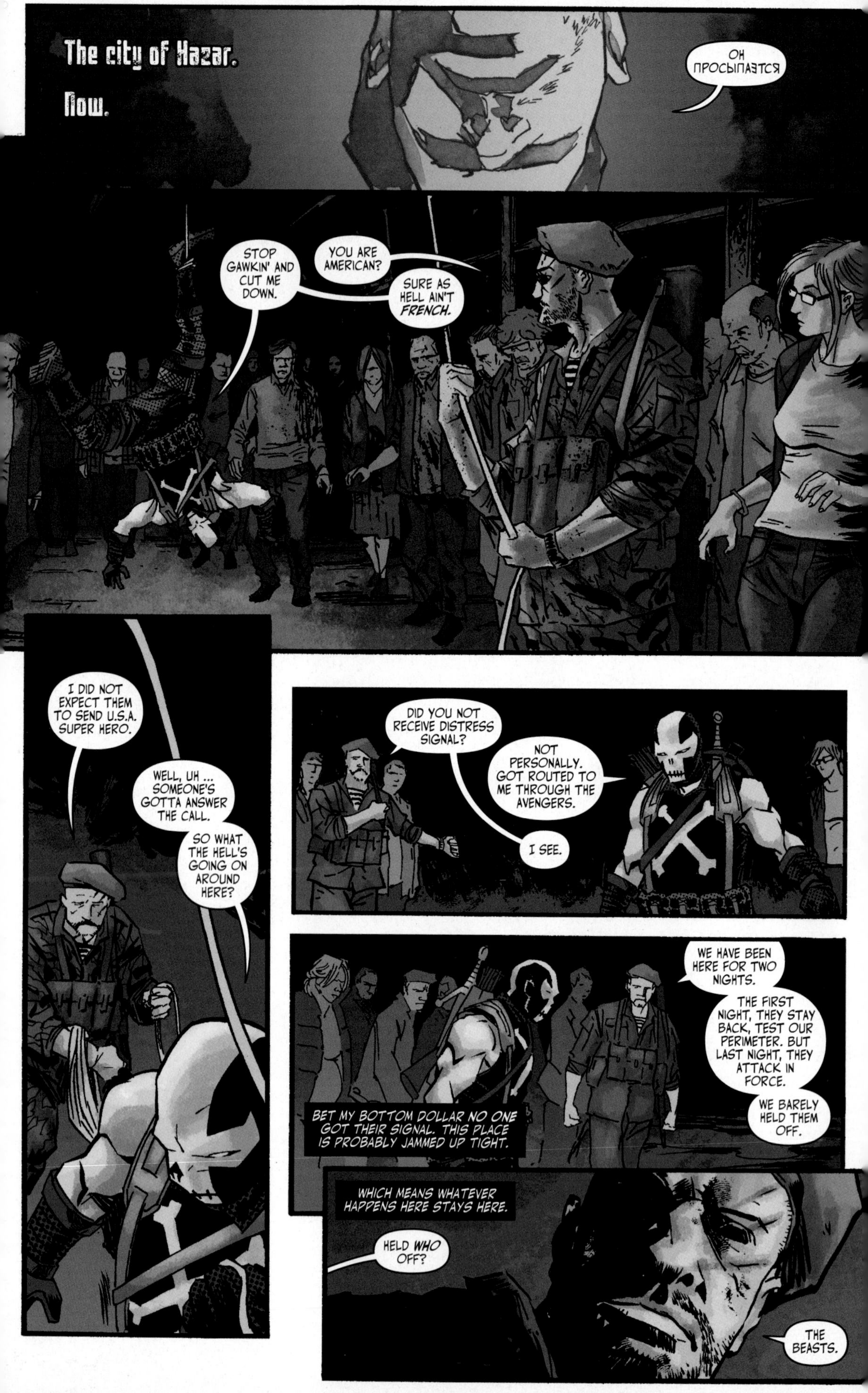
The city of Hazar.
Now.
ОН ПРОСЫПАЭТСЯ
STOP GAWKIN' AND CUT ME DOWN.
YOU ARE AMERICAN?
SURE AS HELL AIN'T FRENCH.
I DID NOT EXPECT THEM TO SEND U.S.A. SUPER HERO.
WELL, UH ... SOMEONE'S GOTTA ANSWER THE CALL.
SO WHAT THE HELL'S GOING ON AROUND HERE?
DID YOU NOT RECEIVE DISTRESS SIGNAL?
NOT PERSONALLY. GOT ROUTED TO ME THROUGH THE AVENGERS.
I SEE.
WE HAVE BEEN HERE FOR TWO NIGHTS.
THE FIRST NIGHT, THEY STAY BACK, TEST OUR PERIMETER. BUT LAST NIGHT, THEY ATTACK IN FORCE.
WE BARELY HELD THEM OFF.
BET MY BOTTOM DOLLAR NO ONE GOT THEIR SIGNAL. THIS PLACE IS PROBABLY JAMMED UP TIGHT.
WHICH MEANS WHATEVER HAPPENS HERE STAYS HERE.
HELD WHO OFF?
THE BEASTS.

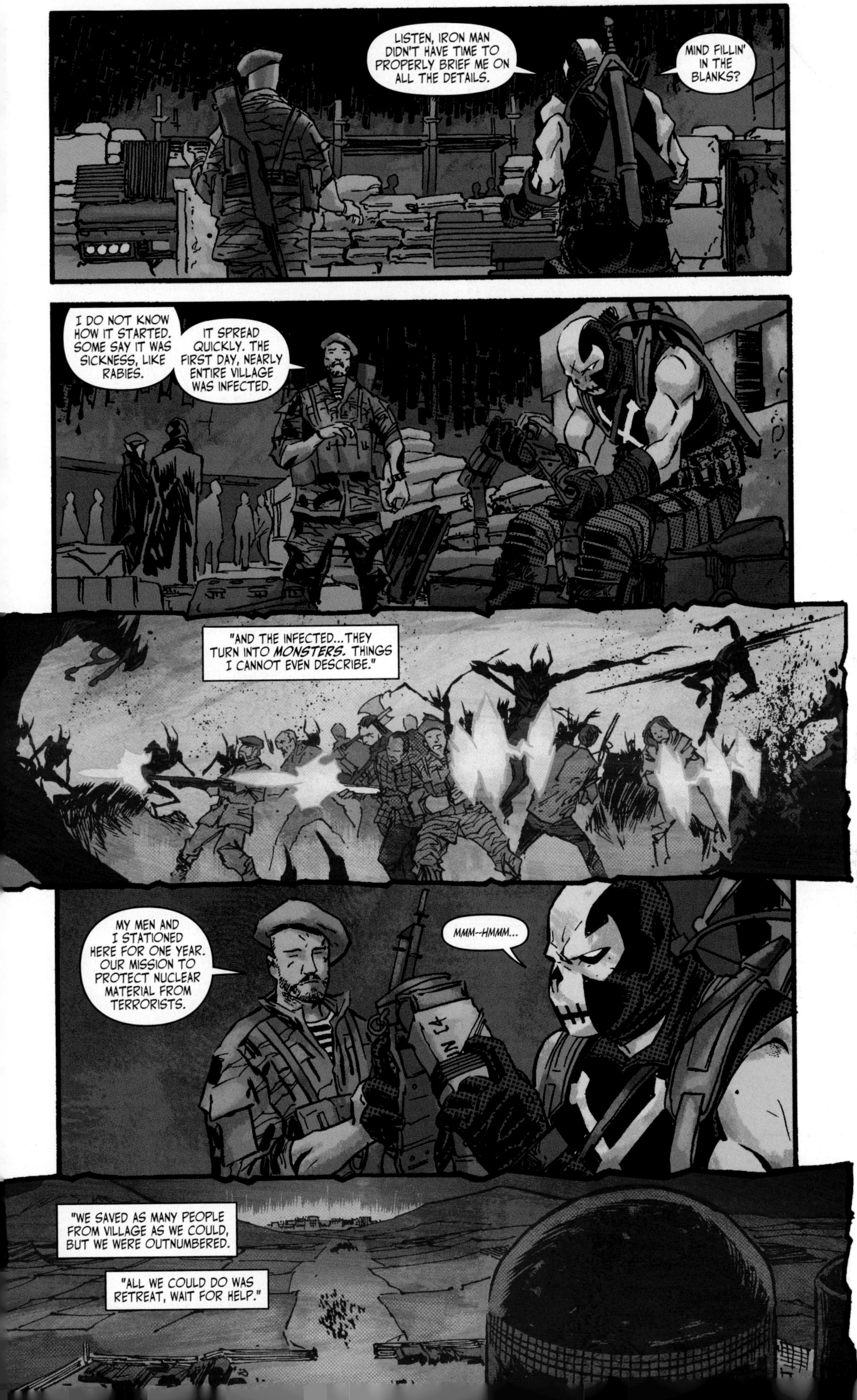
LISTEN, IRON MAN DIDN'T HAVE TIME TO PROPERLY BRIEF ME ON ALL THE DETAILS.
MIND FILLIN' IN THE BLANKS?
I DO NOT KNOW HOW IT STARTED. SOME SAY IT WAS SICKNESS, LIKE RABIES.
IT SPREAD QUICKLY. THE FIRST DAY, NEARLY ENTIRE VILLAGE WAS INFECTED.
"AND THE INFECTED...THEY TURN INTO *MONSTERS.* THINGS I CANNOT EVEN DESCRIBE."
MY MEN AND I STATIONED HERE FOR ONE YEAR. OUR MISSION TO PROTECT NUCLEAR MATERIAL FROM TERRORISTS.
MMM--HMMM...
"WE SAVED AS MANY PEOPLE FROM VILLAGE AS WE COULD, BUT WE WERE OUTNUMBERED.
"ALL WE COULD DO WAS RETREAT, WAIT FOR HELP."

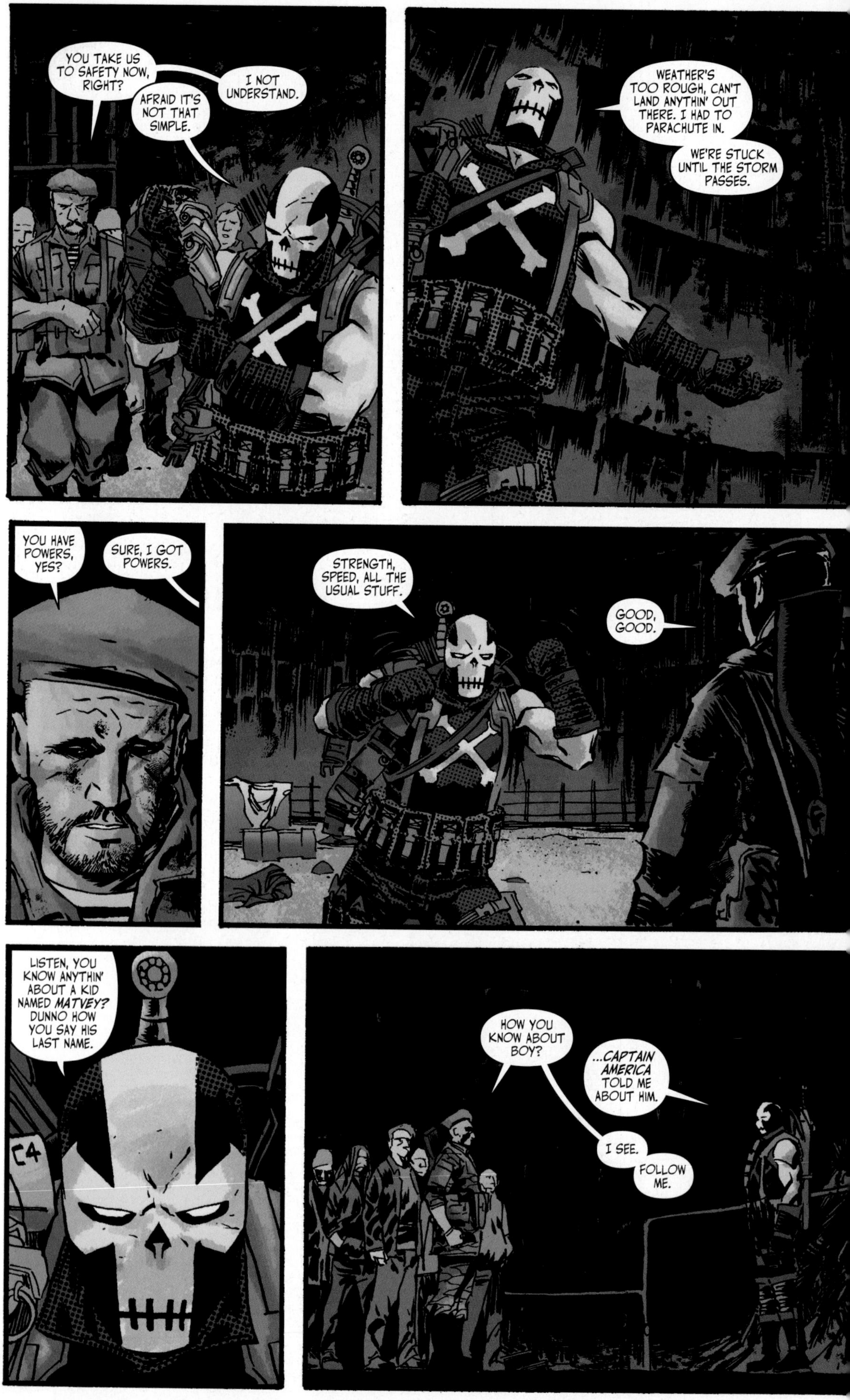
YOU TAKE US TO SAFETY NOW, RIGHT?
AFRAID IT'S NOT THAT SIMPLE.
I NOT UNDERSTAND.
WEATHER'S TOO ROUGH, CAN'T LAND ANYTHIN' OUT THERE. I HAD TO PARACHUTE IN.
WE'RE STUCK UNTIL THE STORM PASSES.
YOU HAVE POWERS, YES?
SURE, I GOT POWERS.
STRENGTH, SPEED, ALL THE USUAL STUFF.
GOOD, GOOD.
LISTEN, YOU KNOW ANYTHIN' ABOUT A KID NAMED *MATVEY?* DUNNO HOW YOU SAY HIS LAST NAME.
C4
HOW YOU KNOW ABOUT BOY?
...*CAPTAIN AMERICA* TOLD ME ABOUT HIM.
I SEE.
FOLLOW ME.

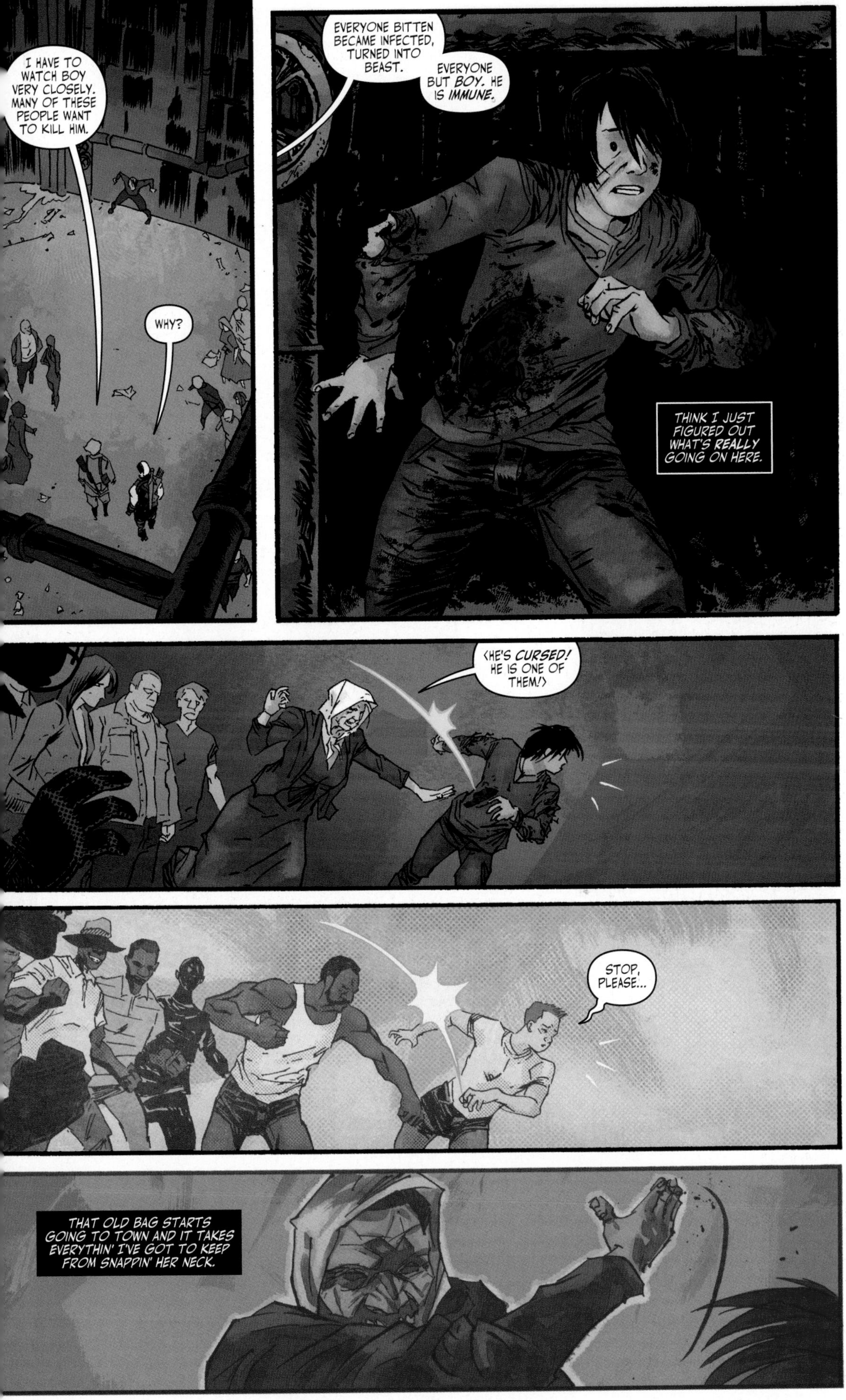
I HAVE TO WATCH BOY VERY CLOSELY. MANY OF THESE PEOPLE WANT TO KILL HIM.
WHY?
EVERYONE BITTEN BECAME INFECTED, TURNED INTO BEAST.
EVERYONE BUT BOY. HE IS IMMUNE.
THINK I JUST FIGURED OUT WHAT'S REALLY GOING ON HERE.
‹HE'S CURSED! HE IS ONE OF THEM!›
STOP, PLEASE...
THAT OLD BAG STARTS GOING TO TOWN AND IT TAKES EVERYTHIN' I'VE GOT TO KEEP FROM SNAPPIN' HER NECK.

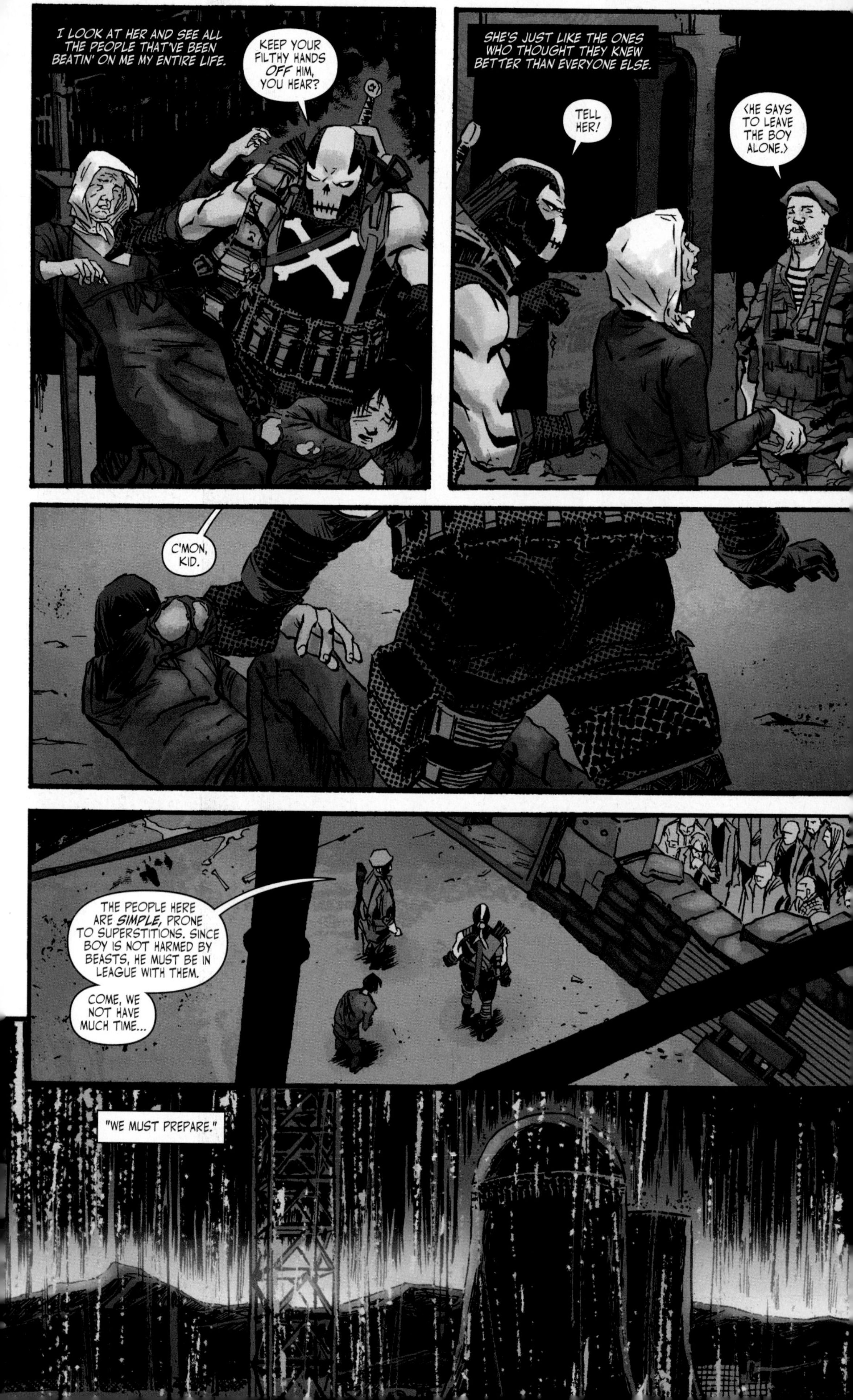
I LOOK AT HER AND SEE ALL THE PEOPLE THAT'VE BEEN BEATIN' ON ME MY ENTIRE LIFE.
KEEP YOUR FILTHY HANDS *OFF* HIM, YOU HEAR?
SHE'S JUST LIKE THE ONES WHO THOUGHT THEY KNEW BETTER THAN EVERYONE ELSE.
TELL HER!
<HE SAYS TO LEAVE THE BOY ALONE.>
C'MON, KID.
THE PEOPLE HERE ARE *SIMPLE,* PRONE TO SUPERSTITIONS. SINCE BOY IS NOT HARMED BY BEASTS, HE MUST BE IN LEAGUE WITH THEM.
COME, WE NOT HAVE MUCH TIME...
"WE MUST PREPARE."

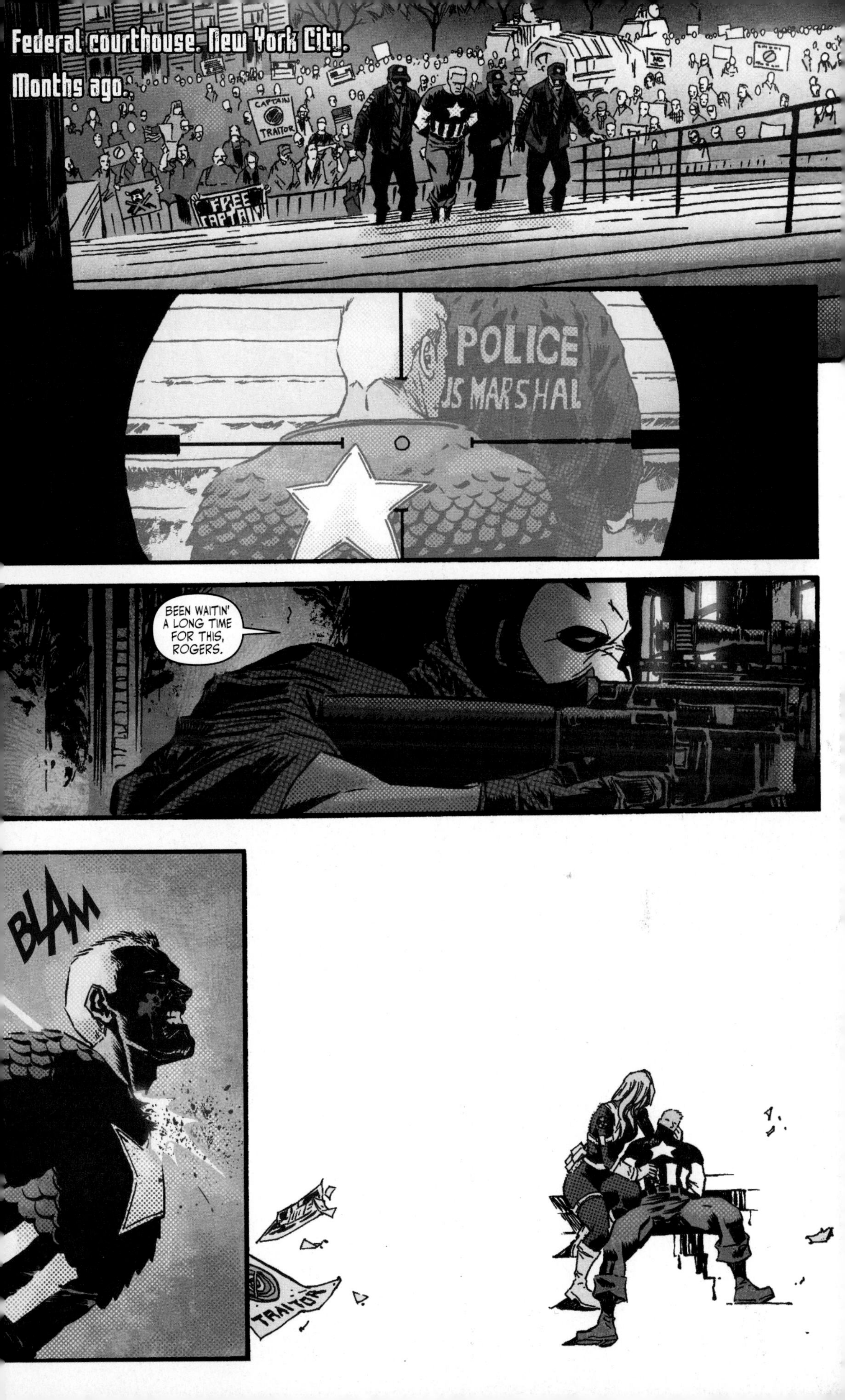
Federal courthouse. New York City.
Months ago.
CAPTAIN TRAITOR
FREE CAPTAIN
POLICE
US MARSHAL
BEEN WAITIN' A LONG TIME FOR THIS, ROGERS.
BLAM
TRAITOR

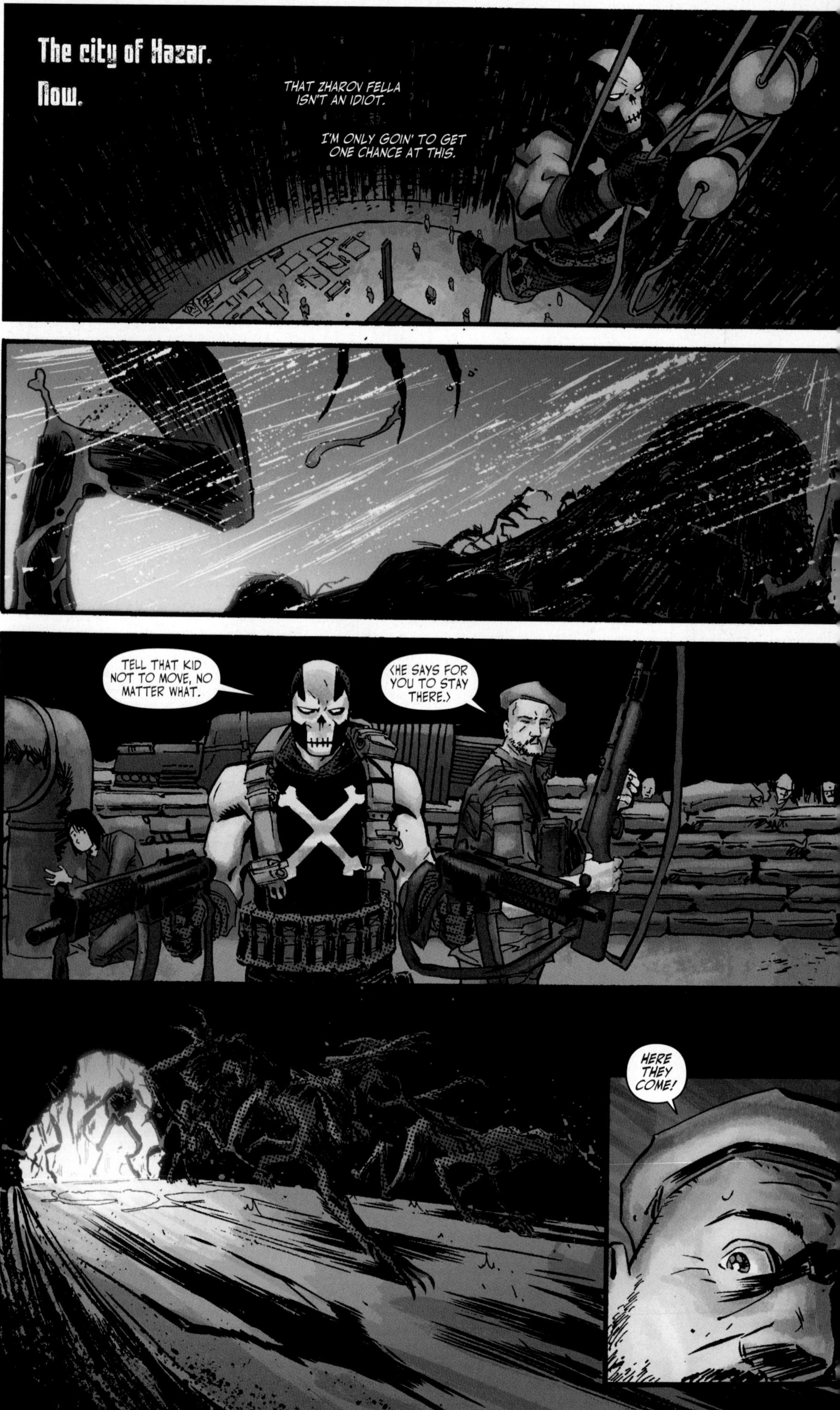

The city of Hazar.
Now.
THAT ZHAROV FELLA ISN'T AN IDIOT.
I'M ONLY GOIN' TO GET ONE CHANCE AT THIS.
TELL THAT KID NOT TO MOVE, NO MATTER WHAT.
<HE SAYS FOR YOU TO STAY THERE.>
HERE THEY COME!

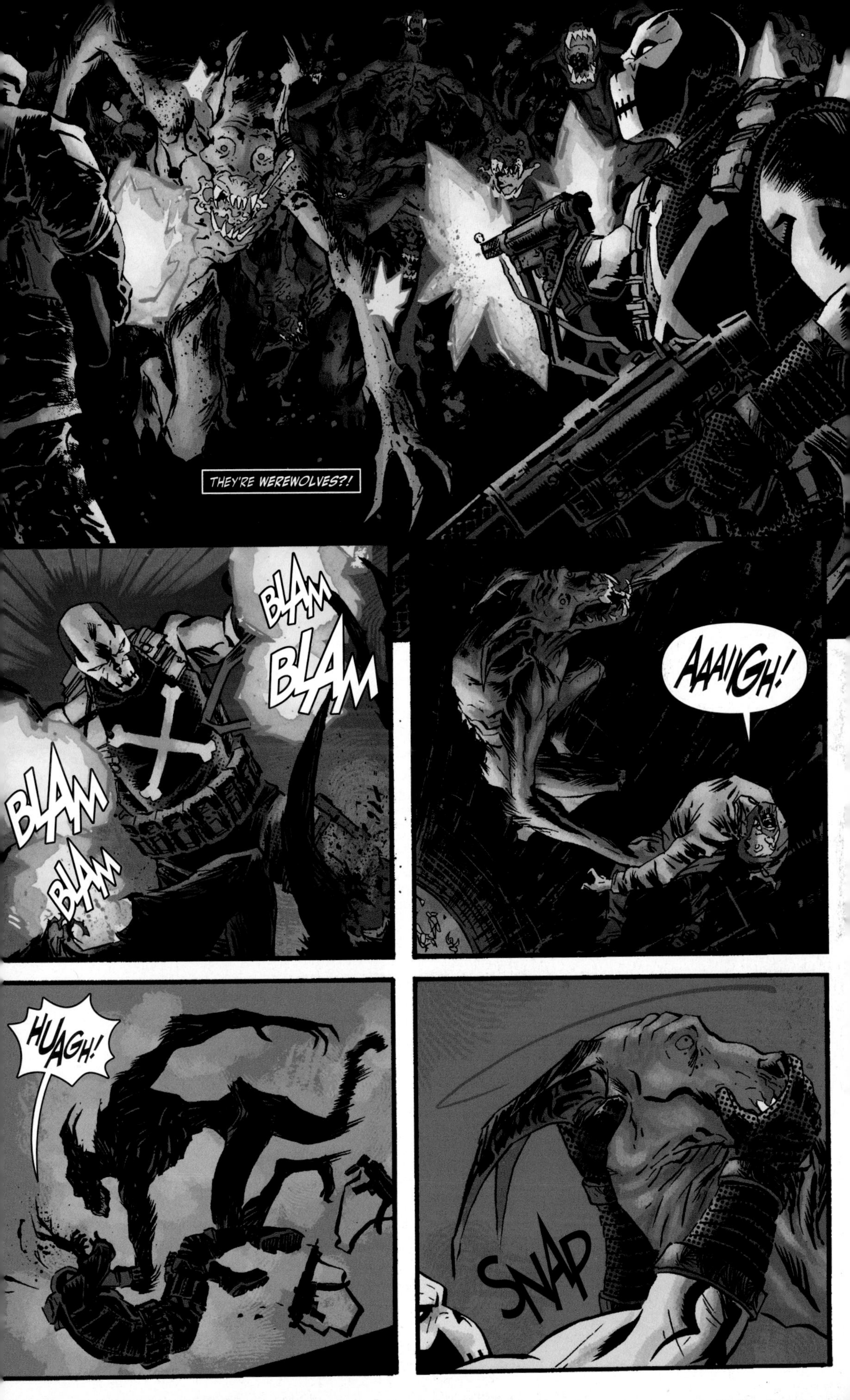
THEY'RE WEREWOLVES?!
BLAM
BLAM
BLAM
BLAM
AAAIIGH!
HUAGH!
SNAP

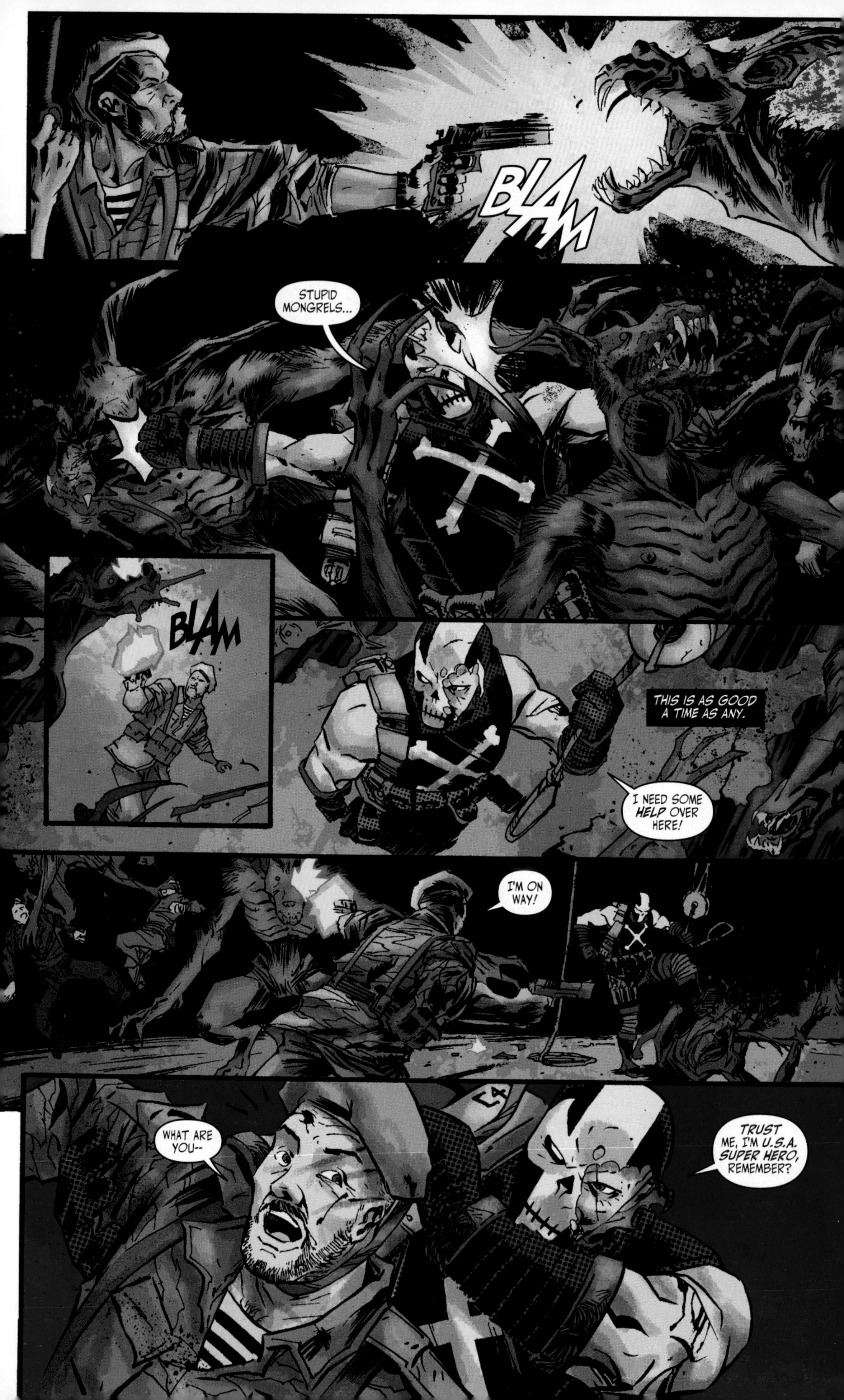
BLAM
STUPID MONGRELS...
BLAM
THIS IS AS GOOD A TIME AS ANY.
I NEED SOME HELP OVER HERE!
I'M ON WAY!
WHAT ARE YOU--
TRUST ME, I'M U.S.A. SUPER HERO, REMEMBER?

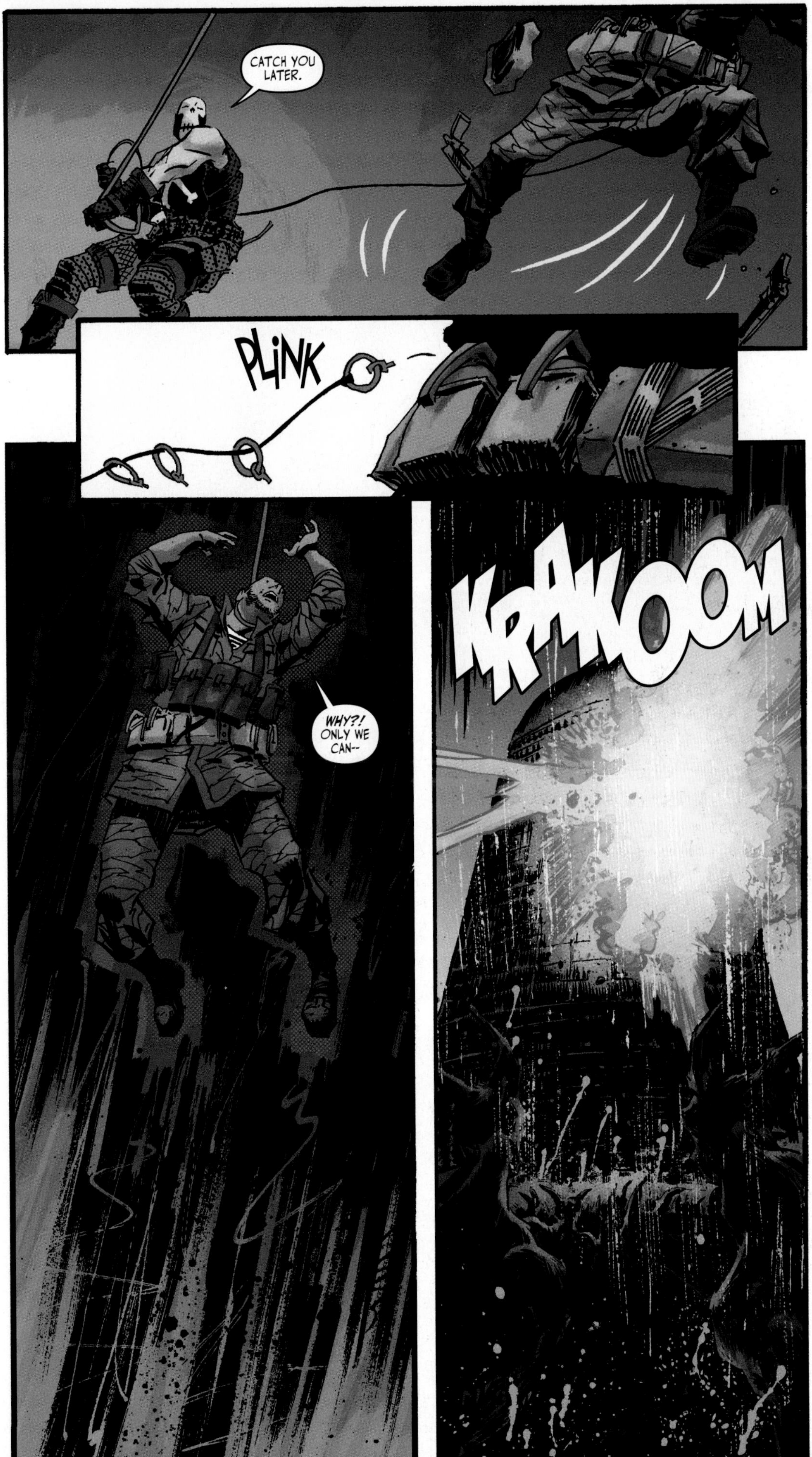
CATCH YOU LATER.
PLINK
WHY?! ONLY WE CAN--
KRAKOOM

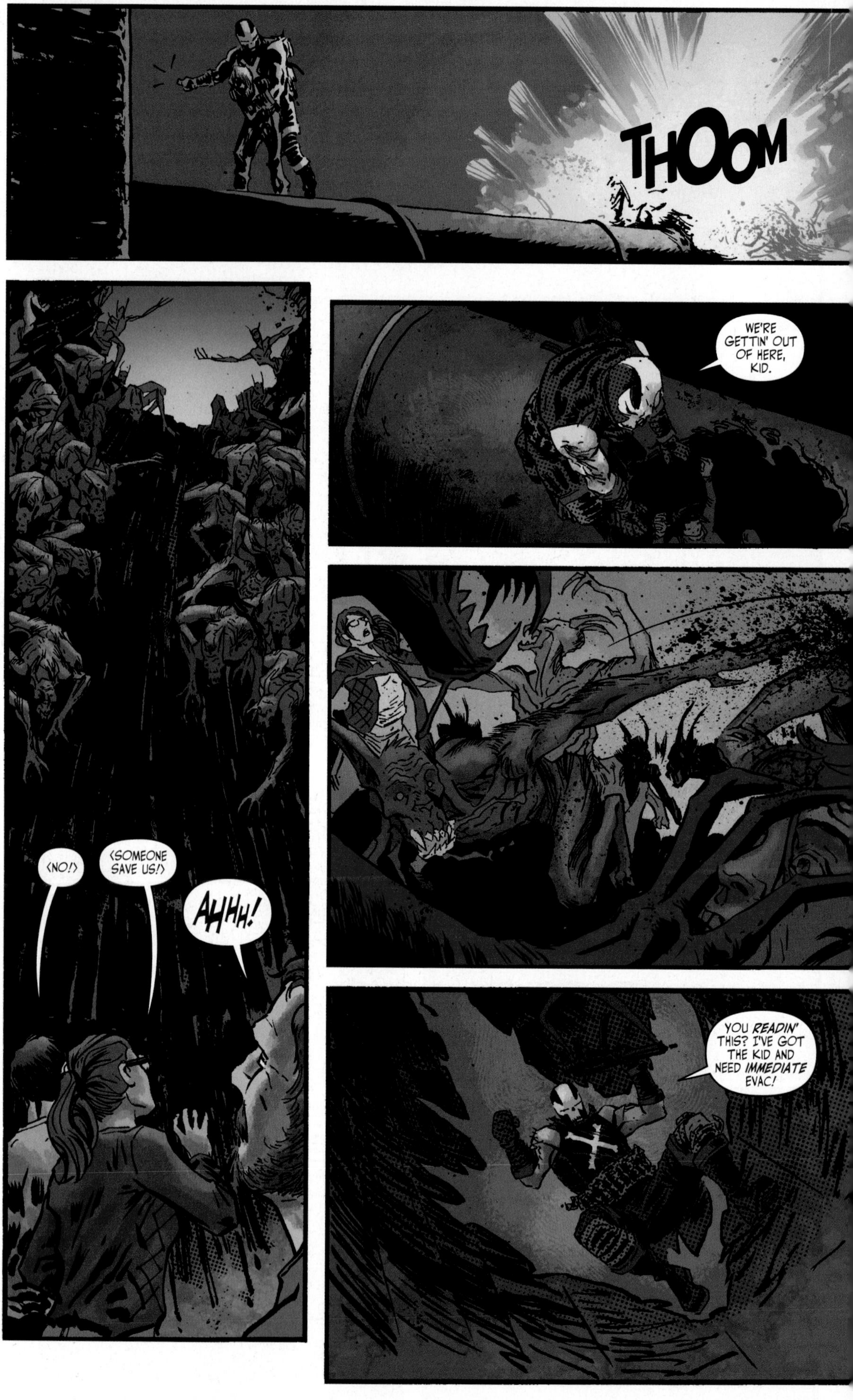
THOOM
WE'RE GETTIN' OUT OF HERE, KID.
<NO!>
<SOMEONE SAVE US!>
AHHH!
YOU READIN' THIS? I'VE GOT THE KID AND NEED IMMEDIATE EVAC!

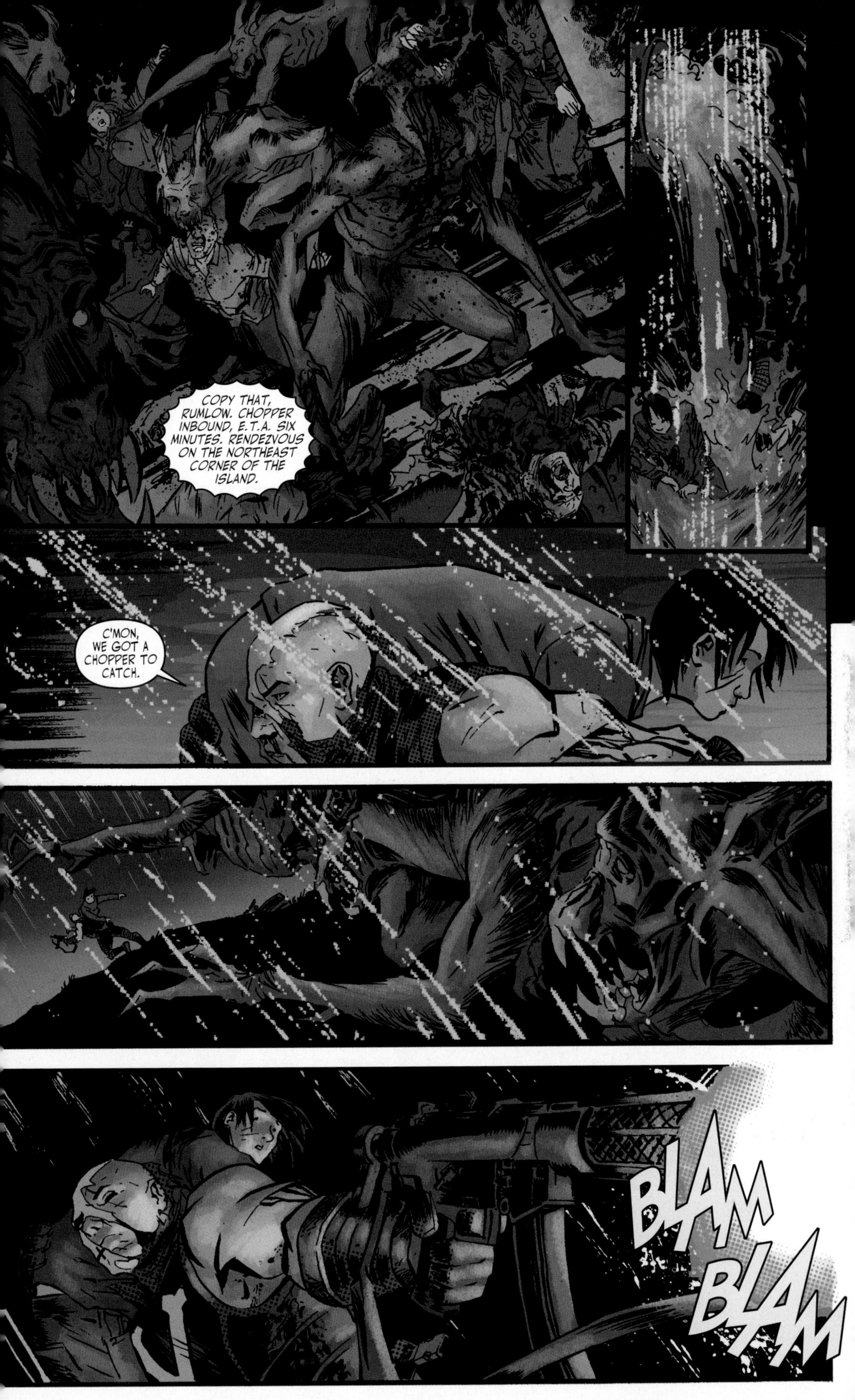
COPY THAT, RUMLOW. CHOPPER INBOUND, E.T.A. SIX MINUTES. RENDEZVOUS ON THE NORTHEAST CORNER OF THE ISLAND.
C'MON, WE GOT A CHOPPER TO CATCH.
BLAM
BLAM

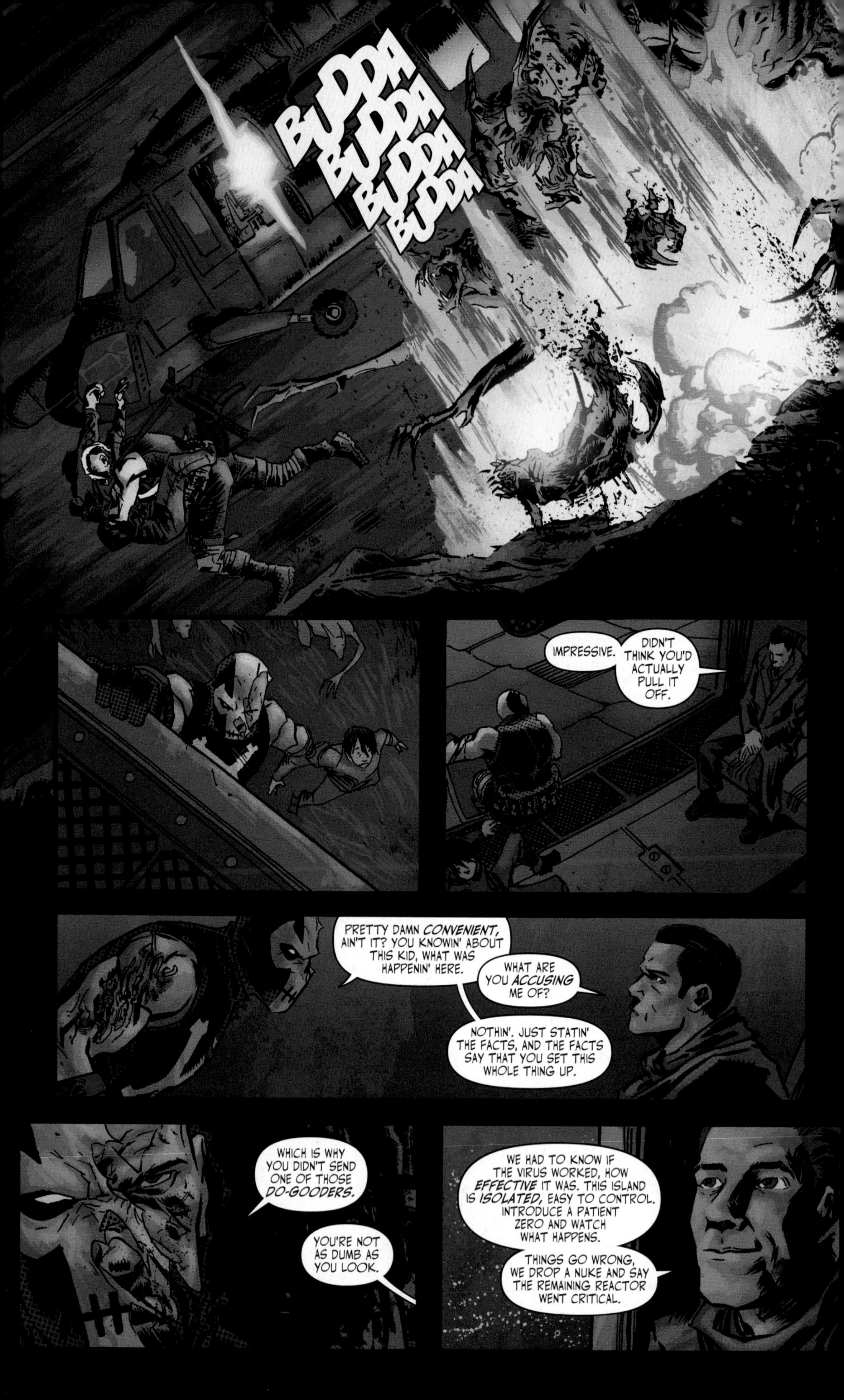
BUDDA BUDDA BUDDA BUDDA
IMPRESSIVE.
DIDN'T THINK YOU'D ACTUALLY PULL IT OFF.
PRETTY DAMN CONVENIENT, AIN'T IT? YOU KNOWIN' ABOUT THIS KID, WHAT WAS HAPPENIN' HERE.
WHAT ARE YOU ACCUSING ME OF?
NOTHIN'. JUST STATIN' THE FACTS, AND THE FACTS SAY THAT YOU SET THIS WHOLE THING UP.
WHICH IS WHY YOU DIDN'T SEND ONE OF THOSE DO-GOODERS.
YOU'RE NOT AS DUMB AS YOU LOOK.
WE HAD TO KNOW IF THE VIRUS WORKED, HOW EFFECTIVE IT WAS. THIS ISLAND IS ISOLATED, EASY TO CONTROL. INTRODUCE A PATIENT ZERO AND WATCH WHAT HAPPENS.
THINGS GO WRONG, WE DROP A NUKE AND SAY THE REMAINING REACTOR WENT CRITICAL.

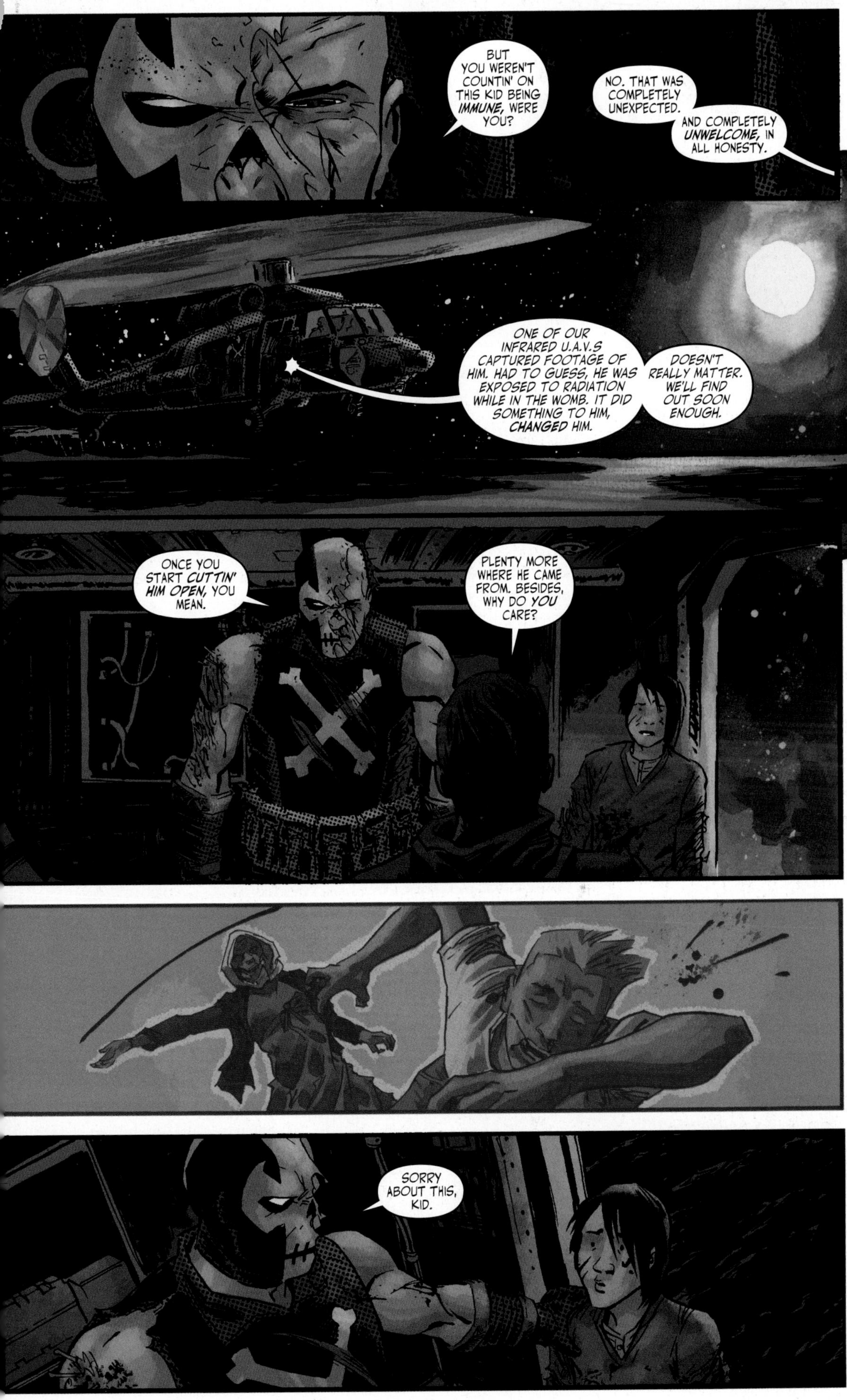
BUT YOU WEREN'T COUNTIN' ON THIS KID BEING *IMMUNE,* WERE YOU?
NO. THAT WAS COMPLETELY UNEXPECTED.
AND COMPLETELY *UNWELCOME,* IN ALL HONESTY.
ONE OF OUR INFRARED U.A.V.S CAPTURED FOOTAGE OF HIM. HAD TO GUESS, HE WAS EXPOSED TO RADIATION WHILE IN THE WOMB. IT DID SOMETHING TO HIM, CHANGED HIM.
DOESN'T REALLY MATTER. WE'LL FIND OUT SOON ENOUGH.
ONCE YOU START *CUTTIN' HIM OPEN,* YOU MEAN.
PLENTY MORE WHERE HE CAME FROM. BESIDES, WHY DO *YOU* CARE?
SORRY ABOUT THIS, KID.

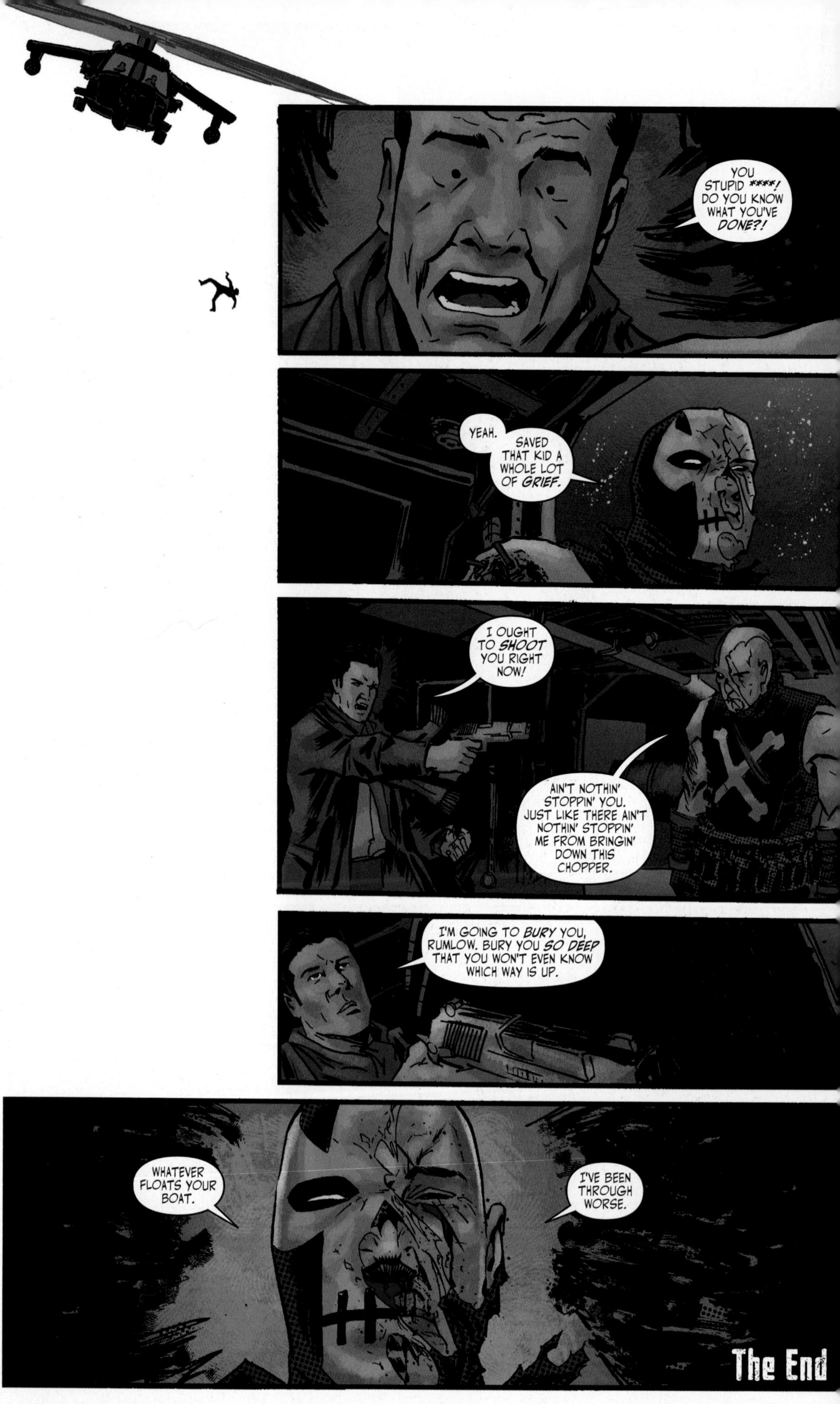
YOU STUPID ****! DO YOU KNOW WHAT YOU'VE DONE?!
YEAH.
SAVED THAT KID A WHOLE LOT OF GRIEF.
I OUGHT TO SHOOT YOU RIGHT NOW!
AIN'T NOTHIN' STOPPIN' YOU. JUST LIKE THERE AIN'T NOTHIN' STOPPIN' ME FROM BRINGIN' DOWN THIS CHOPPER.
I'M GOING TO BURY YOU, RUMLOW. BURY YOU SO DEEP THAT YOU WON'T EVEN KNOW WHICH WAY IS UP.
WHATEVER FLOATS YOUR BOAT.
I'VE BEEN THROUGH WORSE.
The End

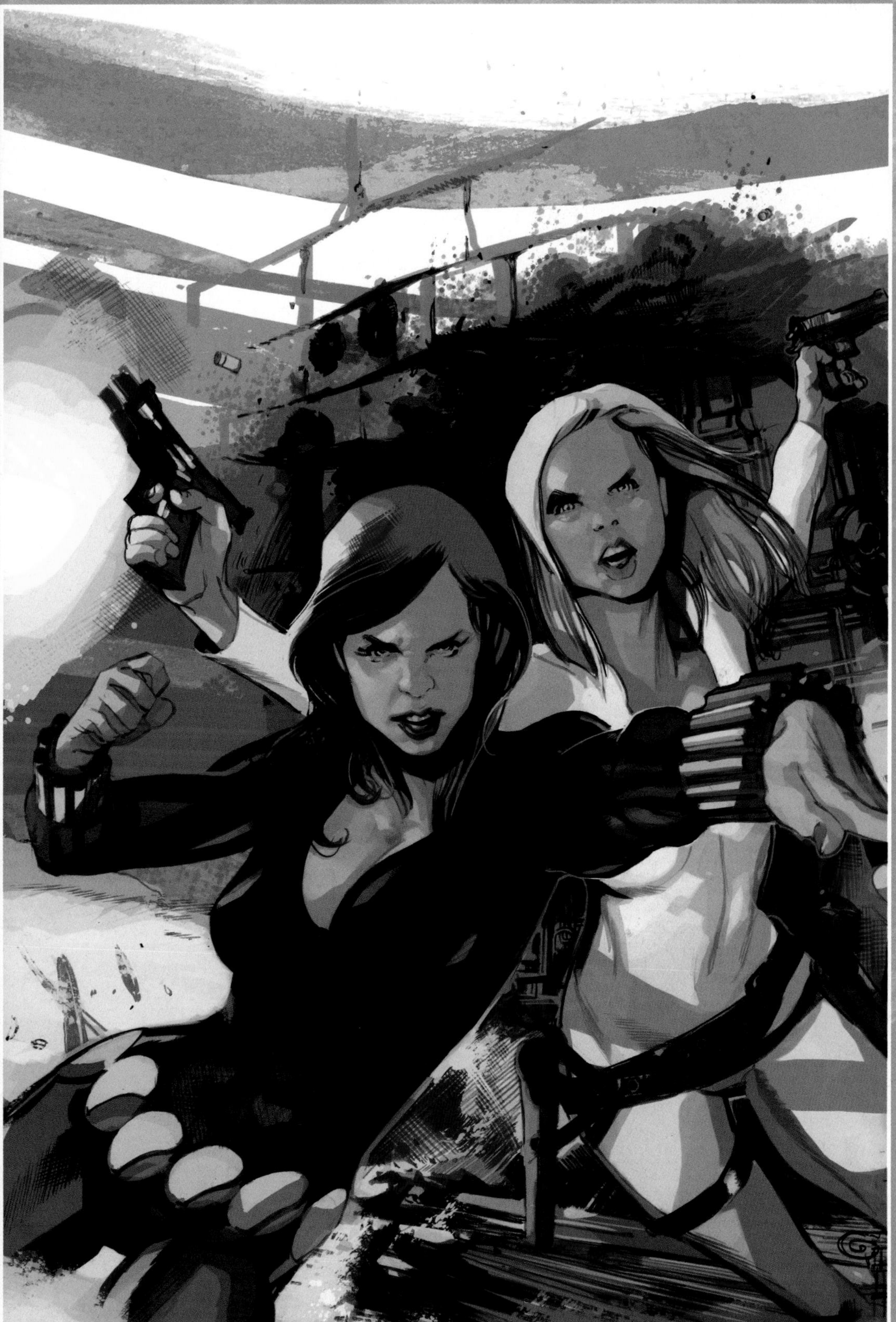

CAPTAIN AMERICA AND THE SECRET AVENGERS

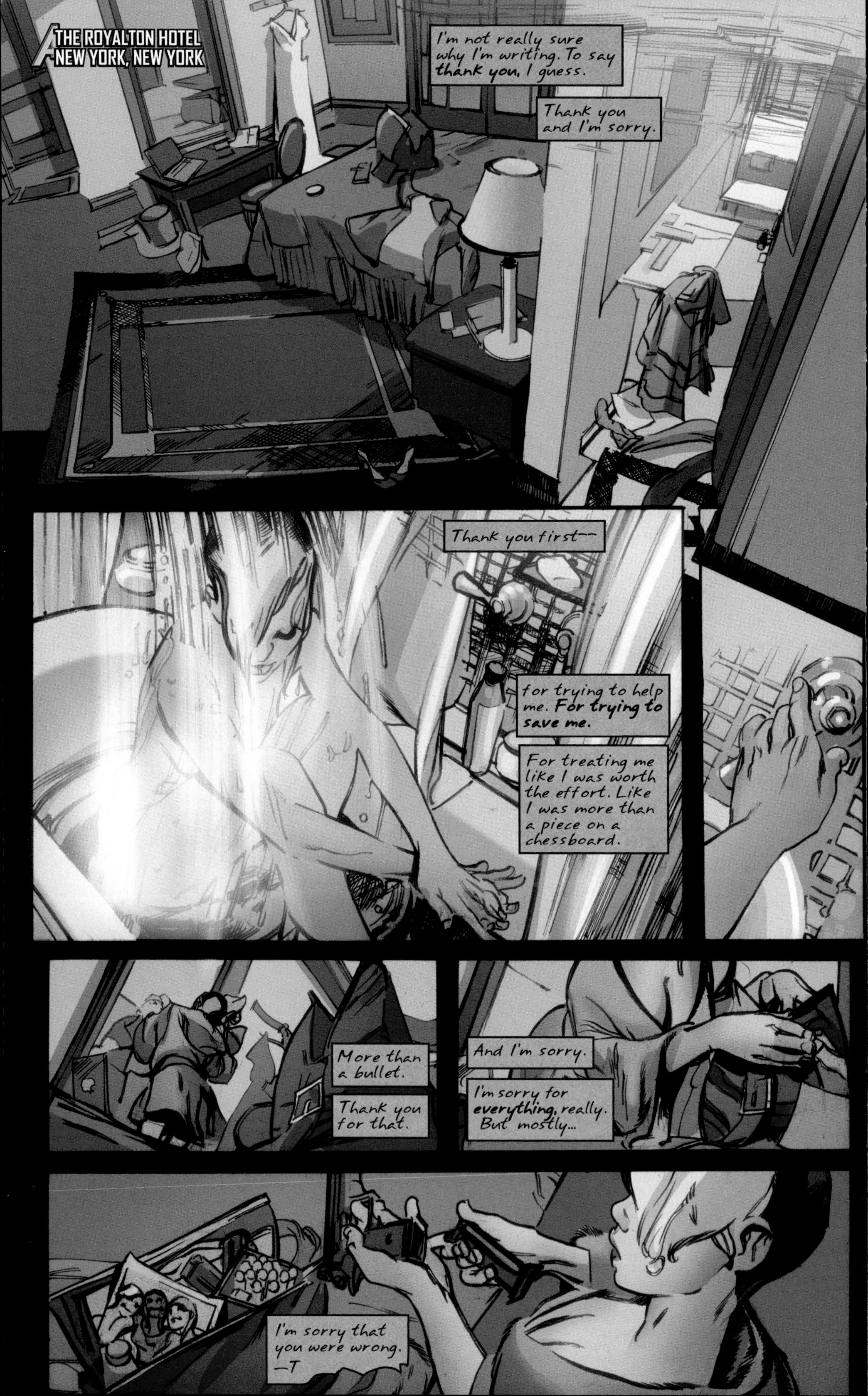
THE ROYALTON HOTEL NEW YORK, NEW YORK
I'm not really sure why I'm writing. To say **thank you**, I guess.
Thank you and I'm sorry.
Thank you first--
for trying to help me. **For trying to save me.**
For treating me like I was worth the effort. Like I was more than a piece on a chessboard.
More than a bullet.
Thank you for that.
And I'm sorry.
I'm sorry for **everything**, really. But mostly...
I'm sorry that you were wrong. —T

As World War II raged on, a young, scrawny Steve Rogers was selected to participate in Project: Rebirth to become the living embodiment of the American Spirit: Captain America!

CAPTAIN ☆ AMERICA

AND THE

SECRET AVENGERS

Brought together by the former Captain America Steve Rogers as a black ops unit to handle the world's deadliest threats, Black Widow, Moon Knight, Beast, Ant-Man and Sharon Carter are the Secret Avengers.

Kelly Sue DeConnick - Writer
Greg Tocchini - Artist
Paul Mounts - Color Artist
Dave Lanphear - Letterer
Greg Tocchini - Cover Art
Taylor Esposito - Production
Lauren Sankovitch - Editor
Tom Brevoort - Executive Editor
Axel Alonso - Editor in Chief
Joe Quesada - Chief Creative Officer
Dan Buckley - Publisher
Alan Fine - Executive Producer

Captain America created by Joe Simon & Jack Kirby.

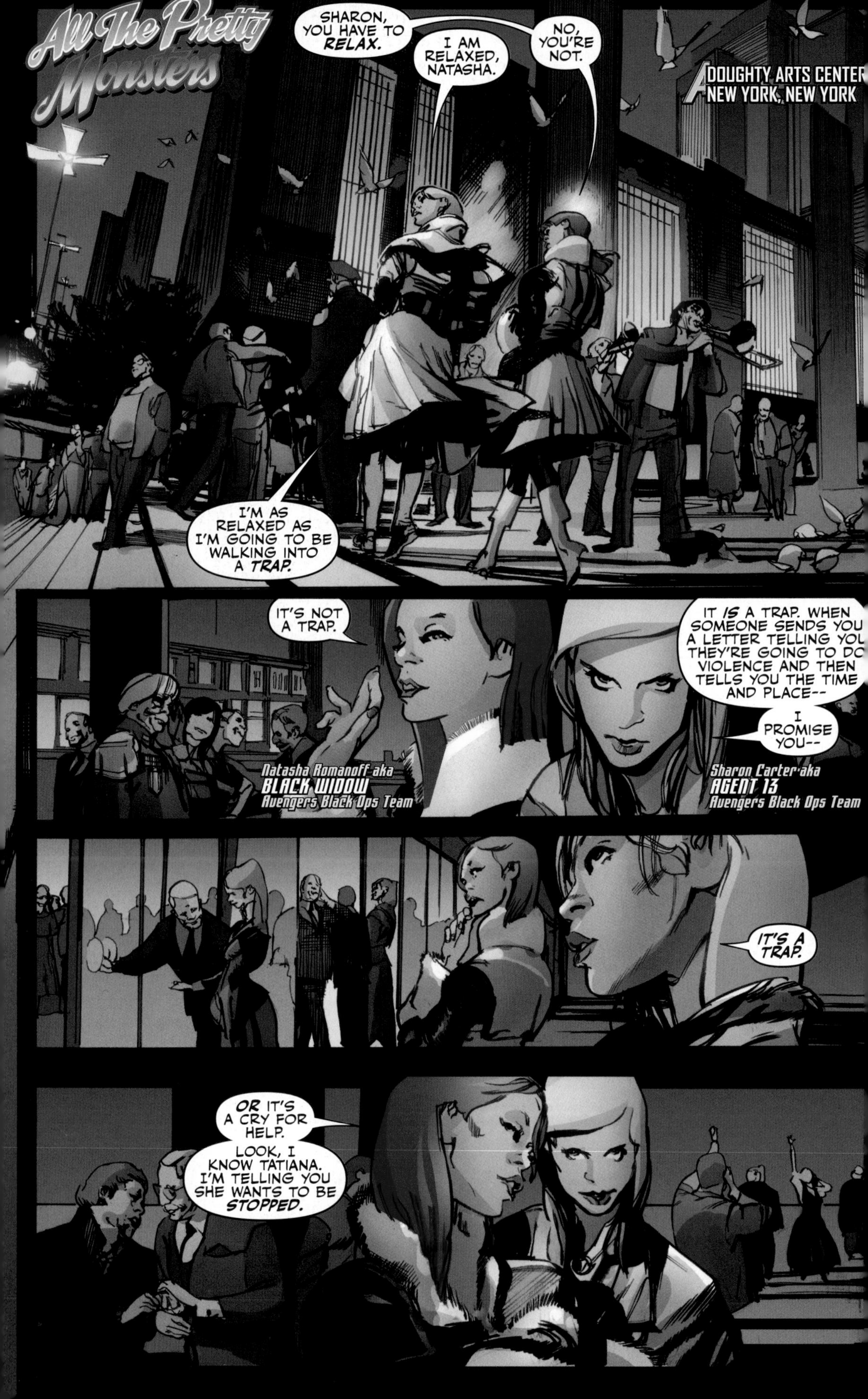

All The Pretty Monsters
SHARON, YOU HAVE TO RELAX.
I AM RELAXED, NATASHA.
NO, YOU'RE NOT.
DOUGHTY ARTS CENTER
NEW YORK, NEW YORK
I'M AS RELAXED AS I'M GOING TO BE WALKING INTO A TRAP.
IT'S NOT A TRAP.
Natasha Romanoff aka
BLACK WIDOW
Avengers Black Ops Team
IT IS A TRAP. WHEN SOMEONE SENDS YOU A LETTER TELLING YOU THEY'RE GOING TO DO VIOLENCE AND THEN TELLS YOU THE TIME AND PLACE--
I PROMISE YOU--
Sharon Carter aka
AGENT 13
Avengers Black Ops Team
IT'S A TRAP.
OR IT'S A CRY FOR HELP.
LOOK, I KNOW TATIANA. I'M TELLING YOU SHE WANTS TO BE STOPPED.

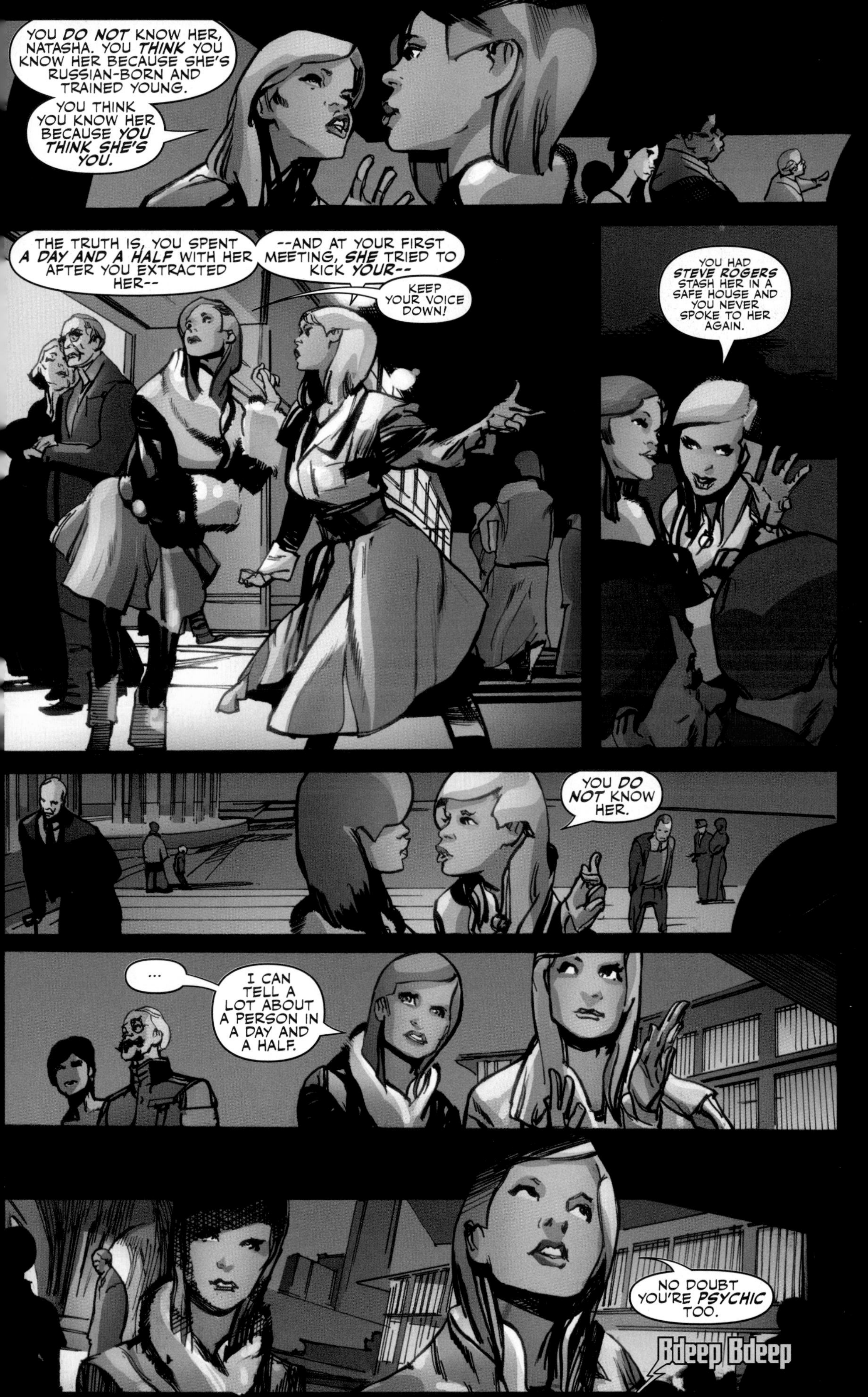
YOU DO NOT KNOW HER, NATASHA. YOU THINK YOU KNOW HER BECAUSE SHE'S RUSSIAN-BORN AND TRAINED YOUNG.
YOU THINK YOU KNOW HER BECAUSE YOU THINK SHE'S YOU.
THE TRUTH IS, YOU SPENT A DAY AND A HALF WITH HER AFTER YOU EXTRACTED HER--
--AND AT YOUR FIRST MEETING, SHE TRIED TO KICK YOUR--
KEEP YOUR VOICE DOWN!
YOU HAD STEVE ROGERS STASH HER IN A SAFE HOUSE AND YOU NEVER SPOKE TO HER AGAIN.
YOU DO NOT KNOW HER.
...
I CAN TELL A LOT ABOUT A PERSON IN A DAY AND A HALF.
NO DOUBT YOU'RE PSYCHIC TOO.
Bdeep Bdeep

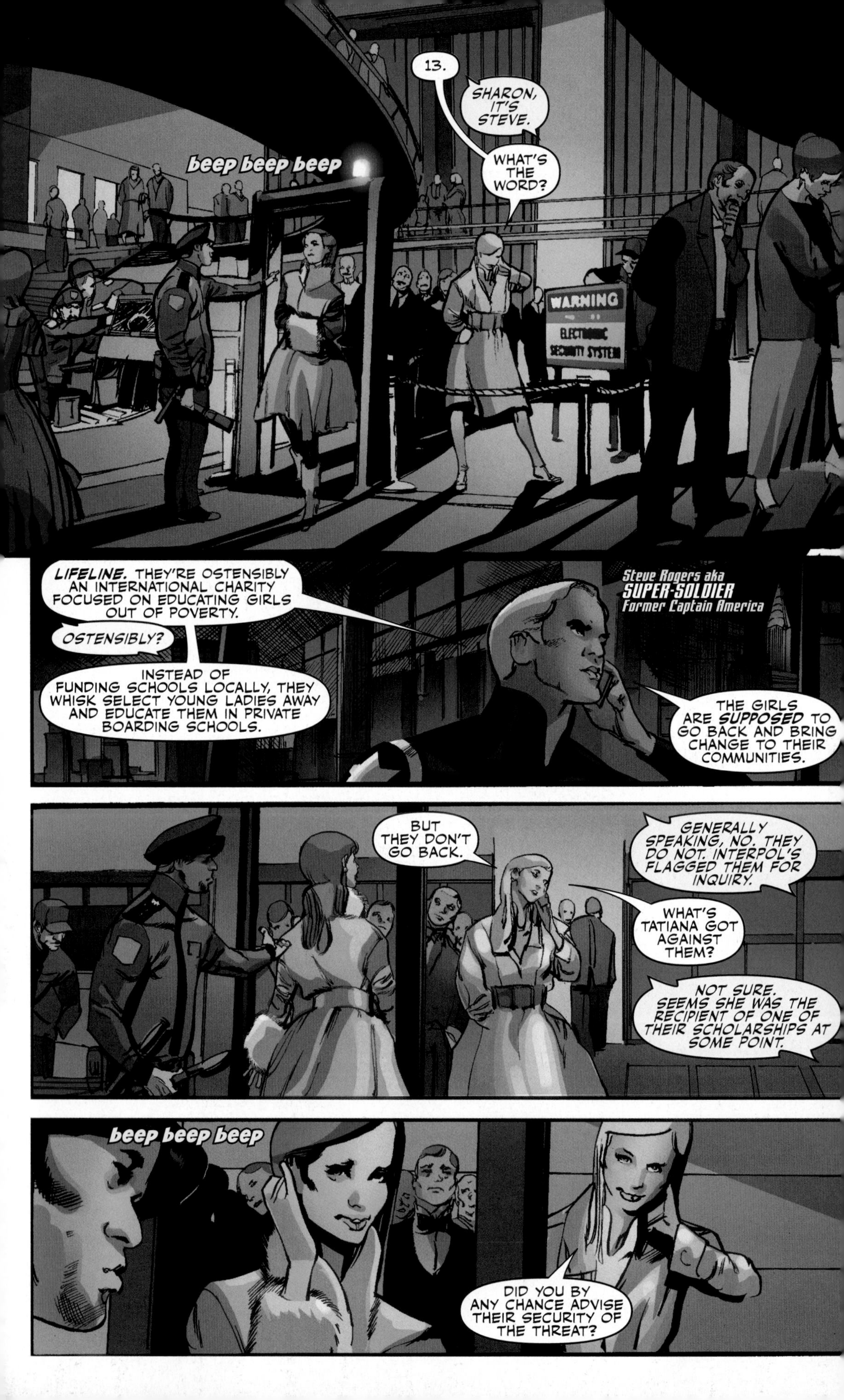
beep beep beep
13.
SHARON, IT'S STEVE.
WHAT'S THE WORD?
WARNING
ELECTRONIC SECURITY SYSTEM
LIFELINE. THEY'RE OSTENSIBLY AN INTERNATIONAL CHARITY FOCUSED ON EDUCATING GIRLS OUT OF POVERTY.
OSTENSIBLY?
INSTEAD OF FUNDING SCHOOLS LOCALLY, THEY WHISK SELECT YOUNG LADIES AWAY AND EDUCATE THEM IN PRIVATE BOARDING SCHOOLS.
Steve Rogers aka SUPER-SOLDIER Former Captain America
THE GIRLS ARE SUPPOSED TO GO BACK AND BRING CHANGE TO THEIR COMMUNITIES.
BUT THEY DON'T GO BACK.
GENERALLY SPEAKING, NO. THEY DO NOT. INTERPOL'S FLAGGED THEM FOR INQUIRY.
WHAT'S TATIANA GOT AGAINST THEM?
NOT SURE. SEEMS SHE WAS THE RECIPIENT OF ONE OF THEIR SCHOLARSHIPS AT SOME POINT.
beep beep beep
DID YOU BY ANY CHANCE ADVISE THEIR SECURITY OF THE THREAT?

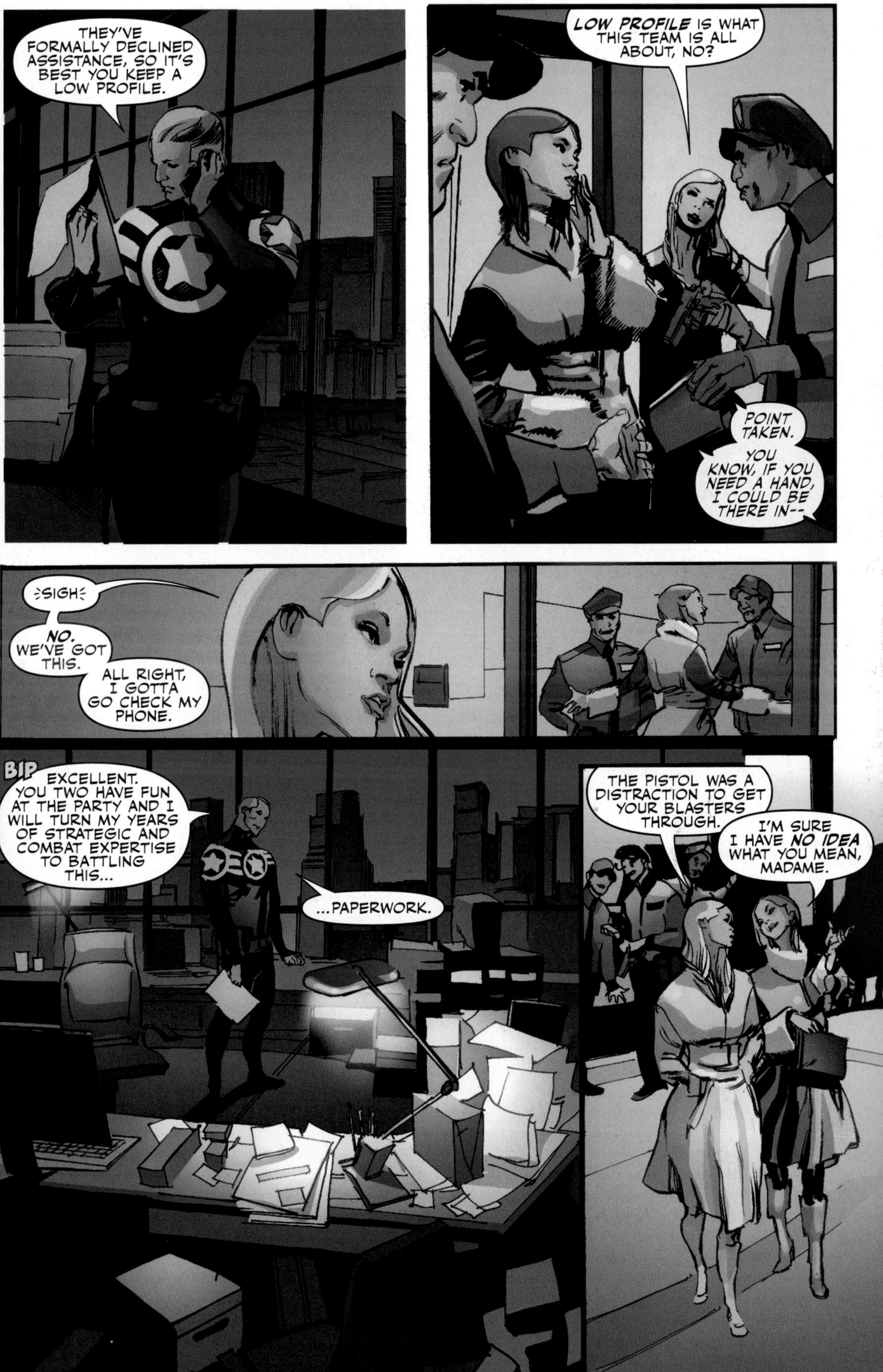
THEY'VE FORMALLY DECLINED ASSISTANCE, SO IT'S BEST YOU KEEP A LOW PROFILE.
LOW PROFILE IS WHAT THIS TEAM IS ALL ABOUT, NO?
POINT TAKEN.
YOU KNOW, IF YOU NEED A HAND, I COULD BE THERE IN--
SIGH
NO. WE'VE GOT THIS.
ALL RIGHT, I GOTTA GO CHECK MY PHONE.
BIP
EXCELLENT. YOU TWO HAVE FUN AT THE PARTY AND I WILL TURN MY YEARS OF STRATEGIC AND COMBAT EXPERTISE TO BATTLING THIS...
...PAPERWORK.
THE PISTOL WAS A DISTRACTION TO GET YOUR BLASTERS THROUGH.
I'M SURE I HAVE NO IDEA WHAT YOU MEAN, MADAME.

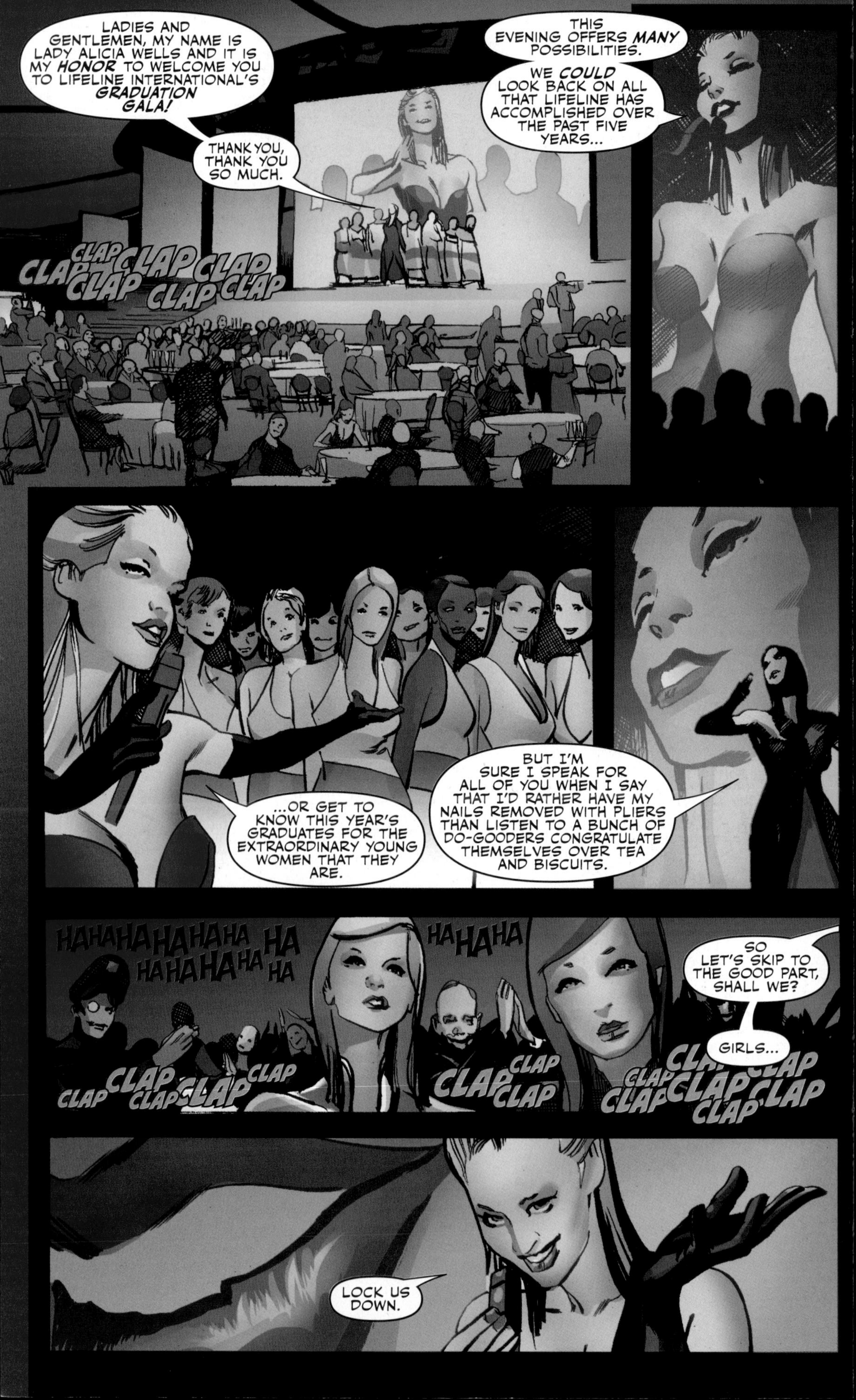
LADIES AND GENTLEMEN, MY NAME IS LADY ALICIA WELLS AND IT IS MY HONOR TO WELCOME YOU TO LIFELINE INTERNATIONAL'S GRADUATION GALA!
THANK YOU, THANK YOU SO MUCH.
CLAP CLAP CLAP CLAP CLAP CLAP CLAP CLAP
THIS EVENING OFFERS MANY POSSIBILITIES.
WE COULD LOOK BACK ON ALL THAT LIFELINE HAS ACCOMPLISHED OVER THE PAST FIVE YEARS...
...OR GET TO KNOW THIS YEAR'S GRADUATES FOR THE EXTRAORDINARY YOUNG WOMEN THAT THEY ARE.
BUT I'M SURE I SPEAK FOR ALL OF YOU WHEN I SAY THAT I'D RATHER HAVE MY NAILS REMOVED WITH PLIERS THAN LISTEN TO A BUNCH OF DO-GOODERS CONGRATULATE THEMSELVES OVER TEA AND BISCUITS.
HAHAHA HAHAHA HAHAHAHAHA HA HA
HAHAHA
SO LET'S SKIP TO THE GOOD PART, SHALL WE?
GIRLS...
CLAP CLAP CLAP CLAP CLAP
CLAP CLAP
CLAP CLAP CLAP CLAP CLAP CLAP CLAP
LOCK US DOWN.

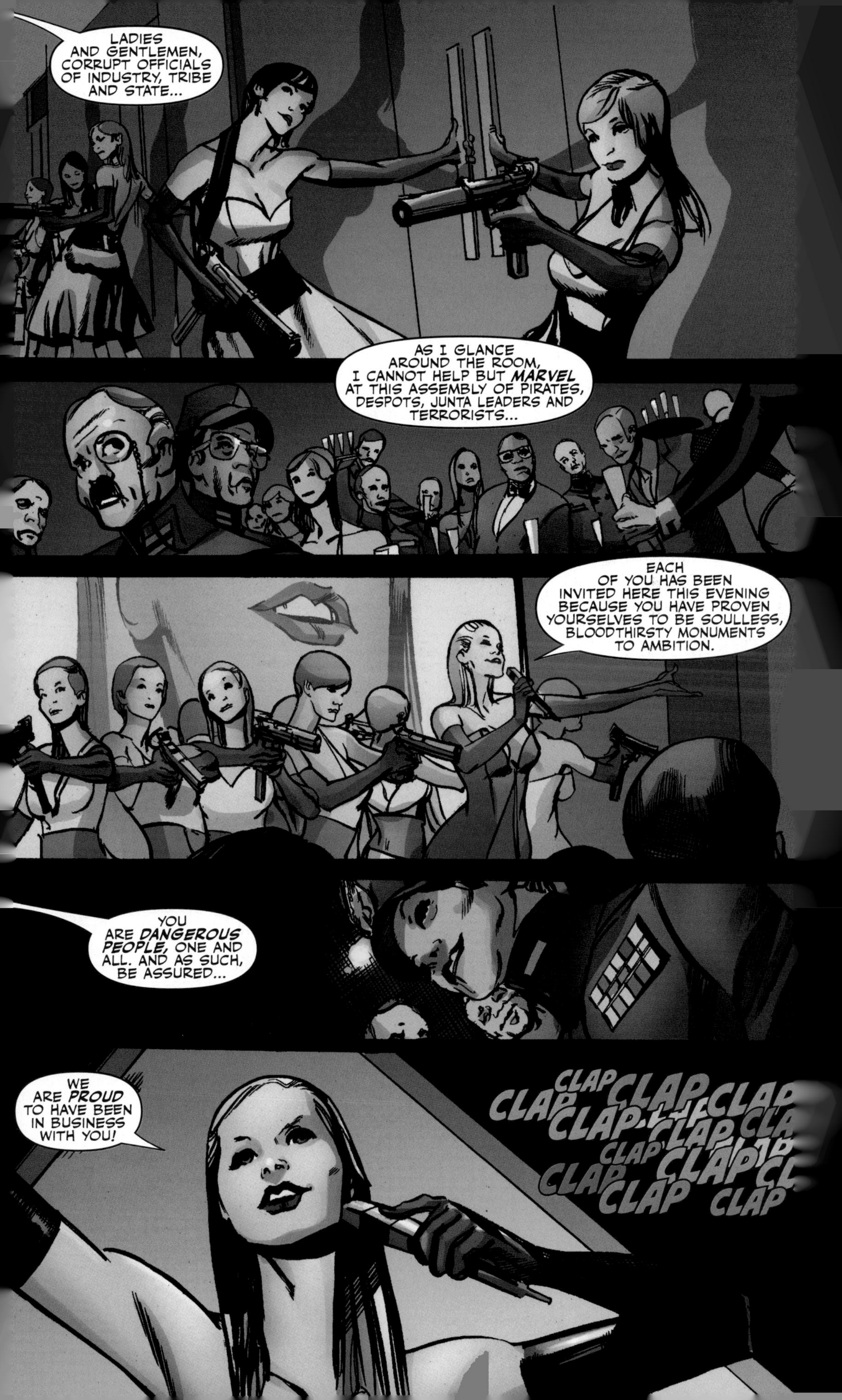

LADIES AND GENTLEMEN, CORRUPT OFFICIALS OF INDUSTRY, TRIBE AND STATE...
AS I GLANCE AROUND THE ROOM, I CANNOT HELP BUT *MARVEL* AT THIS ASSEMBLY OF PIRATES, DESPOTS, JUNTA LEADERS AND TERRORISTS...
EACH OF YOU HAS BEEN INVITED HERE THIS EVENING BECAUSE YOU HAVE PROVEN YOURSELVES TO BE SOULLESS, BLOODTHIRSTY MONUMENTS TO AMBITION.
YOU ARE *DANGEROUS PEOPLE,* ONE AND ALL. AND AS SUCH, BE ASSURED...
WE ARE *PROUD* TO HAVE BEEN IN BUSINESS WITH YOU!
CLAP CLAP CLAP CLAP CLAP CLAP CLAP CLAP CLAP CLAP CLAP CLAP CLAP

REMEMBER WHEN I SAID THIS WAS A TRAP?

SHH.

FIVE YEARS AGO, I APPROACHED A SMALL GROUP OF FORWARD THINKING INVESTORS ABOUT FORMING LIFELINE, NOT AS A *CHARITY*--

BUT AS A *FRONT* AND A *RECRUITING ORGANIZATION* FOR A SECOND *FOR-PROFIT* ENDEAVOR. HAVE CHOSEN TO CALL L.A.S.S.E.S.--

L.A.S.S.E.S.
LADY ALICIA'S SWEET SIXTEEN EXECUTIONER'S SCHOOL

LADY ALICIA'S SWEET SIXTEEN EXECUTIONER'S SCHOOL.

BECAUSE-- LET'S BE HONEST-- I AM A SLAVE TO WHIMSY.

- ART
- MUSIC
- HISTORY
- HAND-TO-HAND COMBAT
- BODY DISPOSAL
- CHEMISTRY

FOR HALF A DECADE, SELECT GIRLS HAVE PARTICIPATED IN A SPECIAL EDUCATION PROGRAM WHEREIN THEY HAVE MASTERED NOT ONLY THE ARTS OF *ELOCUTION* AND *DIPLOMACY*, BUT ALSO *SEDUCTION* AND *ASSASSINATION*.

FOR THE RIGHT PRICE, GRADUATES OF OUR PROGRAM COULD KILL A MAN WITH A TOOTHPICK AND LEAVE NO EVIDENCE BUT *THE SMILE ON HIS FACE.*

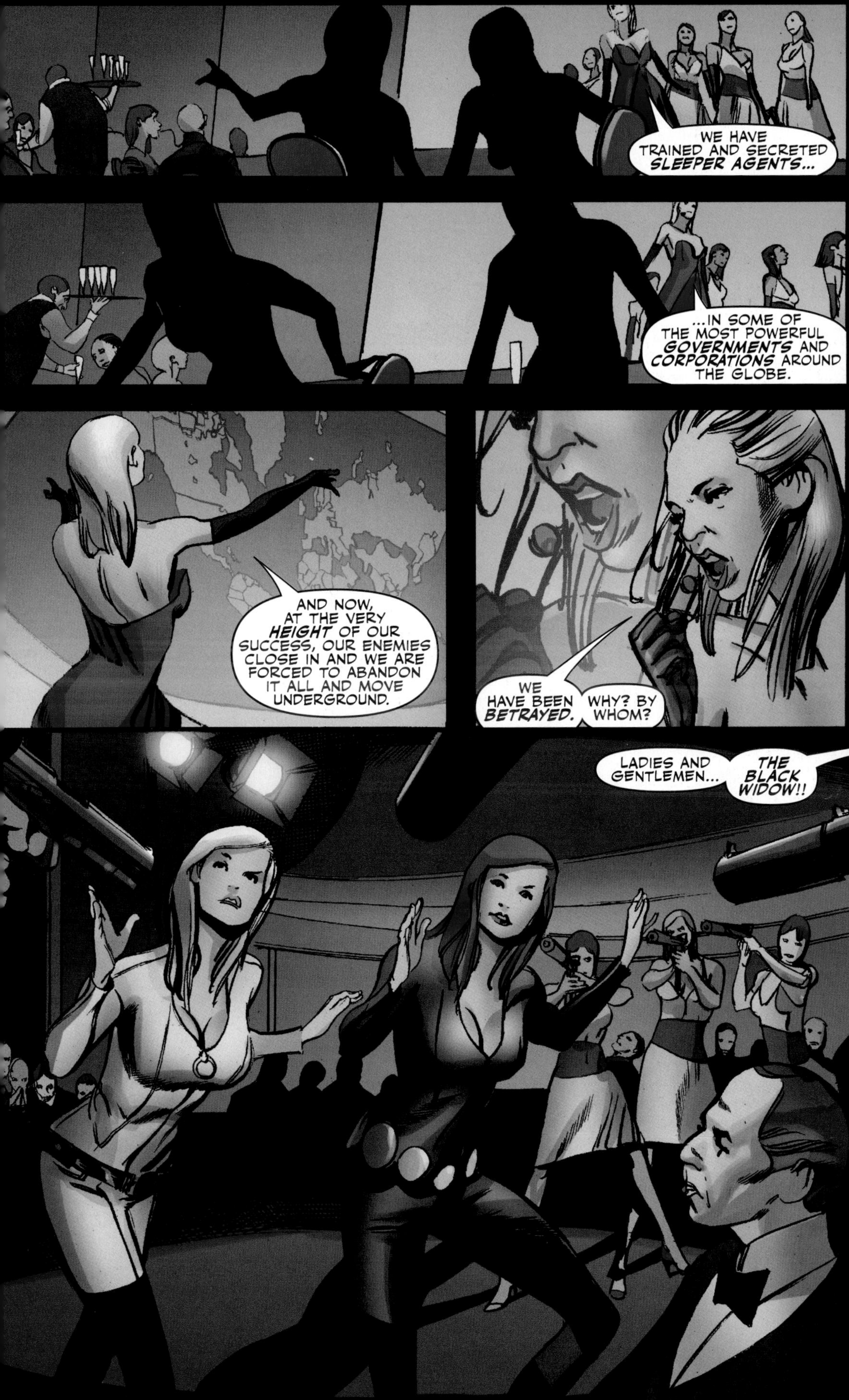
WE HAVE TRAINED AND SECRETED SLEEPER AGENTS...
...IN SOME OF THE MOST POWERFUL GOVERNMENTS AND CORPORATIONS AROUND THE GLOBE.
AND NOW, AT THE VERY HEIGHT OF OUR SUCCESS, OUR ENEMIES CLOSE IN AND WE ARE FORCED TO ABANDON IT ALL AND MOVE UNDERGROUND.
WE HAVE BEEN BETRAYED.
WHY? BY WHOM?
LADIES AND GENTLEMEN...
THE BLACK WIDOW!!

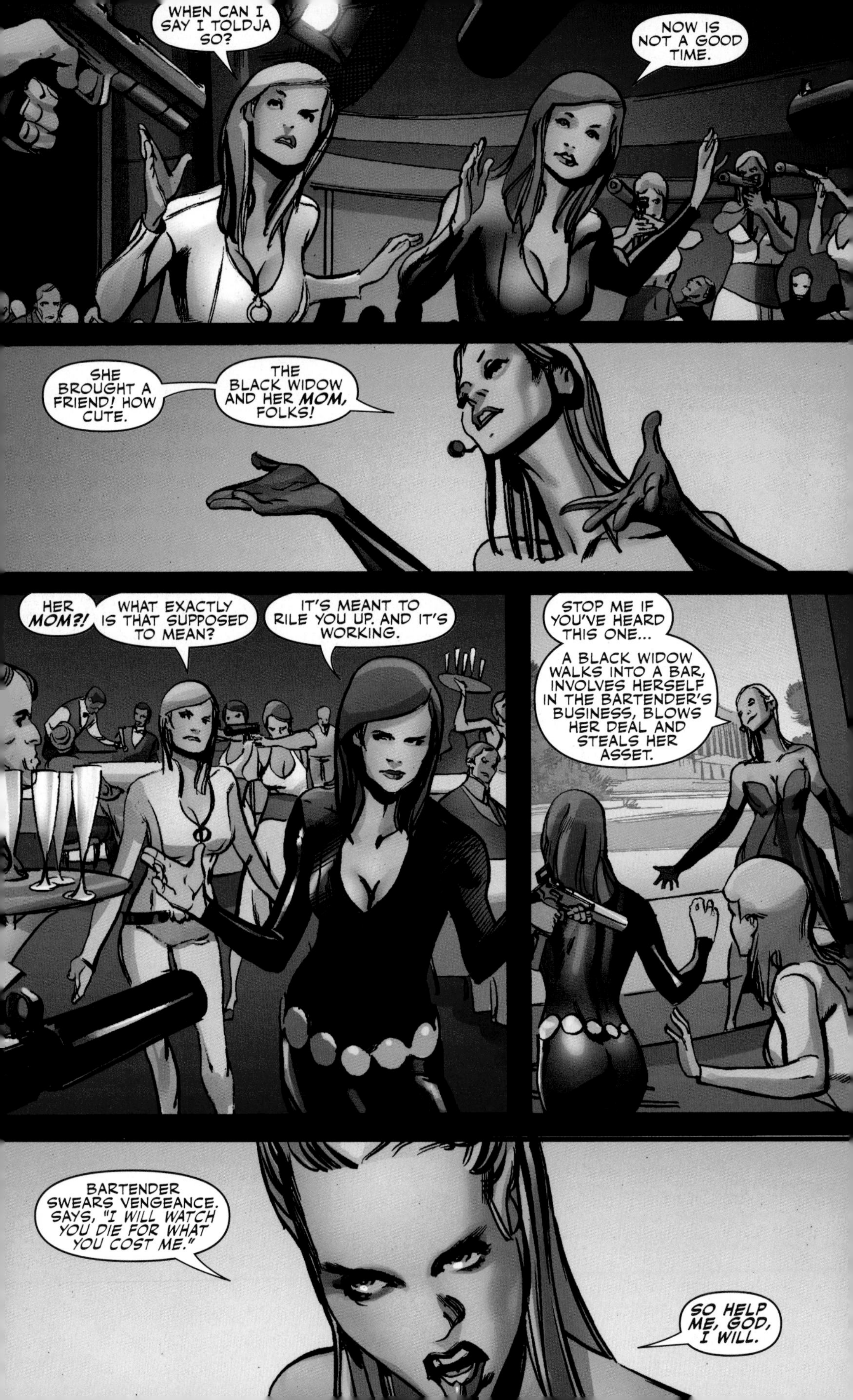
WHEN CAN I SAY I TOLDJA SO?
NOW IS NOT A GOOD TIME.
THE BLACK WIDOW AND HER *MOM,* FOLKS!
SHE BROUGHT A FRIEND! HOW CUTE.
HER *MOM?!*
WHAT EXACTLY IS THAT SUPPOSED TO MEAN?
IT'S MEANT TO RILE YOU UP. AND IT'S WORKING.
STOP ME IF YOU'VE HEARD THIS ONE...
A BLACK WIDOW WALKS INTO A BAR, INVOLVES HERSELF IN THE BARTENDER'S BUSINESS, BLOWS HER DEAL AND STEALS HER ASSET.
BARTENDER SWEARS VENGEANCE. SAYS, *"I WILL WATCH YOU DIE FOR WHAT YOU COST ME."*
SO HELP ME, GOD, I WILL.

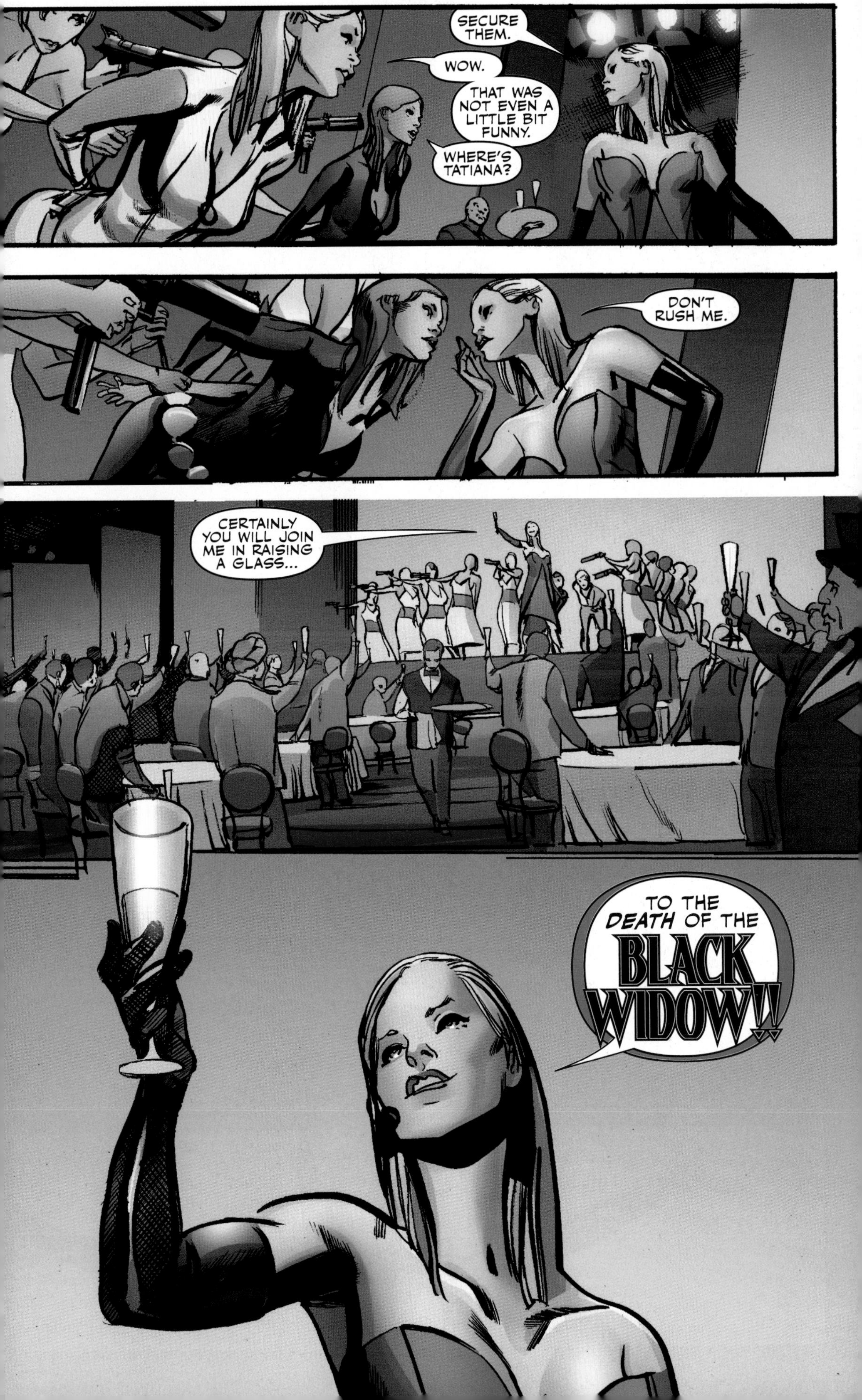
SECURE THEM.
WOW.
THAT WAS NOT EVEN A LITTLE BIT FUNNY.
WHERE'S TATIANA?
DON'T RUSH ME.
CERTAINLY YOU WILL JOIN ME IN RAISING A GLASS...
TO THE DEATH OF THE BLACK WIDOW!!

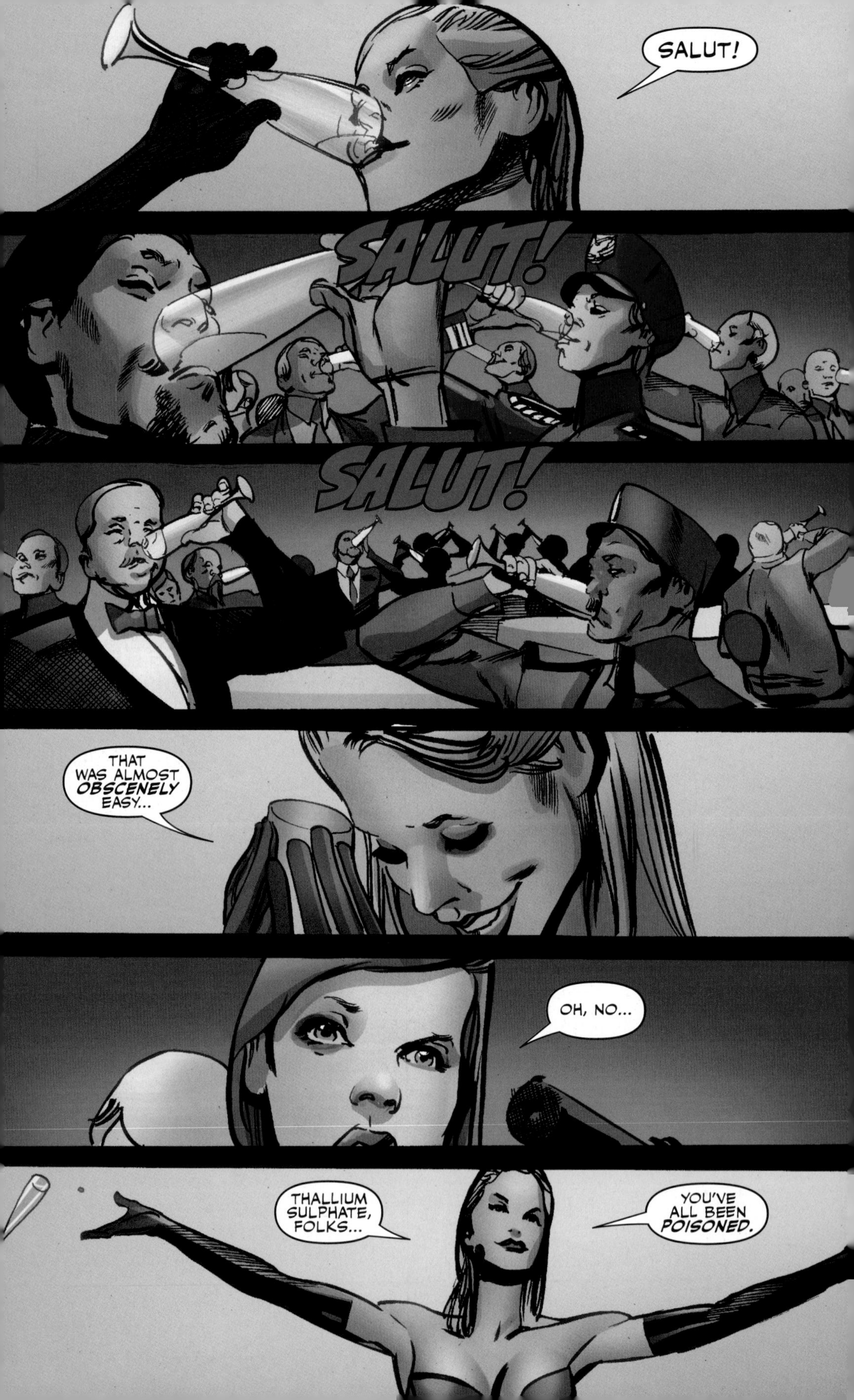
SALUT!
SALUT!
SALUT!
THAT WAS ALMOST OBSCENELY EASY...
OH, NO...
THALLIUM SULPHATE, FOLKS...
YOU'VE ALL BEEN POISONED.

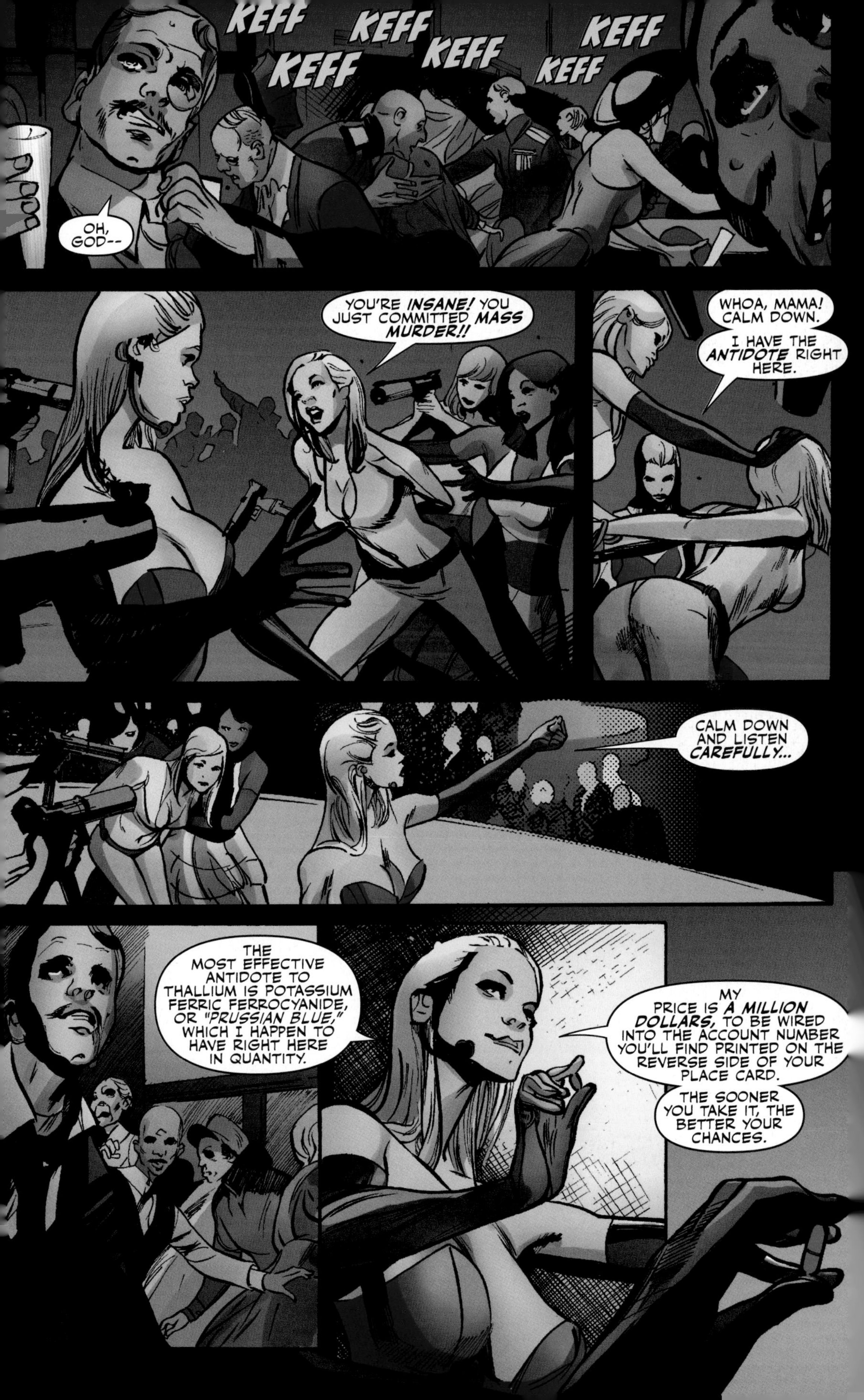
KEFF
KEFF
KEFF
KEFF
KEFF
KEFF
OH, GOD--
YOU'RE *INSANE!* YOU JUST COMMITTED *MASS MURDER!!*
WHOA, MAMA! CALM DOWN.
I HAVE THE *ANTIDOTE* RIGHT HERE.
CALM DOWN AND LISTEN *CAREFULLY...*
THE MOST EFFECTIVE ANTIDOTE TO THALLIUM IS POTASSIUM FERRIC FERROCYANIDE, OR *"PRUSSIAN BLUE,"* WHICH I HAPPEN TO HAVE RIGHT HERE IN QUANTITY.
MY PRICE IS *A MILLION DOLLARS,* TO BE WIRED INTO THE ACCOUNT NUMBER YOU'LL FIND PRINTED ON THE REVERSE SIDE OF YOUR PLACE CARD.
THE SOONER YOU TAKE IT, THE BETTER YOUR CHANCES.

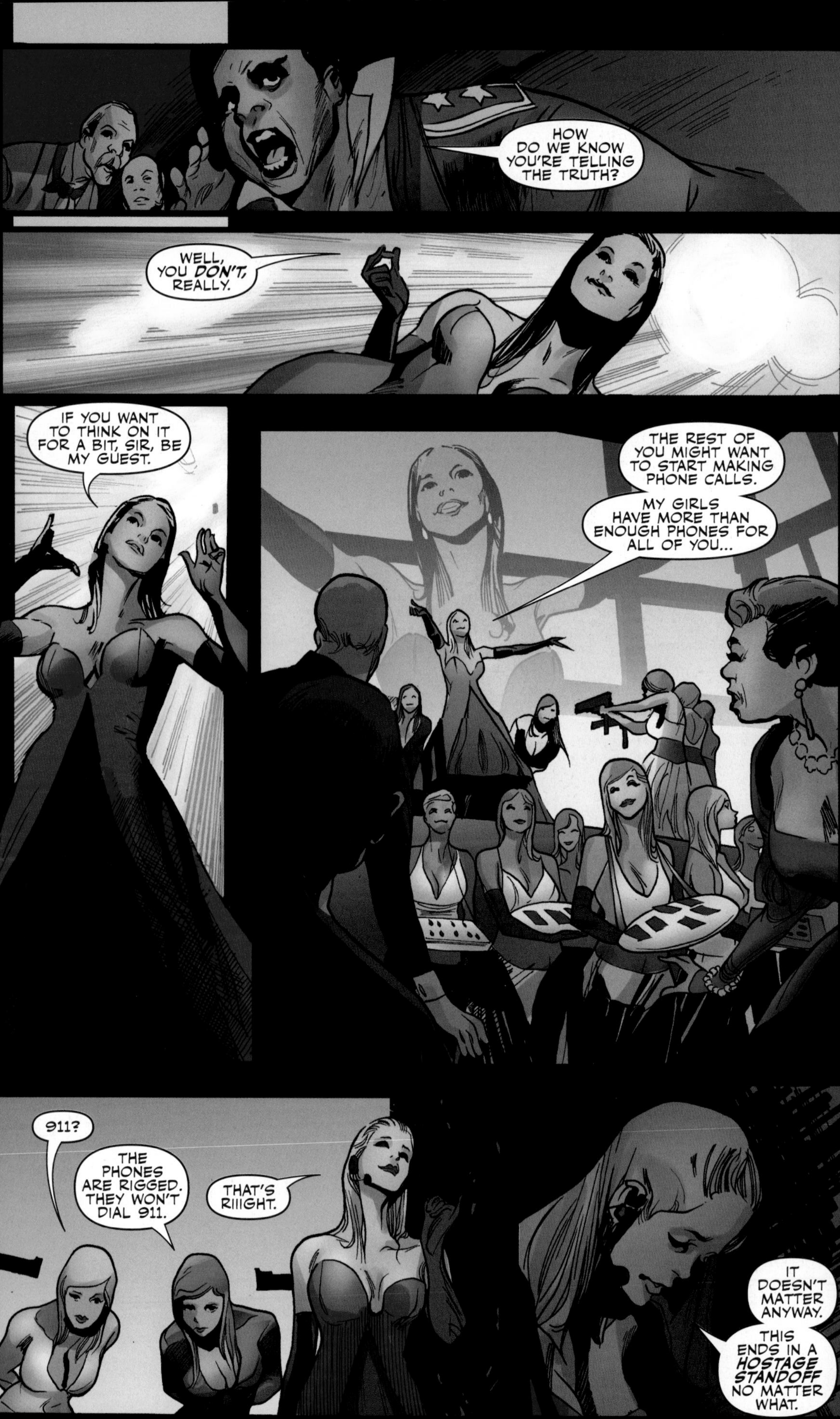
HOW DO WE KNOW YOU'RE TELLING THE TRUTH?
WELL, YOU *DON'T*, REALLY.
IF YOU WANT TO THINK ON IT FOR A BIT, SIR, BE MY GUEST.
THE REST OF YOU MIGHT WANT TO START MAKING PHONE CALLS.
MY GIRLS HAVE MORE THAN ENOUGH PHONES FOR ALL OF YOU...
911?
THE PHONES ARE RIGGED. THEY WON'T DIAL 911.
THAT'S RIIIGHT.
IT DOESN'T MATTER ANYWAY.
THIS ENDS IN A ***HOSTAGE STANDOFF*** NO MATTER WHAT.

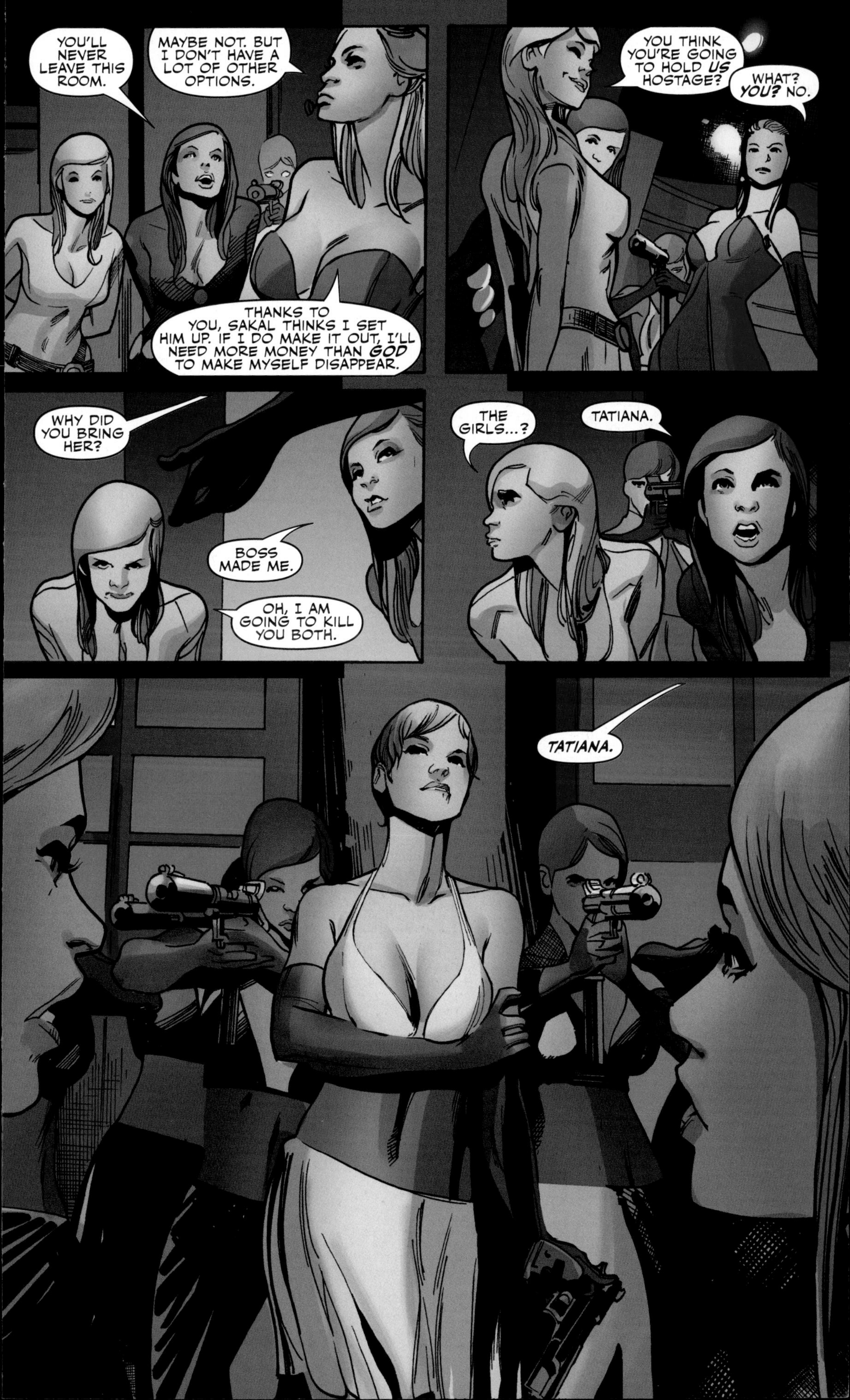
YOU'LL NEVER LEAVE THIS ROOM.
MAYBE NOT. BUT I DON'T HAVE A LOT OF OTHER OPTIONS.
THANKS TO YOU, SAKAL THINKS I SET HIM UP. IF I DO MAKE IT OUT, I'LL NEED MORE MONEY THAN *GOD* TO MAKE MYSELF DISAPPEAR.
YOU THINK YOU'RE GOING TO HOLD *US* HOSTAGE?
WHAT? *YOU?* NO.
WHY DID YOU BRING HER?
BOSS MADE ME.
OH, I AM GOING TO KILL YOU BOTH.
THE GIRLS...?
TATIANA.
TATIANA.

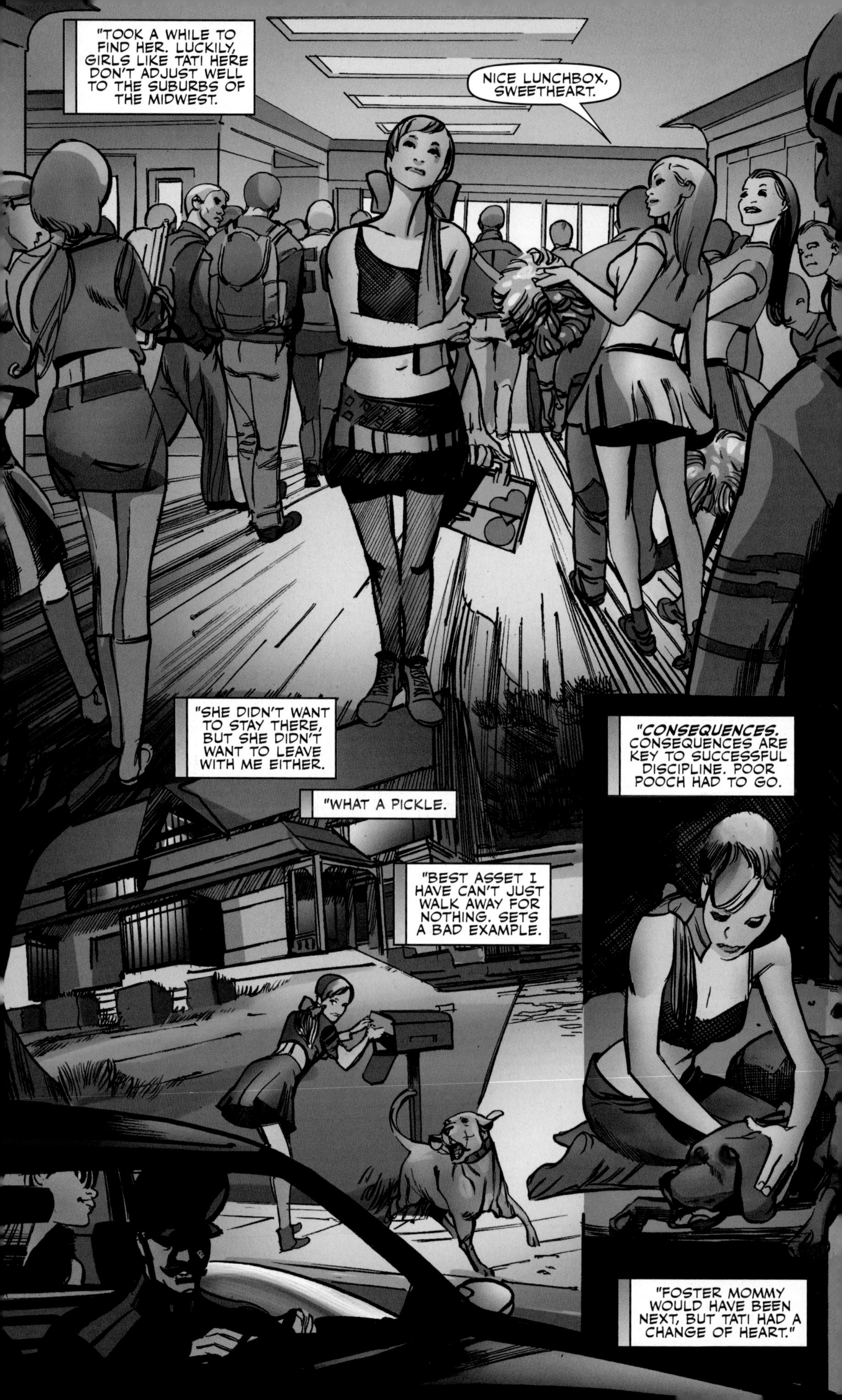
"TOOK A WHILE TO FIND HER. LUCKILY, GIRLS LIKE TATI HERE DON'T ADJUST WELL TO THE SUBURBS OF THE MIDWEST.
NICE LUNCHBOX, SWEETHEART.
"SHE DIDN'T WANT TO STAY THERE, BUT SHE DIDN'T WANT TO LEAVE WITH ME EITHER.
"WHAT A PICKLE.
"BEST ASSET I HAVE CAN'T JUST WALK AWAY FOR NOTHING. SETS A BAD EXAMPLE.
"CONSEQUENCES. CONSEQUENCES ARE KEY TO SUCCESSFUL DISCIPLINE. POOR POOCH HAD TO GO.
"FOSTER MOMMY WOULD HAVE BEEN NEXT, BUT TATI HAD A CHANGE OF HEART."

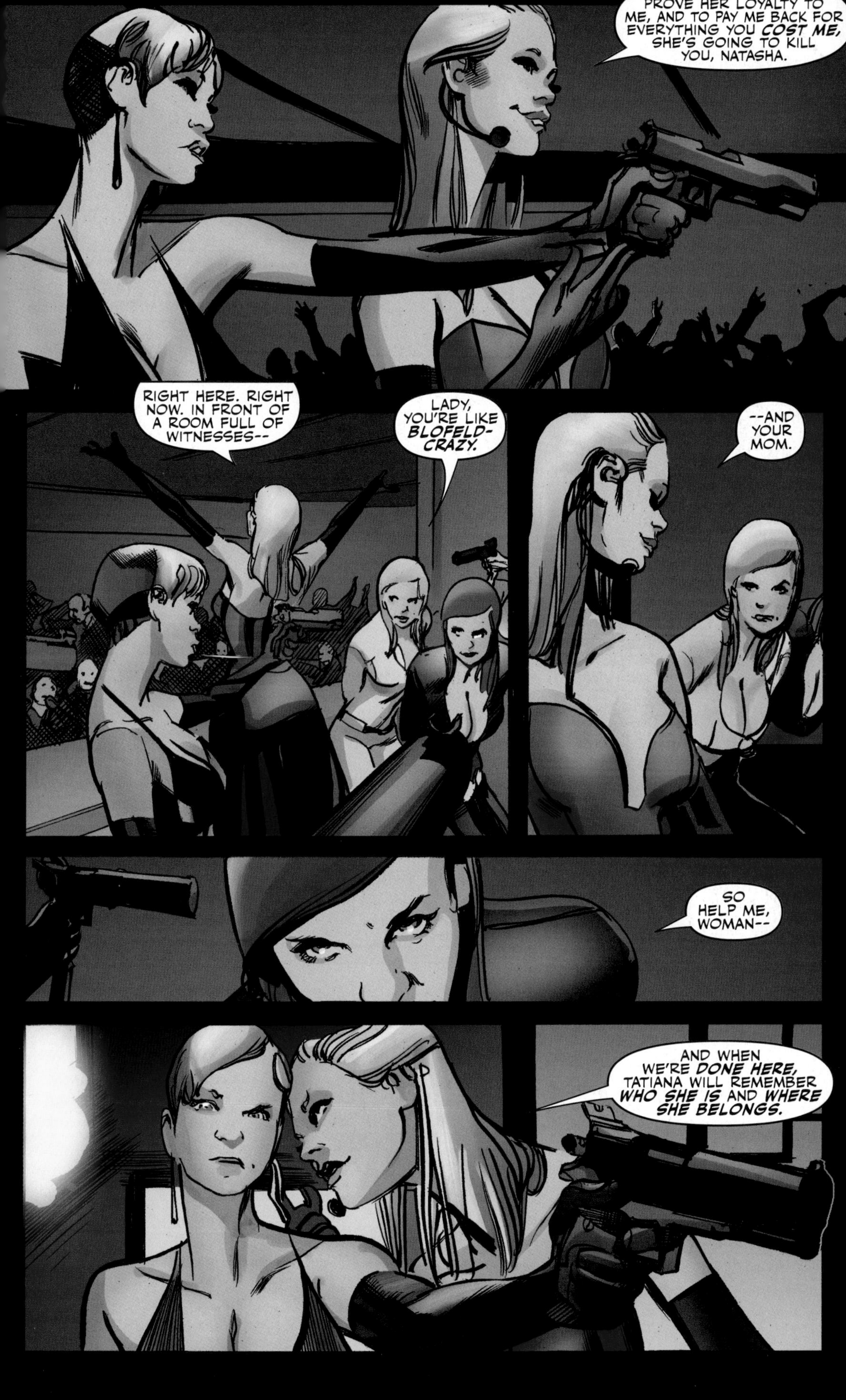
AND NOW, TO PROVE HER LOYALTY TO ME, AND TO PAY ME BACK FOR EVERYTHING YOU *COST ME,* SHE'S GOING TO KILL YOU, NATASHA.
RIGHT HERE. RIGHT NOW. IN FRONT OF A ROOM FULL OF WITNESSES--
LADY, YOU'RE LIKE *BLOFELD-CRAZY.*
--AND YOUR MOM.
SO HELP ME, WOMAN--
AND WHEN WE'RE *DONE HERE,* TATIANA WILL REMEMBER *WHO SHE IS* AND *WHERE SHE BELONGS.*

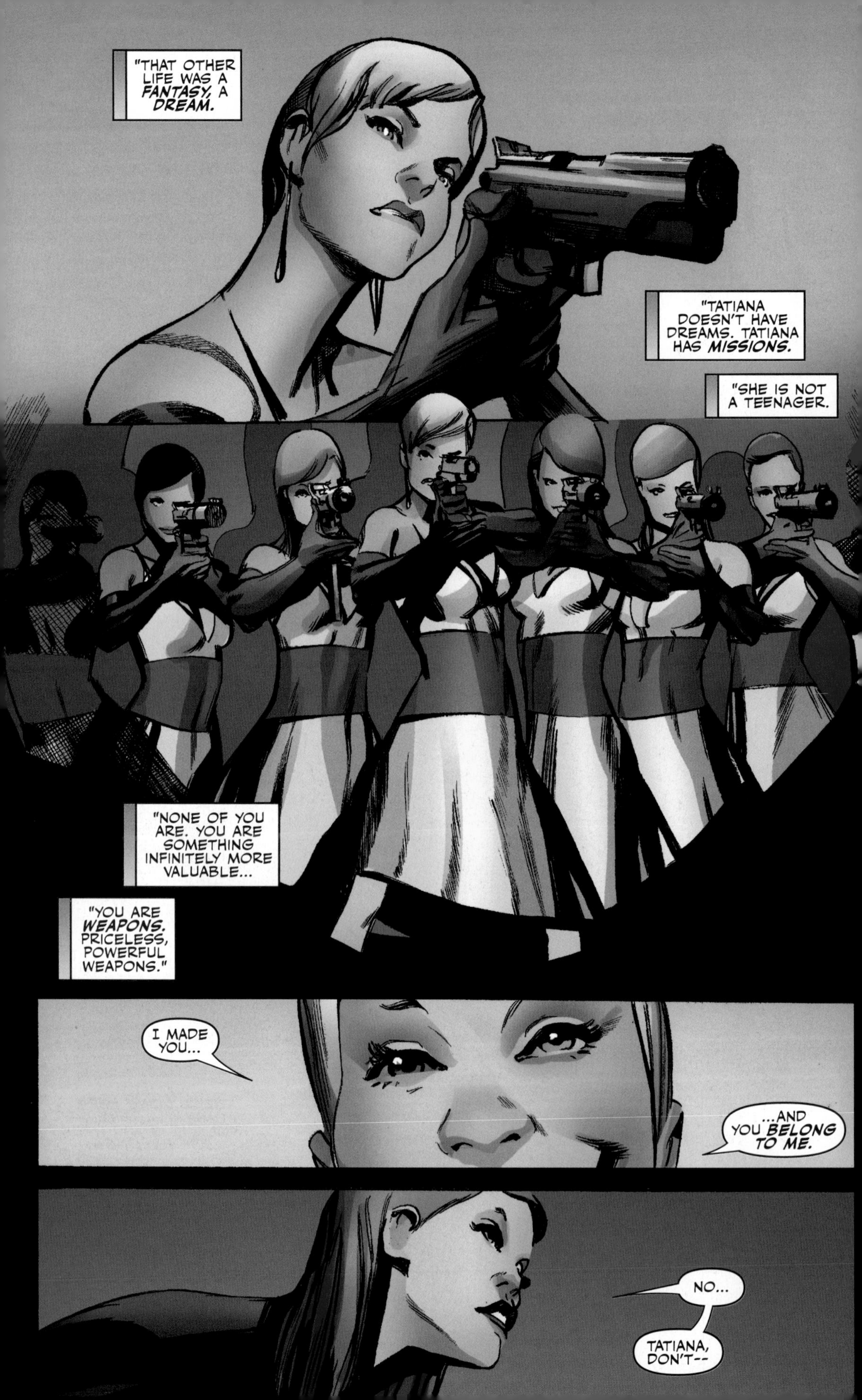
"THAT OTHER LIFE WAS A *FANTASY*, A *DREAM*.
"TATIANA DOESN'T HAVE DREAMS. TATIANA HAS *MISSIONS*.
"SHE IS NOT A TEENAGER.
"NONE OF YOU ARE. YOU ARE SOMETHING INFINITELY MORE VALUABLE...
"YOU ARE *WEAPONS*. PRICELESS, POWERFUL WEAPONS."
I MADE YOU...
...AND YOU *BELONG TO ME*.
NO...
TATIANA, DON'T--

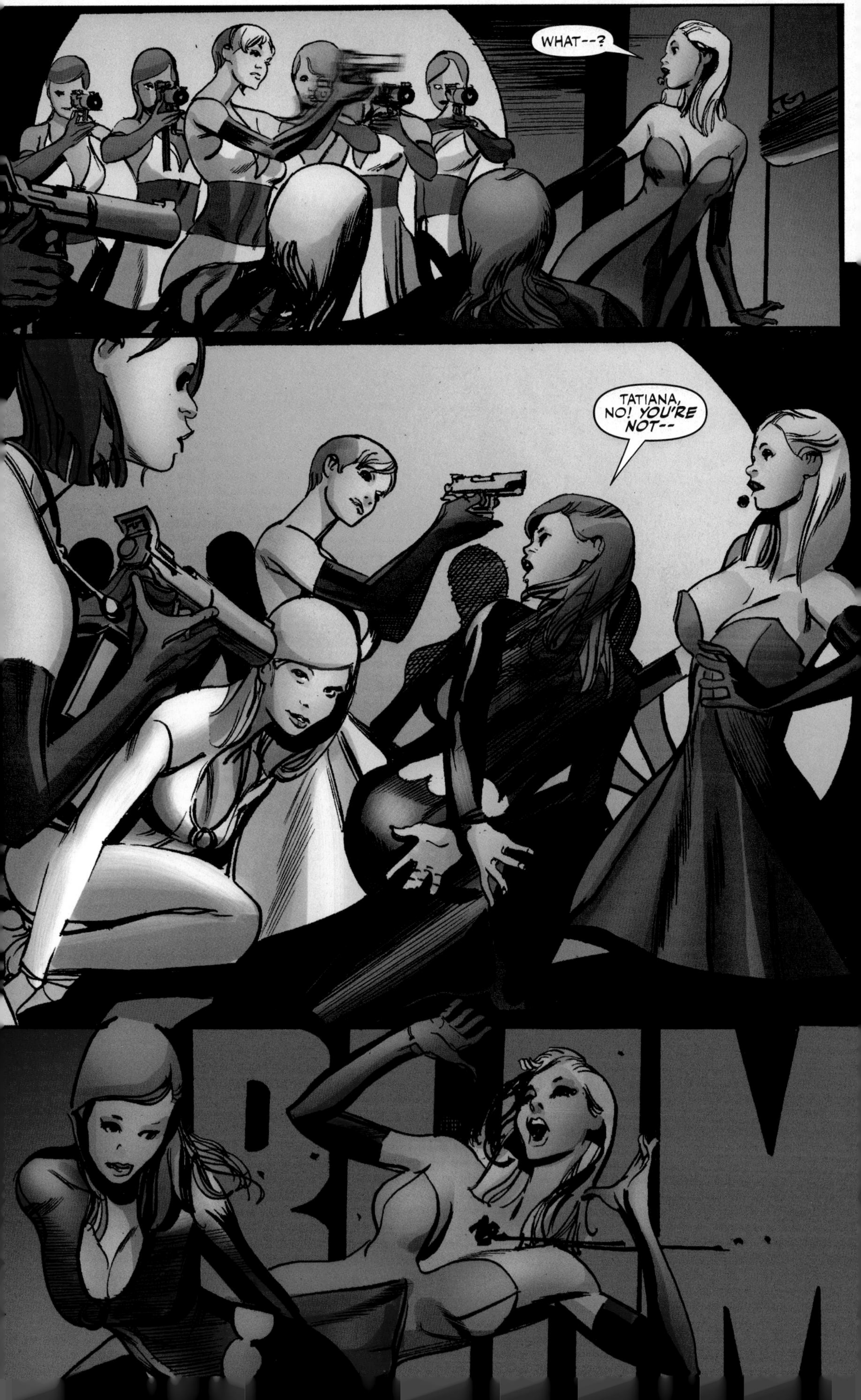
WHAT--?
TATIANA, NO! YOU'RE NOT--

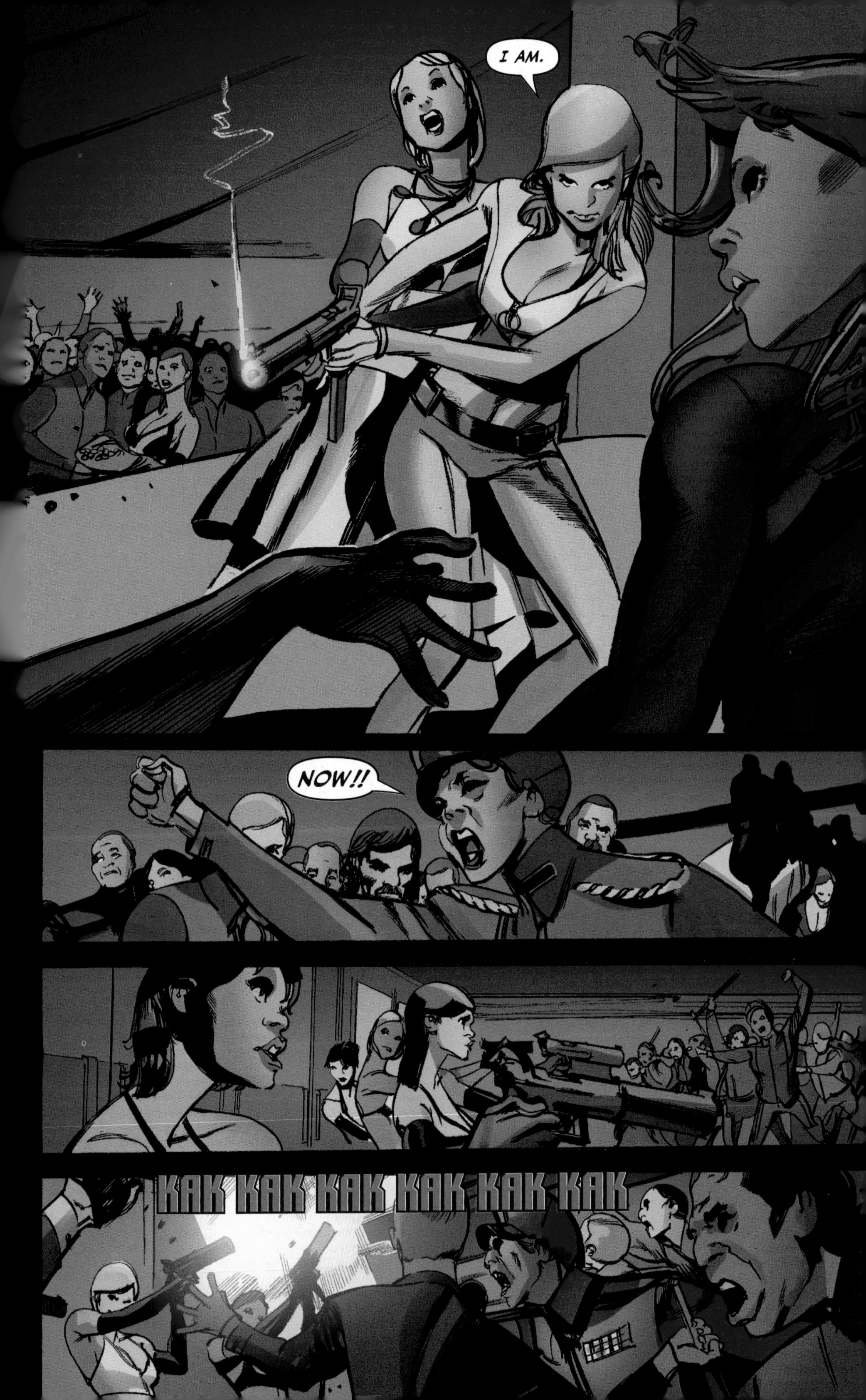
I AM.
NOW!!
KAK KAK KAK KAK KAK KAK

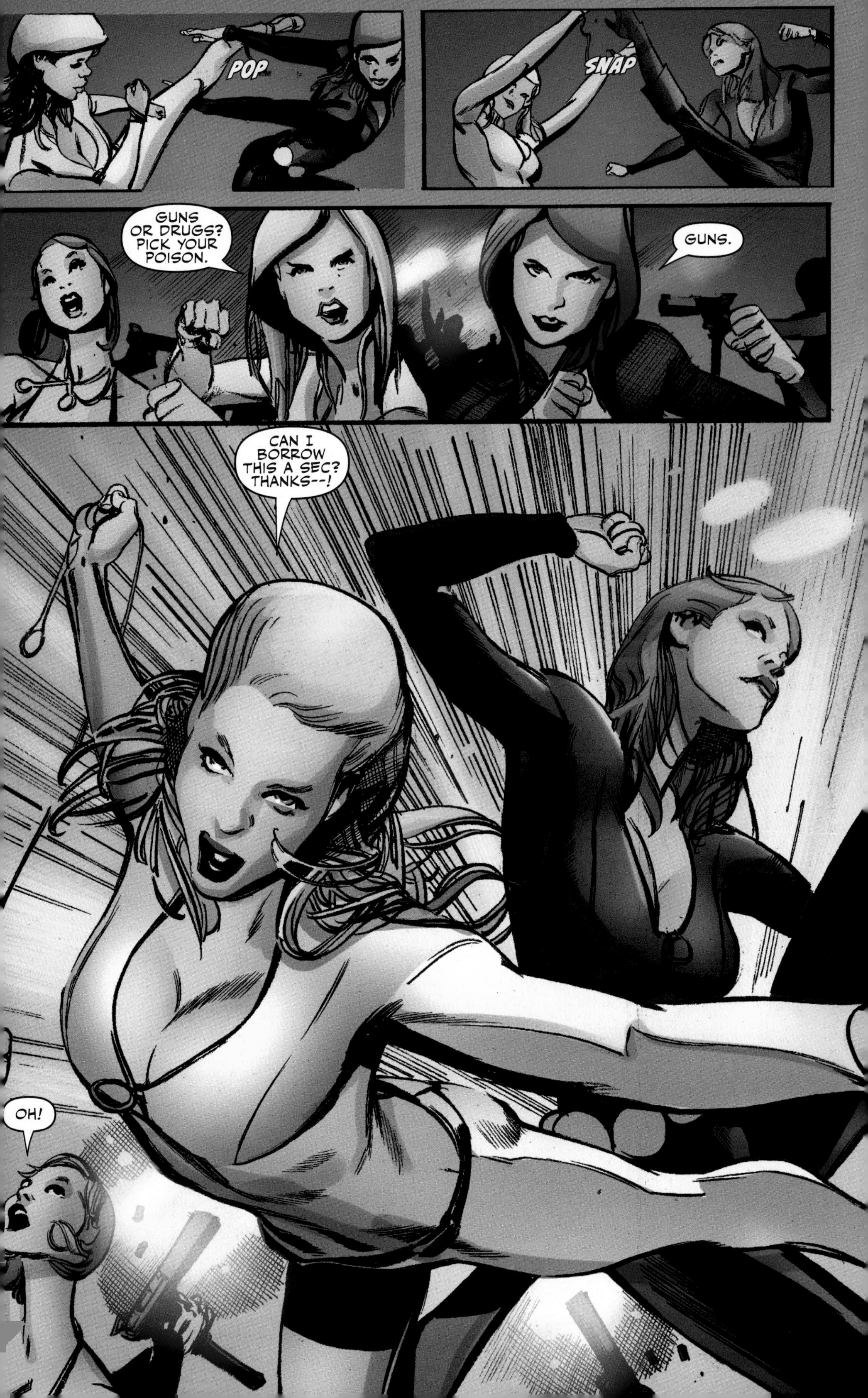
POP
SNAP
GUNS OR DRUGS? PICK YOUR POISON.
GUNS.
CAN I BORROW THIS A SEC? THANKS--!
OH!

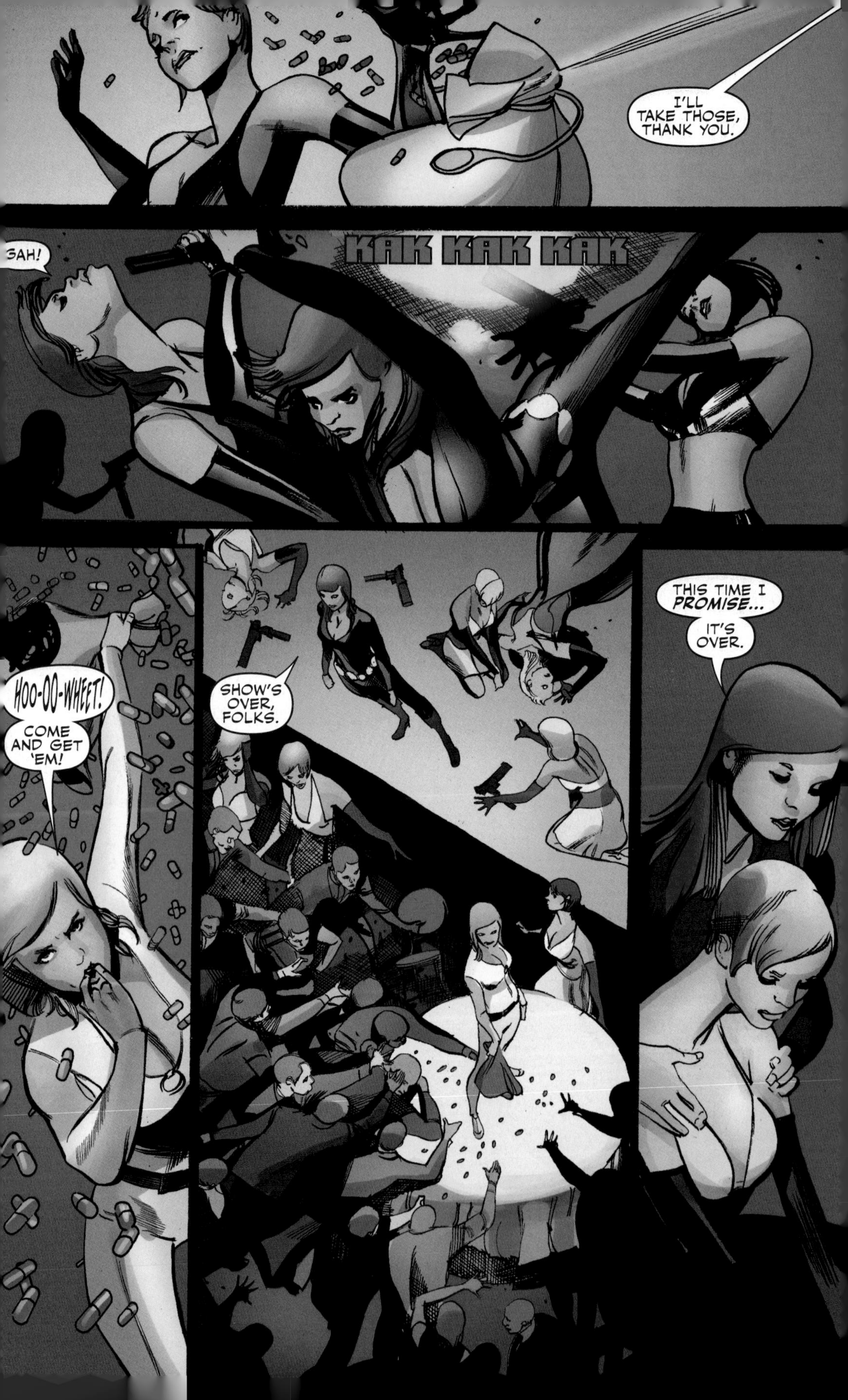
I'LL TAKE THOSE, THANK YOU.
GAH!
KAK KAK KAK
HOO-OO-WHEET!
COME AND GET 'EM!
SHOW'S OVER, FOLKS.
THIS TIME I PROMISE...
IT'S OVER.

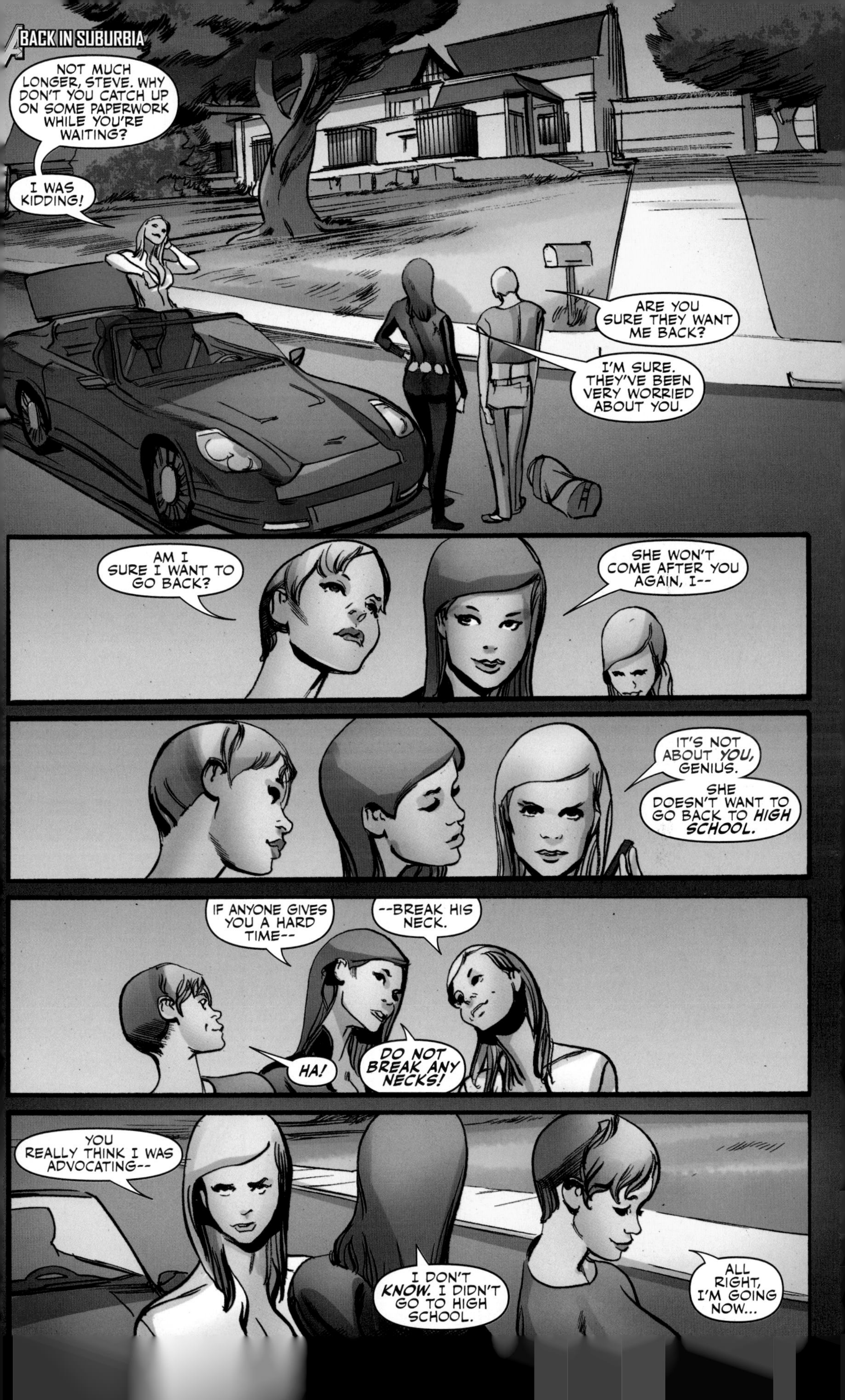
BACK IN SUBURBIA
NOT MUCH LONGER, STEVE. WHY DON'T YOU CATCH UP ON SOME PAPERWORK WHILE YOU'RE WAITING?
I WAS KIDDING!
ARE YOU SURE THEY WANT ME BACK?
I'M SURE. THEY'VE BEEN VERY WORRIED ABOUT YOU.
AM I SURE I WANT TO GO BACK?
SHE WON'T COME AFTER YOU AGAIN, I--
IT'S NOT ABOUT YOU, GENIUS.
SHE DOESN'T WANT TO GO BACK TO HIGH SCHOOL.
IF ANYONE GIVES YOU A HARD TIME--
--BREAK HIS NECK.
HA!
DO NOT BREAK ANY NECKS!
YOU REALLY THINK I WAS ADVOCATING--
I DON'T KNOW. I DIDN'T GO TO HIGH SCHOOL.
ALL RIGHT, I'M GOING NOW...

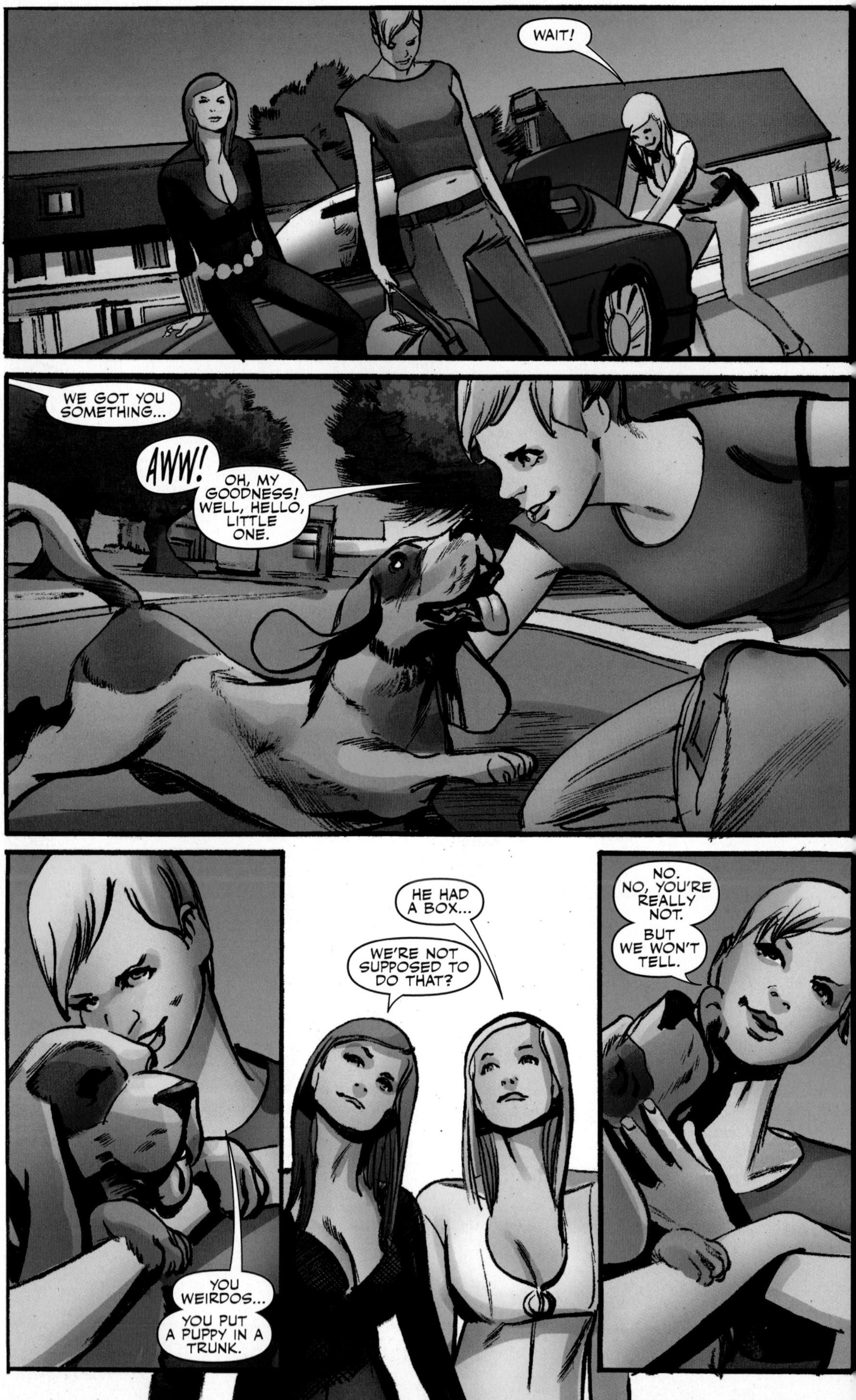
WAIT!
WE GOT YOU SOMETHING...
AWW!
OH, MY GOODNESS! WELL, HELLO, LITTLE ONE.
YOU WEIRDOS...
YOU PUT A PUPPY IN A TRUNK.
HE HAD A BOX...
WE'RE NOT SUPPOSED TO DO THAT?
NO. NO, YOU'RE REALLY NOT.
BUT WE WON'T TELL.

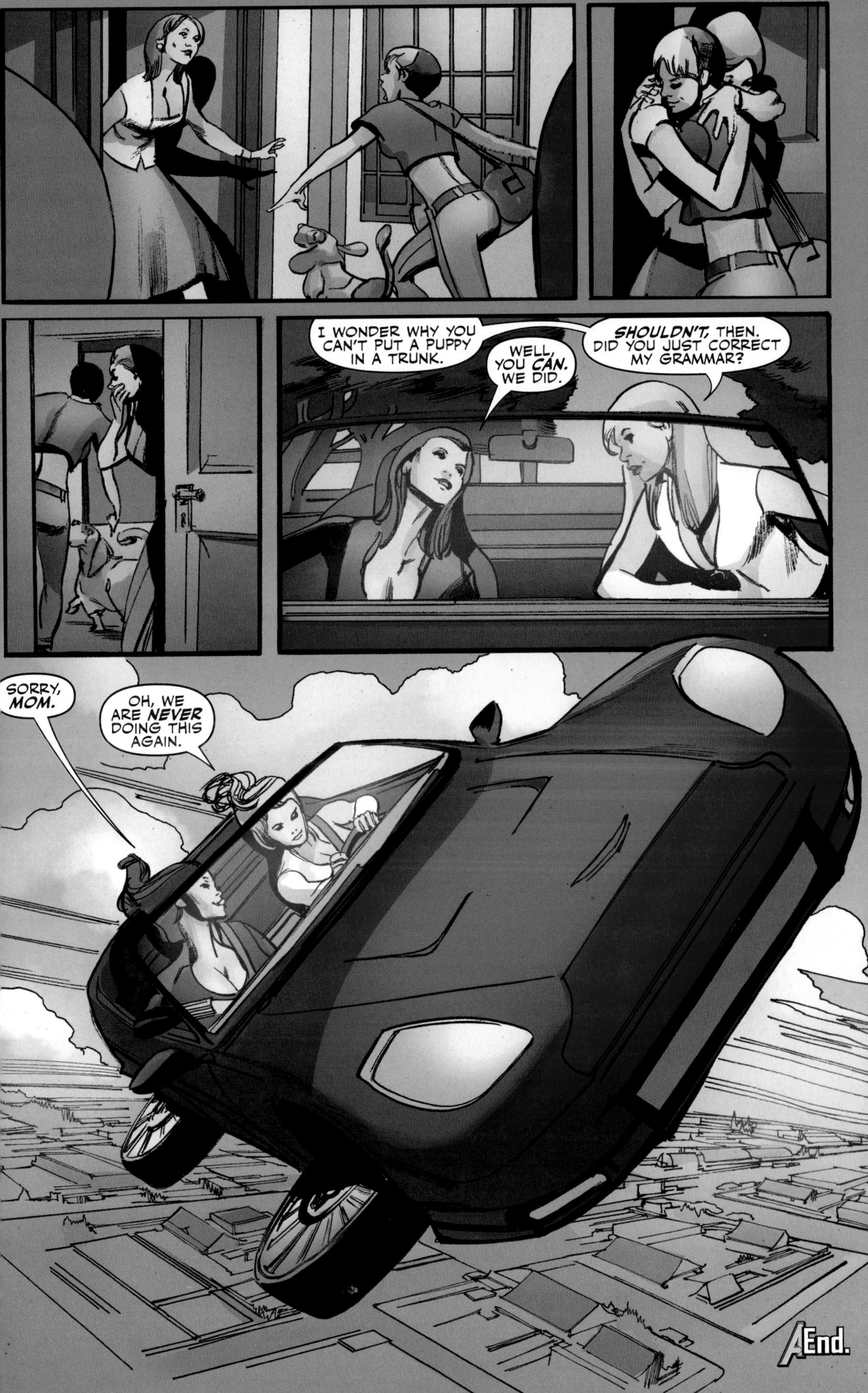
I WONDER WHY YOU CAN'T PUT A PUPPY IN A TRUNK.
WELL, YOU ***CAN.*** WE DID.
SHOULDN'T, THEN. DID YOU JUST CORRECT MY GRAMMAR?
SORRY, ***MOM.***
OH, WE ARE ***NEVER*** DOING THIS AGAIN.
End.

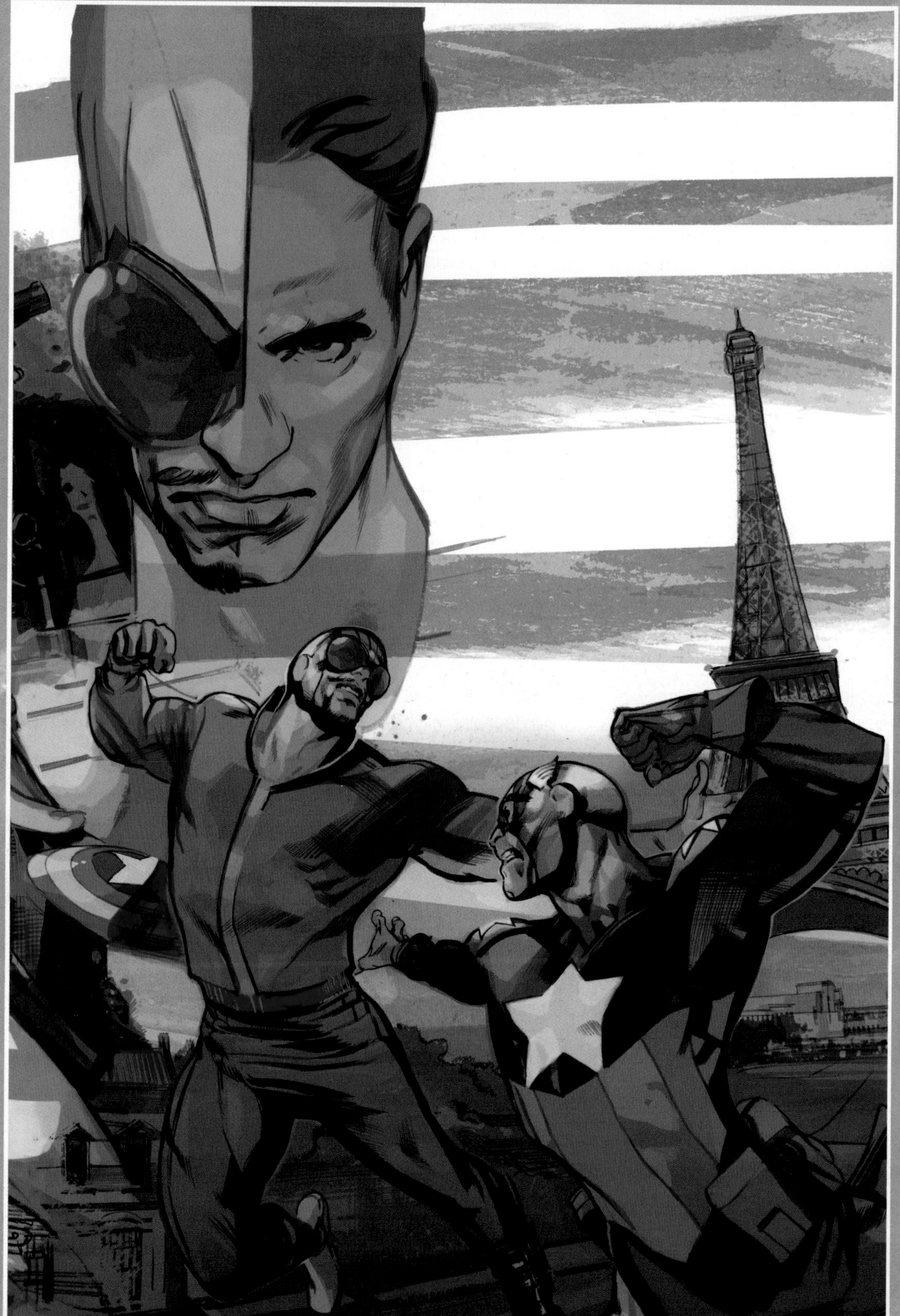

CAPTAIN AMERICA AND BATROC

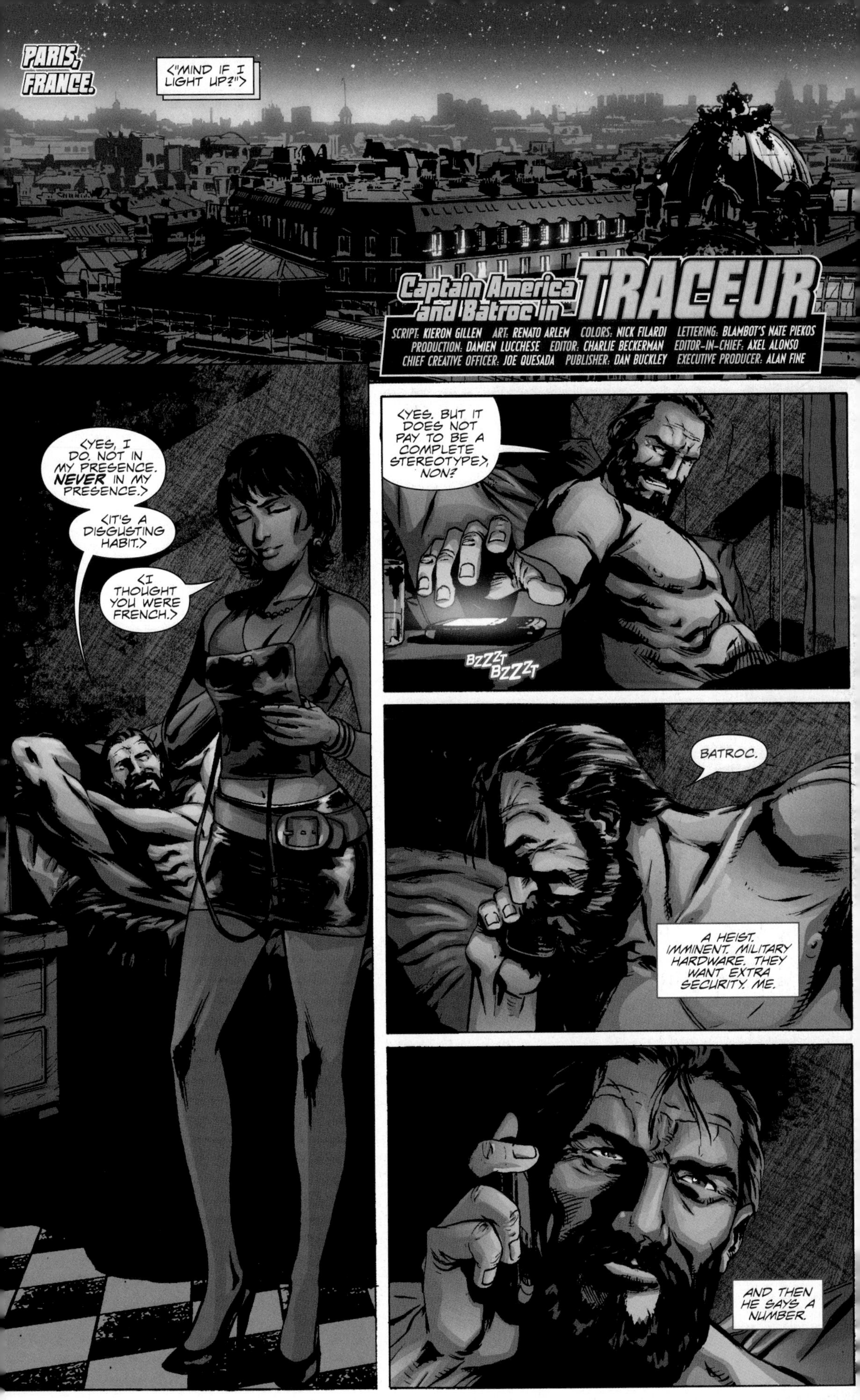
PARIS, FRANCE.
<"MIND IF I LIGHT UP?">
Captain America and Batroc in TRACEUR
SCRIPT: KIERON GILLEN ART: RENATO ARLEM COLORS: NICK FILARDI LETTERING: BLAMBOT'S NATE PIEKOS
PRODUCTION: DAMIEN LUCCHESE EDITOR: CHARLIE BECKERMAN EDITOR-IN-CHIEF: AXEL ALONSO
CHIEF CREATIVE OFFICER: JOE QUESADA PUBLISHER: DAN BUCKLEY EXECUTIVE PRODUCER: ALAN FINE
<YES, I DO. NOT IN MY PRESENCE. NEVER IN MY PRESENCE.>
<IT'S A DISGUSTING HABIT.>
<I THOUGHT YOU WERE FRENCH.>
<YES. BUT IT DOES NOT PAY TO BE A COMPLETE STEREOTYPE>, NON?
BZZZT BZZZT
BATROC.
A HEIST. IMMINENT. MILITARY HARDWARE. THEY WANT EXTRA SECURITY. ME.
AND THEN HE SAYS A NUMBER.

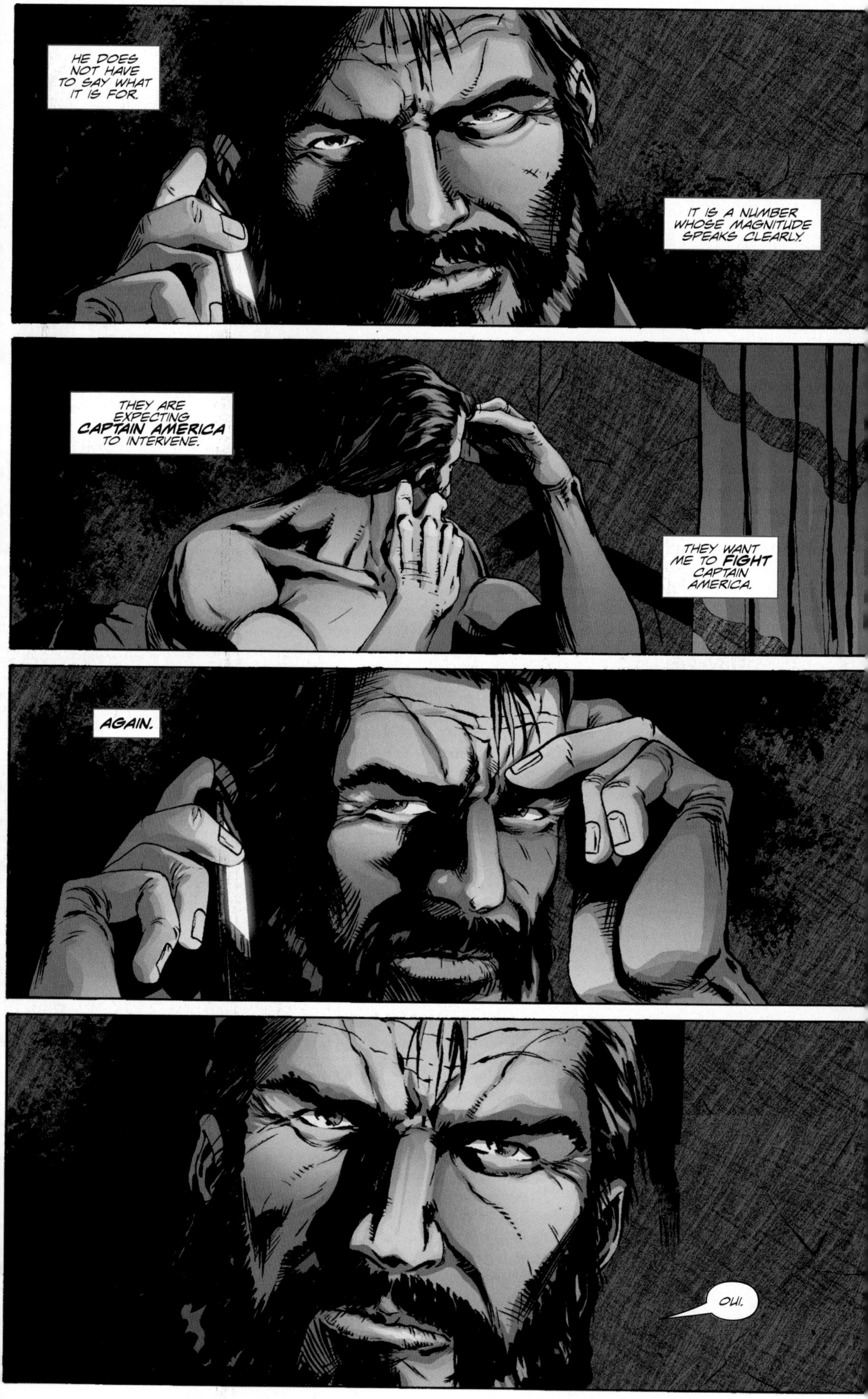
HE DOES NOT HAVE TO SAY WHAT IT IS FOR.
IT IS A NUMBER WHOSE MAGNITUDE SPEAKS CLEARLY.
THEY ARE EXPECTING CAPTAIN AMERICA TO INTERVENE.
THEY WANT ME TO FIGHT CAPTAIN AMERICA.
AGAIN.
OUI.

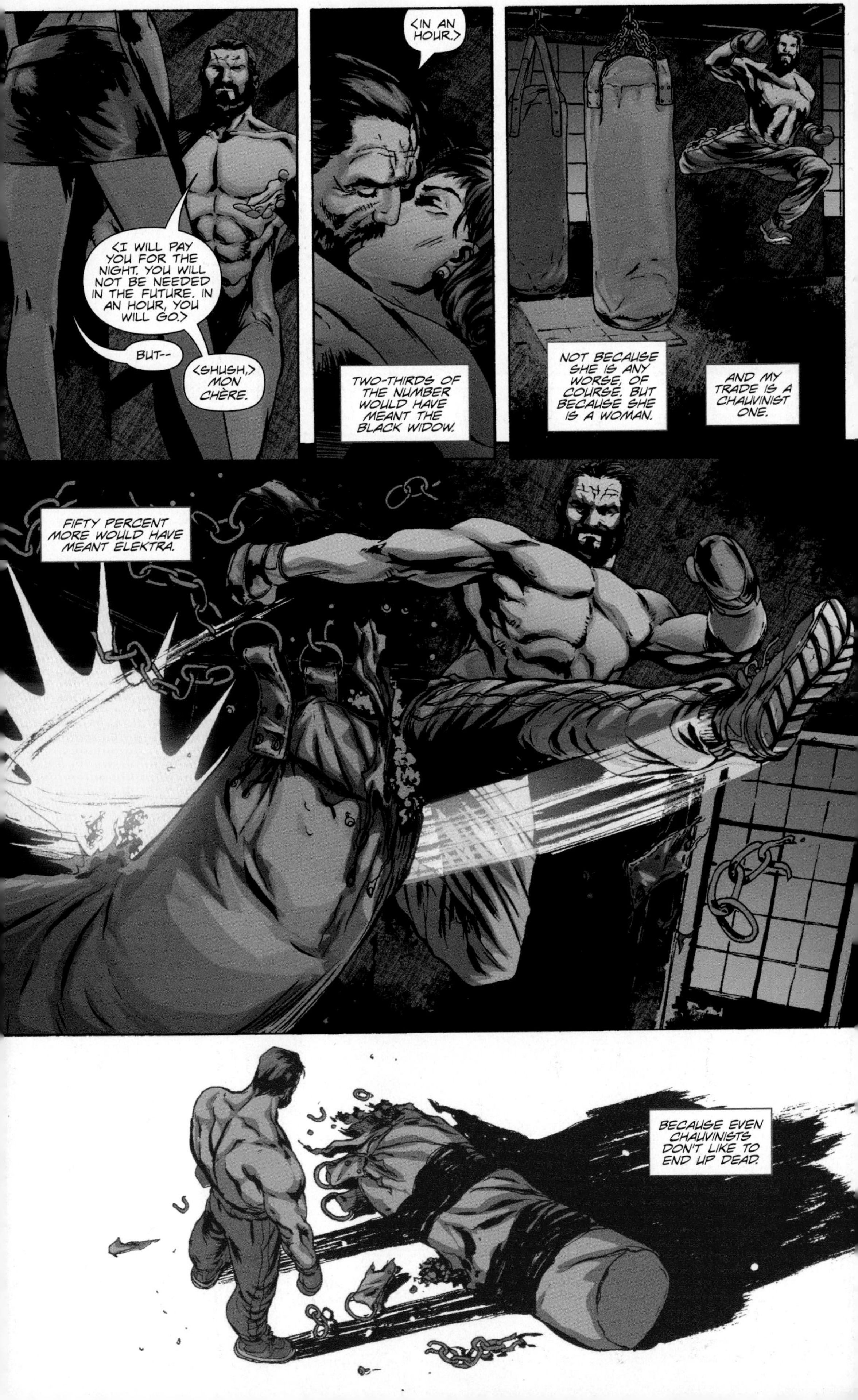

<I WILL PAY YOU FOR THE NIGHT. YOU WILL NOT BE NEEDED IN THE FUTURE. IN AN HOUR, YOU WILL GO.>
BUT--
<SHUSH,> MON CHÈRE.
<IN AN HOUR.>
TWO-THIRDS OF THE NUMBER WOULD HAVE MEANT THE BLACK WIDOW.
NOT BECAUSE SHE IS ANY WORSE, OF COURSE. BUT BECAUSE SHE IS A WOMAN.
AND MY TRADE IS A CHAUVINIST ONE.
FIFTY PERCENT MORE WOULD HAVE MEANT ELEKTRA.
BECAUSE EVEN CHAUVINISTS DON'T LIKE TO END UP DEAD.

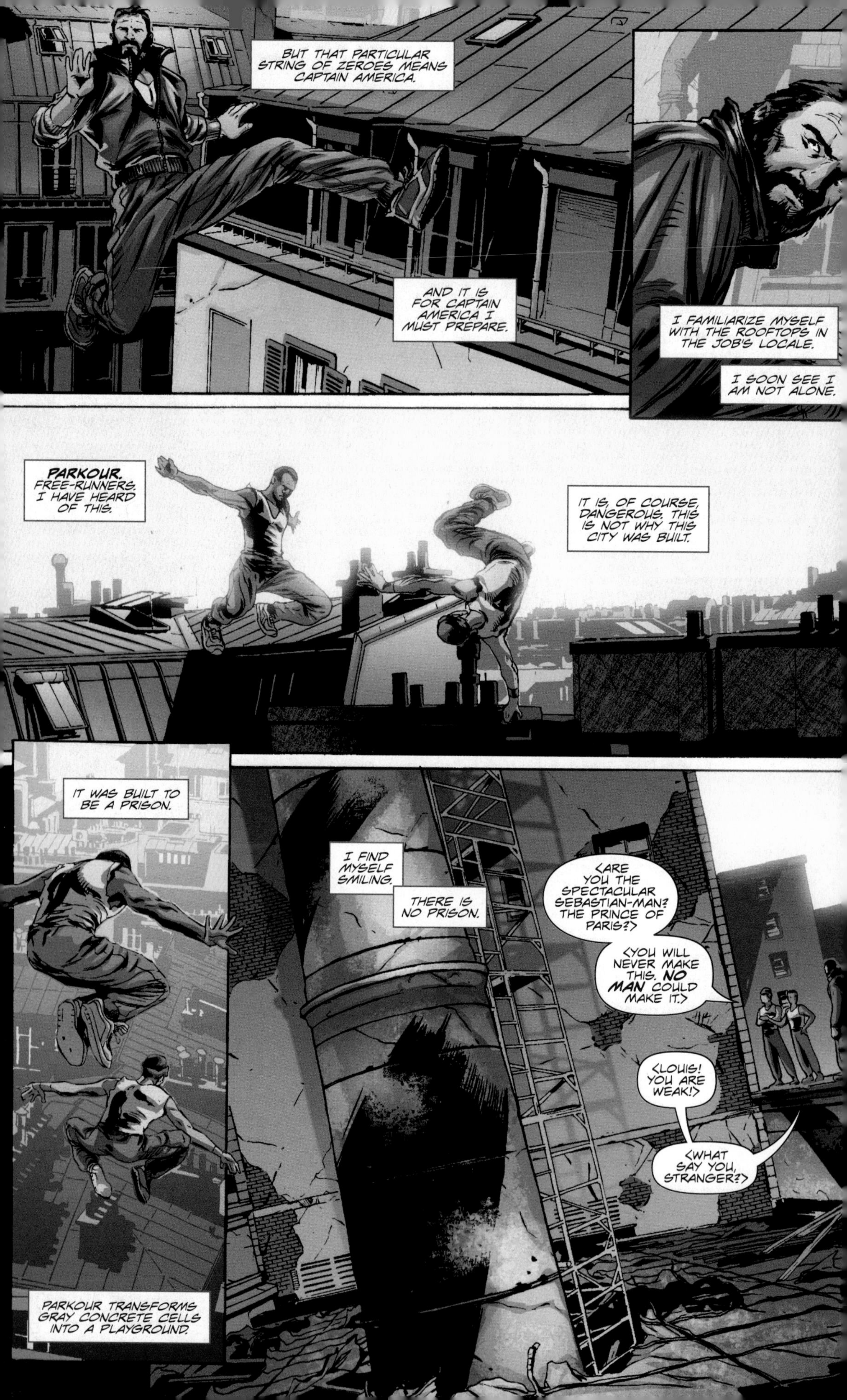
BUT THAT PARTICULAR STRING OF ZEROES MEANS CAPTAIN AMERICA.
AND IT IS FOR CAPTAIN AMERICA I MUST PREPARE.
I FAMILIARIZE MYSELF WITH THE ROOFTOPS IN THE JOB'S LOCALE.
I SOON SEE I AM NOT ALONE.
PARKOUR. FREE-RUNNERS. I HAVE HEARD OF THIS.
IT IS, OF COURSE, DANGEROUS. THIS IS NOT WHY THIS CITY WAS BUILT.
IT WAS BUILT TO BE A PRISON.
PARKOUR TRANSFORMS GRAY CONCRETE CELLS INTO A PLAYGROUND.
I FIND MYSELF SMILING.
THERE IS NO PRISON.
<ARE YOU THE SPECTACULAR SEBASTIAN-MAN? THE PRINCE OF PARIS?>
<YOU WILL NEVER MAKE THIS. NO MAN COULD MAKE IT.>
<LOUIS! YOU ARE WEAK!>
<WHAT SAY YOU, STRANGER?>

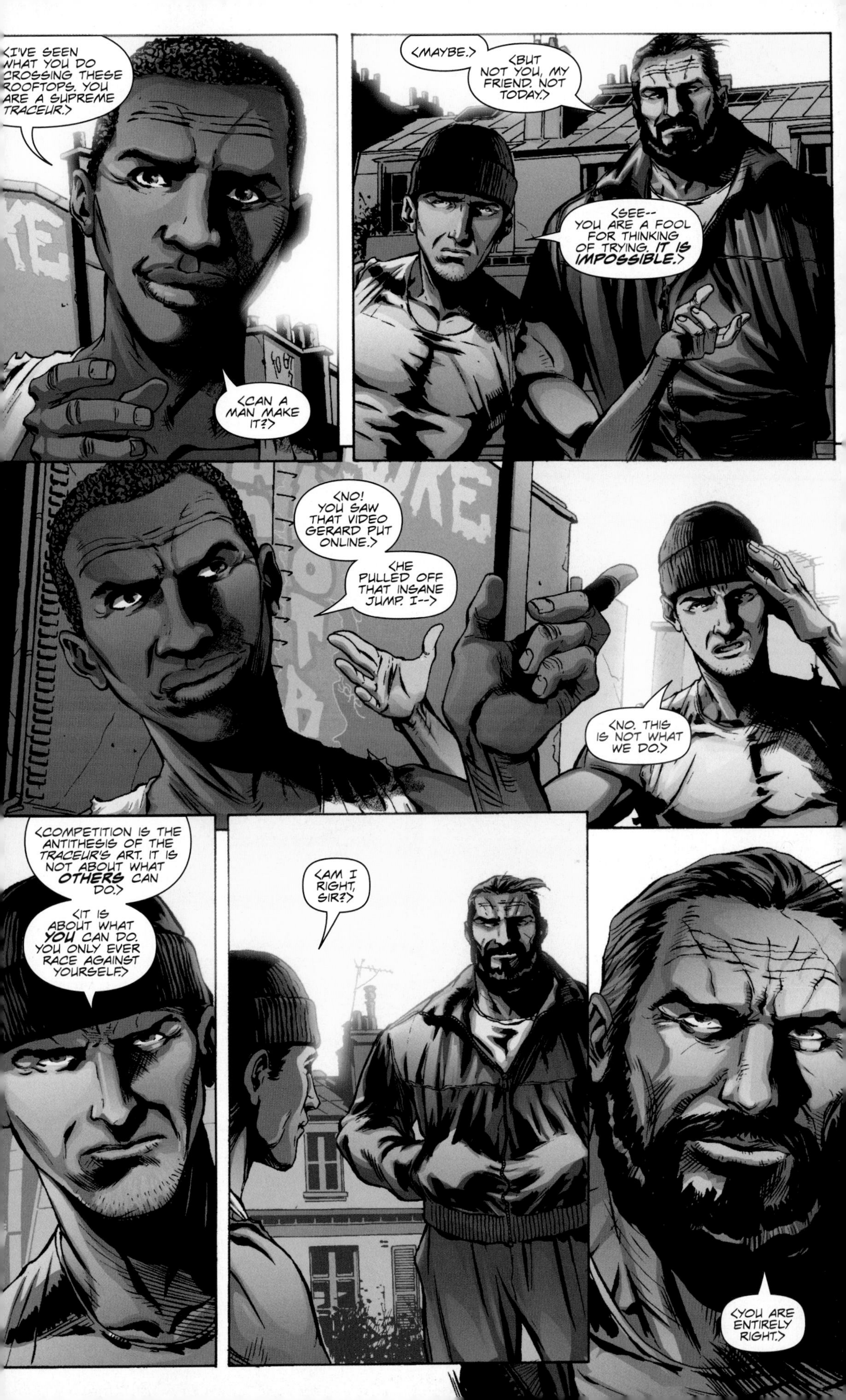

<I'VE SEEN WHAT YOU DO CROSSING THESE ROOFTOPS. YOU ARE A SUPREME TRACEUR.>
<CAN A MAN MAKE IT?>
<MAYBE.>
<BUT NOT YOU, MY FRIEND. NOT TODAY.>
<SEE-- YOU ARE A FOOL FOR THINKING OF TRYING. IT IS IMPOSSIBLE.>
<NO! YOU SAW THAT VIDEO GERARD PUT ONLINE.>
<HE PULLED OFF THAT INSANE JUMP. I-->
<NO. THIS IS NOT WHAT WE DO.>
<COMPETITION IS THE ANTITHESIS OF THE TRACEUR'S ART. IT IS NOT ABOUT WHAT OTHERS CAN DO.>
<IT IS ABOUT WHAT YOU CAN DO. YOU ONLY EVER RACE AGAINST YOURSELF.>
<AM I RIGHT, SIR?>
<YOU ARE ENTIRELY RIGHT.>

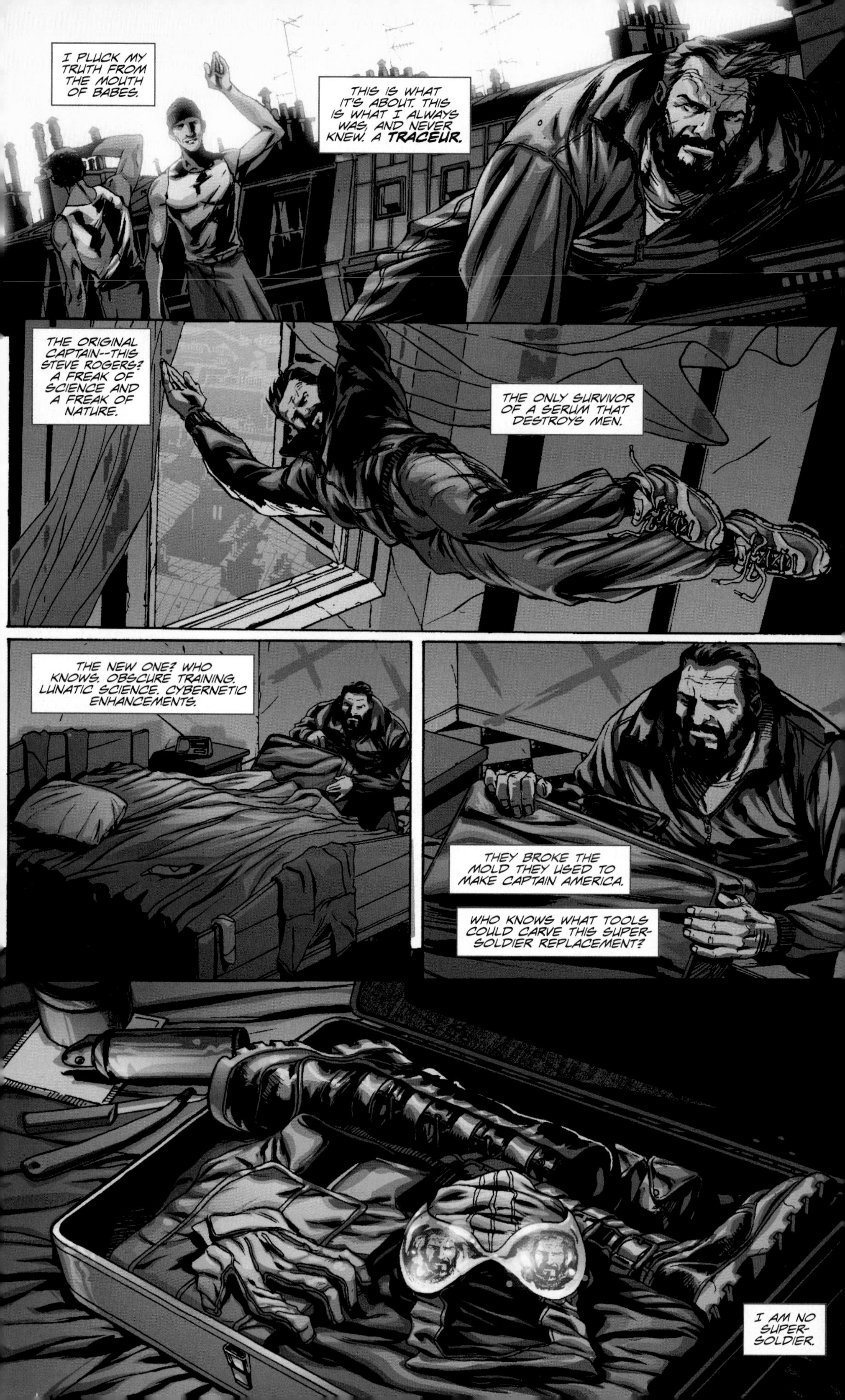
I PLUCK MY TRUTH FROM THE MOUTH OF BABES.
THIS IS WHAT IT'S ABOUT. THIS IS WHAT I ALWAYS WAS, AND NEVER KNEW. A TRACEUR.
THE ORIGINAL CAPTAIN--THIS STEVE ROGERS? A FREAK OF SCIENCE AND A FREAK OF NATURE.
THE ONLY SURVIVOR OF A SERUM THAT DESTROYS MEN.
THE NEW ONE? WHO KNOWS. OBSCURE TRAINING. LUNATIC SCIENCE. CYBERNETIC ENHANCEMENTS.
THEY BROKE THE MOLD THEY USED TO MAKE CAPTAIN AMERICA.
WHO KNOWS WHAT TOOLS COULD CARVE THIS SUPER-SOLDIER REPLACEMENT?
I AM NO SUPER-SOLDIER.

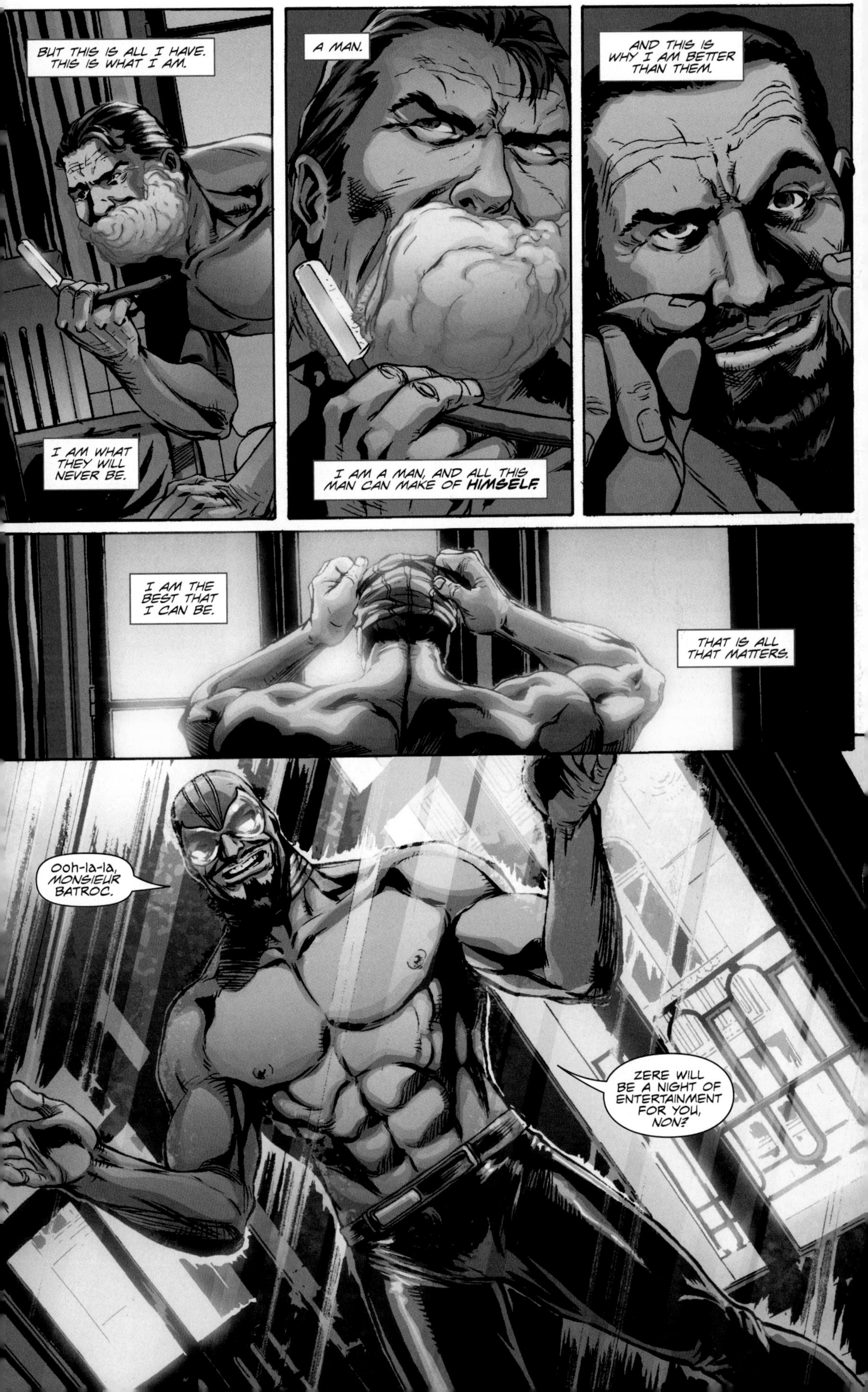
BUT THIS IS ALL I HAVE. THIS IS WHAT I AM.
I AM WHAT THEY WILL NEVER BE.
A MAN.
I AM A MAN, AND ALL THIS MAN CAN MAKE OF HIMSELF.
AND THIS IS WHY I AM BETTER THAN THEM.
I AM THE BEST THAT I CAN BE.
THAT IS ALL THAT MATTERS.
Ooh-la-la, MONSIEUR BATROC.
ZERE WILL BE A NIGHT OF ENTERTAINMENT FOR YOU, NON?

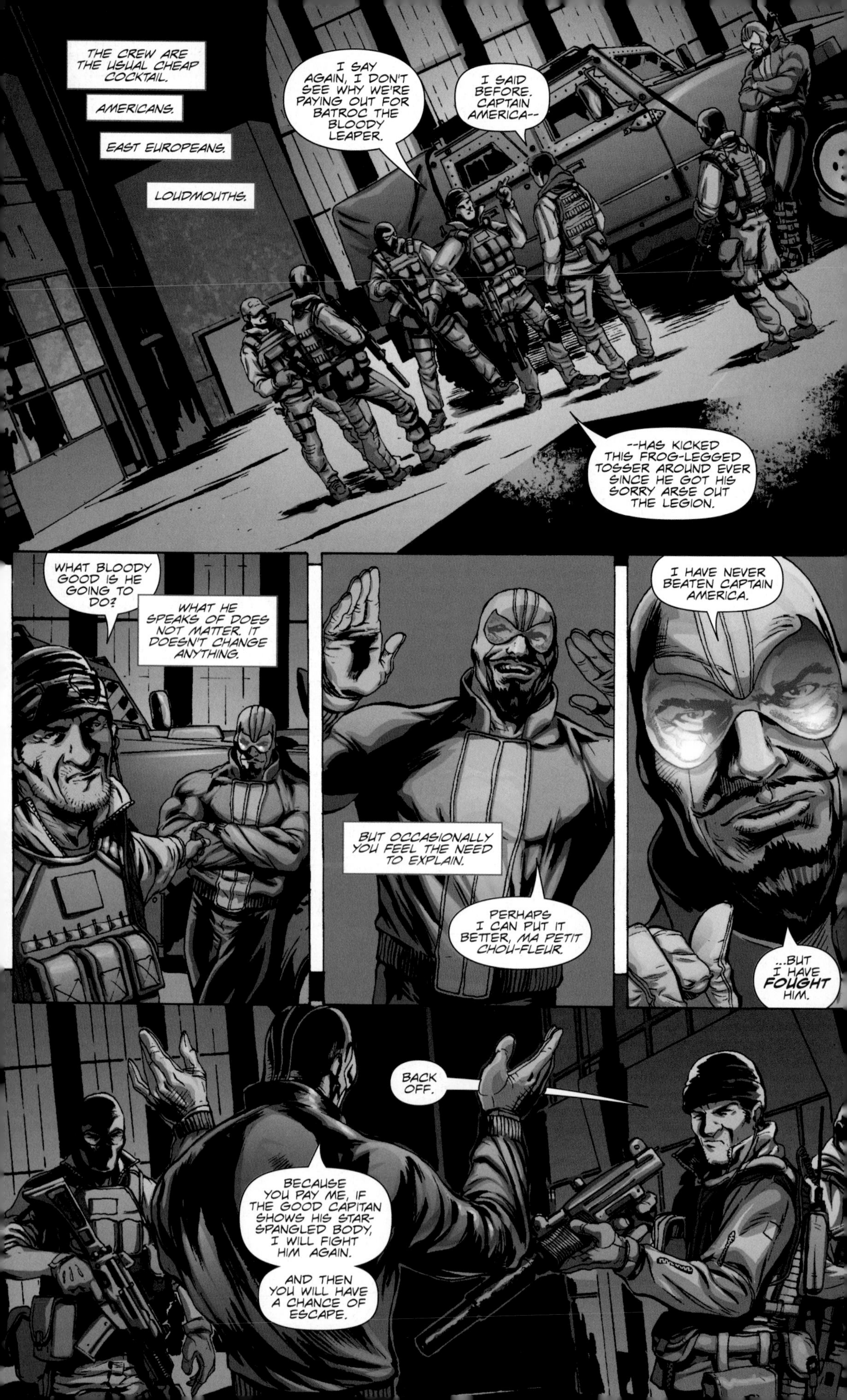
THE CREW ARE THE USUAL CHEAP COCKTAIL.
AMERICANS.
EAST EUROPEANS.
LOUDMOUTHS.
I SAY AGAIN, I DON'T SEE WHY WE'RE PAYING OUT FOR BATROC THE BLOODY LEAPER.
I SAID BEFORE. CAPTAIN AMERICA--
--HAS KICKED THIS FROG-LEGGED TOSSER AROUND EVER SINCE HE GOT HIS SORRY ARSE OUT THE LEGION.
WHAT BLOODY GOOD IS HE GOING TO DO?
WHAT HE SPEAKS OF DOES NOT MATTER. IT DOESN'T CHANGE ANYTHING.
BUT OCCASIONALLY YOU FEEL THE NEED TO EXPLAIN.
PERHAPS I CAN PUT IT BETTER, MA PETIT CHOU-FLEUR.
I HAVE NEVER BEATEN CAPTAIN AMERICA.
...BUT I HAVE FOUGHT HIM.
BACK OFF.
BECAUSE YOU PAY ME, IF THE GOOD CAPITAN SHOWS HIS STAR-SPANGLED BODY, I WILL FIGHT HIM AGAIN.
AND THEN YOU WILL HAVE A CHANCE OF ESCAPE.

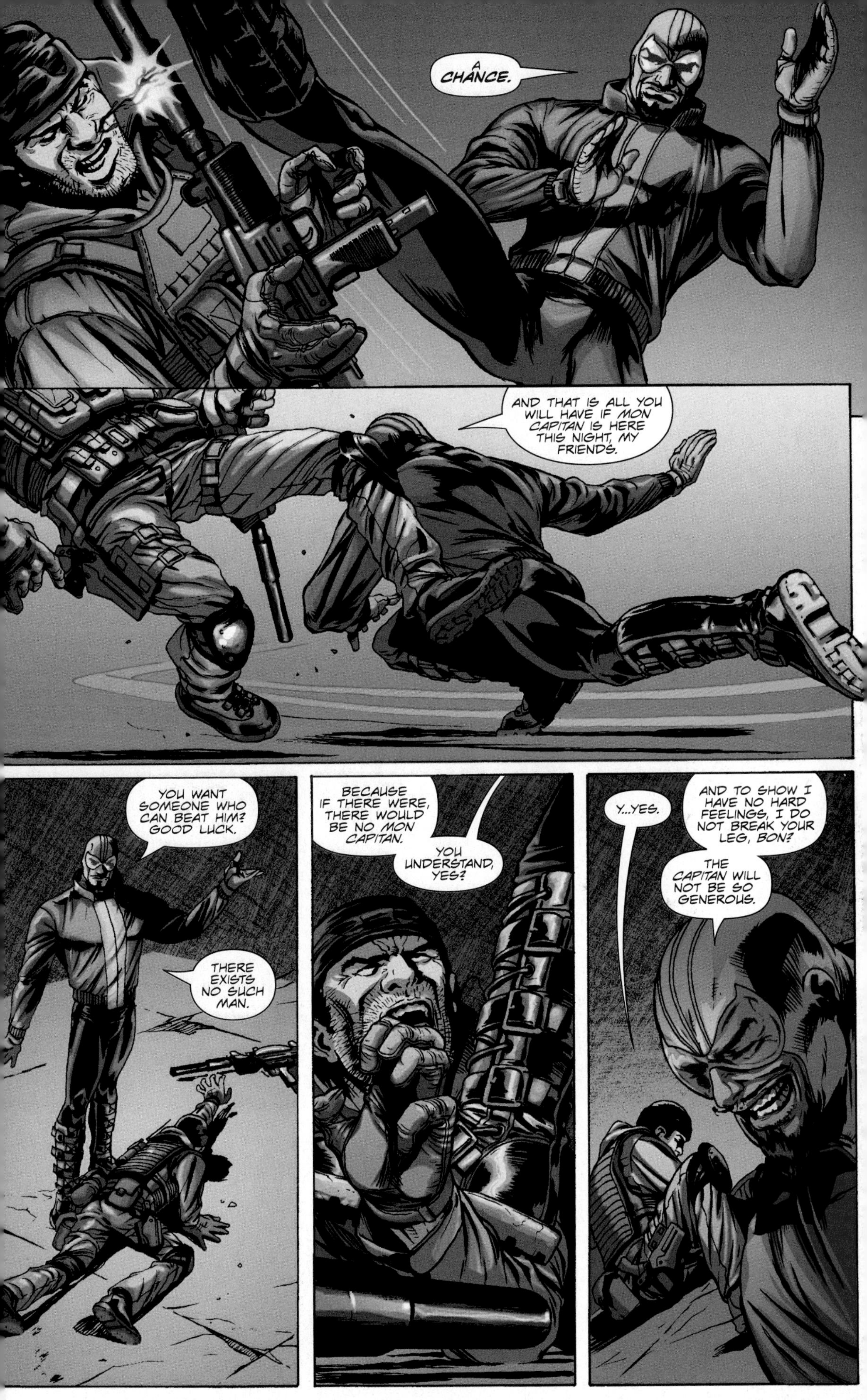
A CHANCE.
AND THAT IS ALL YOU WILL HAVE IF MON CAPITAN IS HERE THIS NIGHT, MY FRIENDS.
YOU WANT SOMEONE WHO CAN BEAT HIM? GOOD LUCK.
THERE EXISTS NO SUCH MAN.
BECAUSE IF THERE WERE, THERE WOULD BE NO MON CAPITAN.
YOU UNDERSTAND, YES?
Y...YES.
AND TO SHOW I HAVE NO HARD FEELINGS, I DO NOT BREAK YOUR LEG, BON?
THE CAPITAN WILL NOT BE SO GENEROUS.

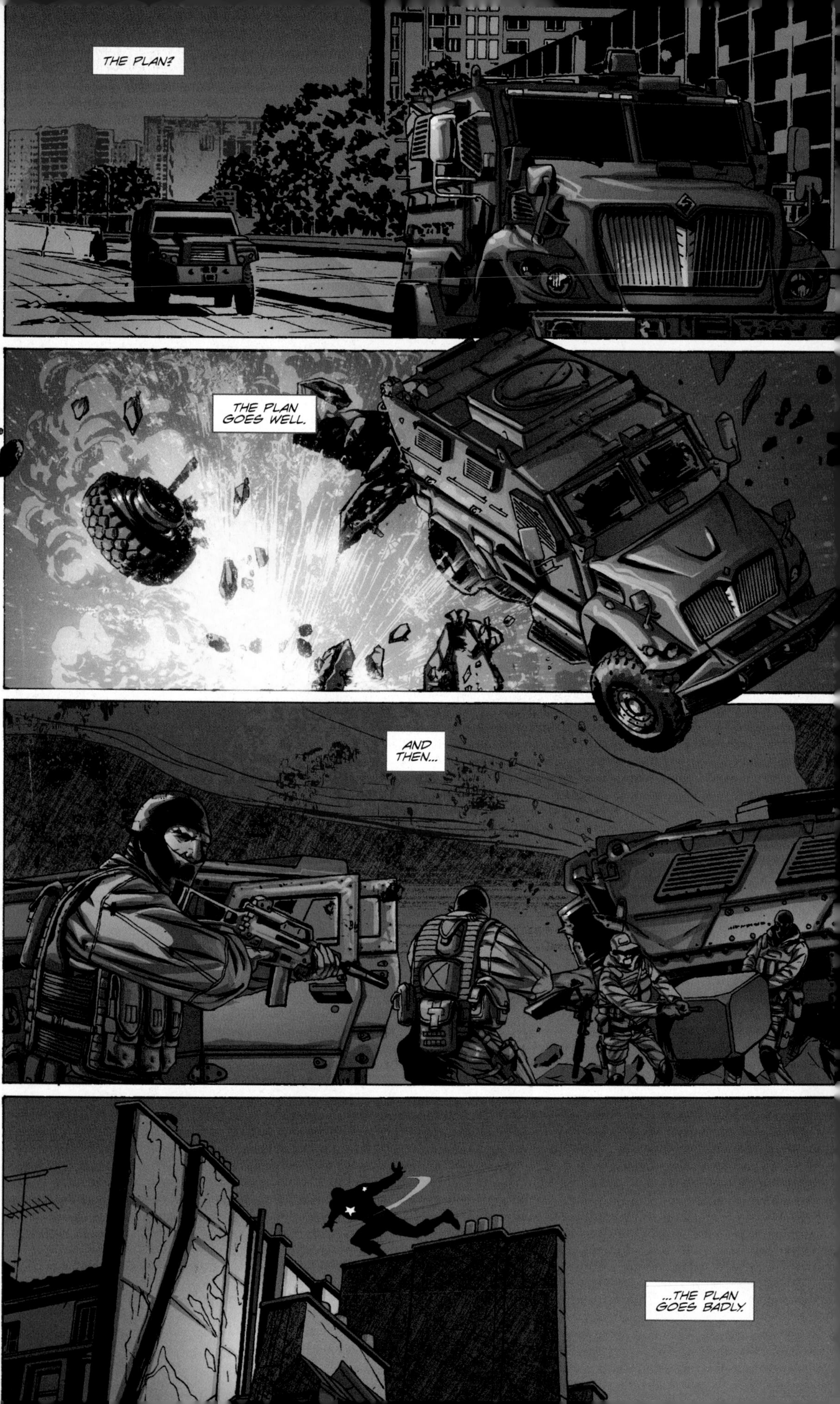
THE PLAN?
THE PLAN GOES WELL.
AND THEN...
...THE PLAN GOES BADLY.

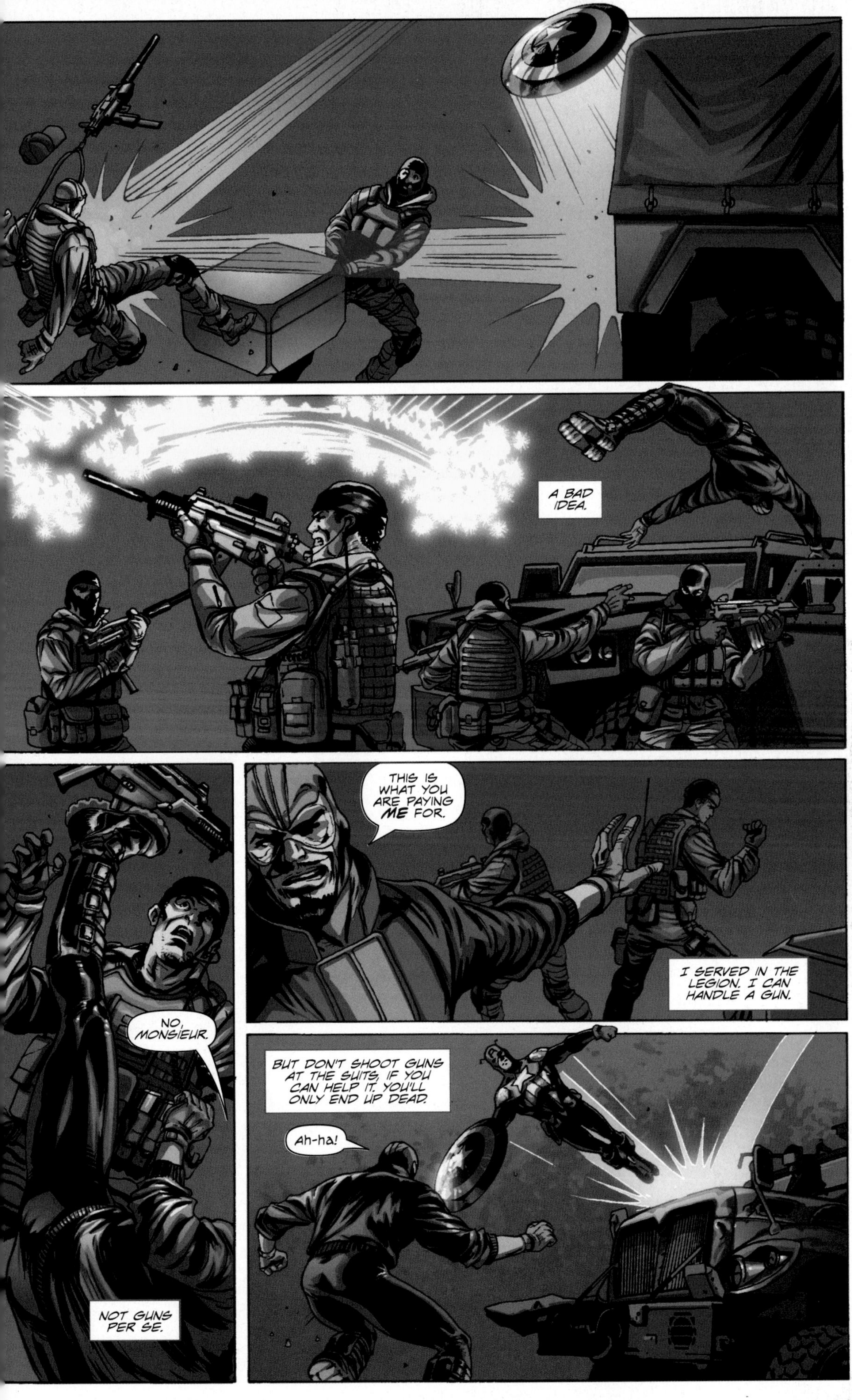
A BAD IDEA.
THIS IS WHAT YOU ARE PAYING ME FOR.
I SERVED IN THE LEGION. I CAN HANDLE A GUN.
NO, MONSIEUR.
NOT GUNS PER SE.
BUT DON'T SHOOT GUNS AT THE SUITS, IF YOU CAN HELP IT. YOU'LL ONLY END UP DEAD.
Ah-ha!

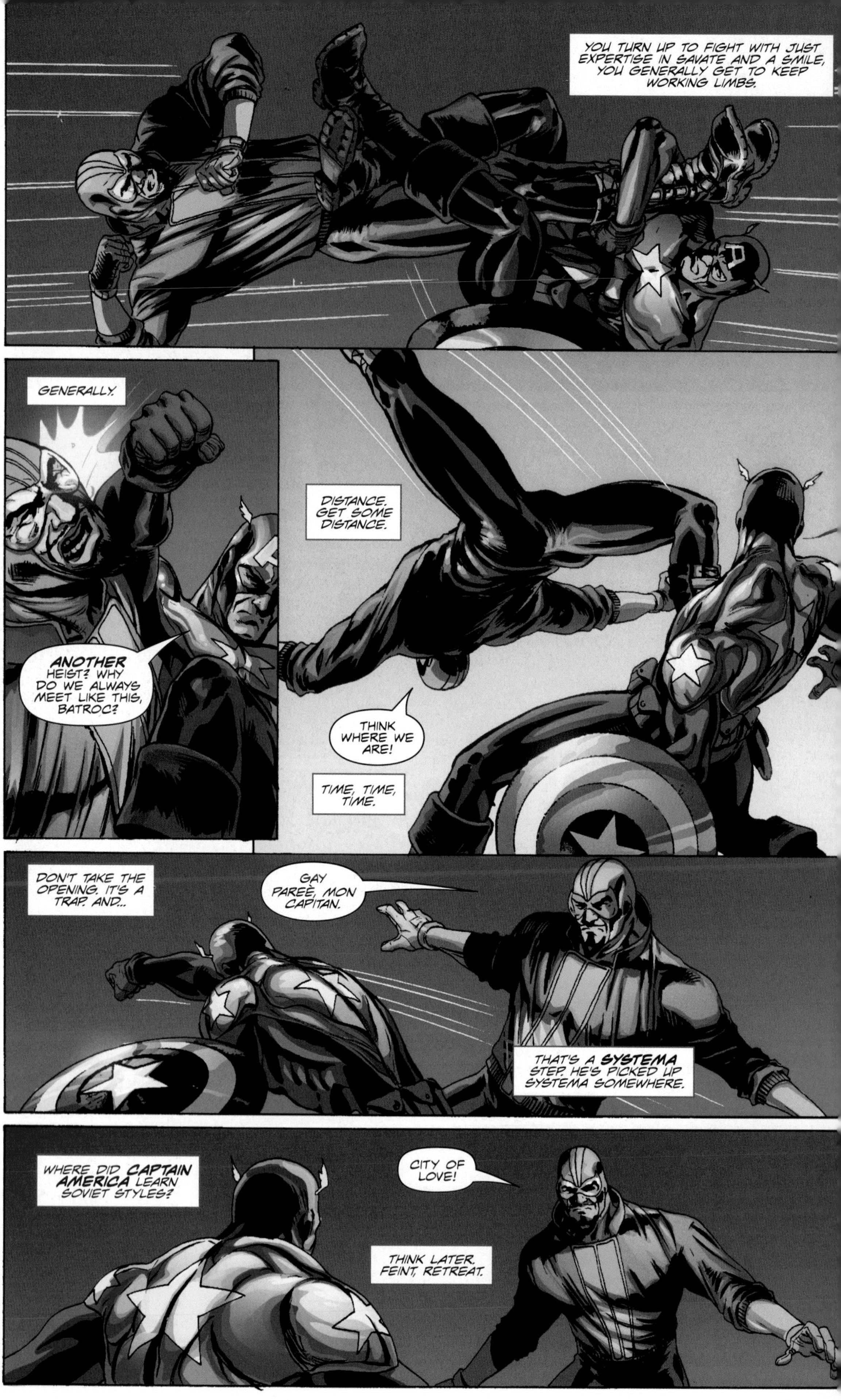
YOU TURN UP TO FIGHT WITH JUST EXPERTISE IN SAVATE AND A SMILE, YOU GENERALLY GET TO KEEP WORKING LIMBS.
GENERALLY.
ANOTHER HEIST? WHY DO WE ALWAYS MEET LIKE THIS, BATROC?
DISTANCE. GET SOME DISTANCE.
THINK WHERE WE ARE!
TIME, TIME, TIME.
DON'T TAKE THE OPENING. IT'S A TRAP. AND...
GAY PAREÈ, MON CAPITAN.
THAT'S A SYSTEMA STEP. HE'S PICKED UP SYSTEMA SOMEWHERE.
WHERE DID CAPTAIN AMERICA LEARN SOVIET STYLES?
CITY OF LOVE!
THINK LATER. FEINT, RETREAT.

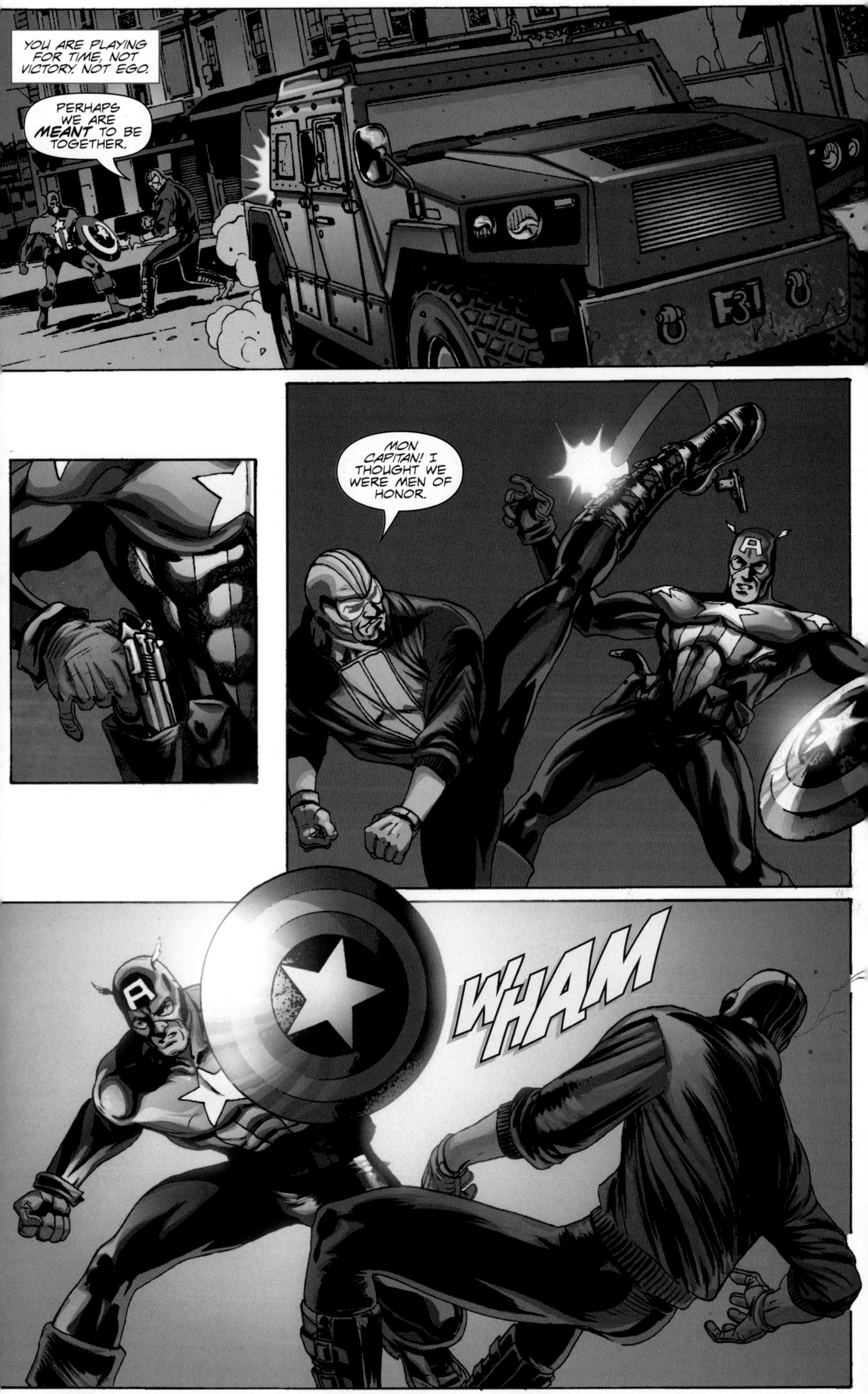
YOU ARE PLAYING FOR TIME, NOT VICTORY. NOT EGO.
PERHAPS WE ARE MEANT TO BE TOGETHER.
MON CAPITAN! I THOUGHT WE WERE MEN OF HONOR.
WHAM

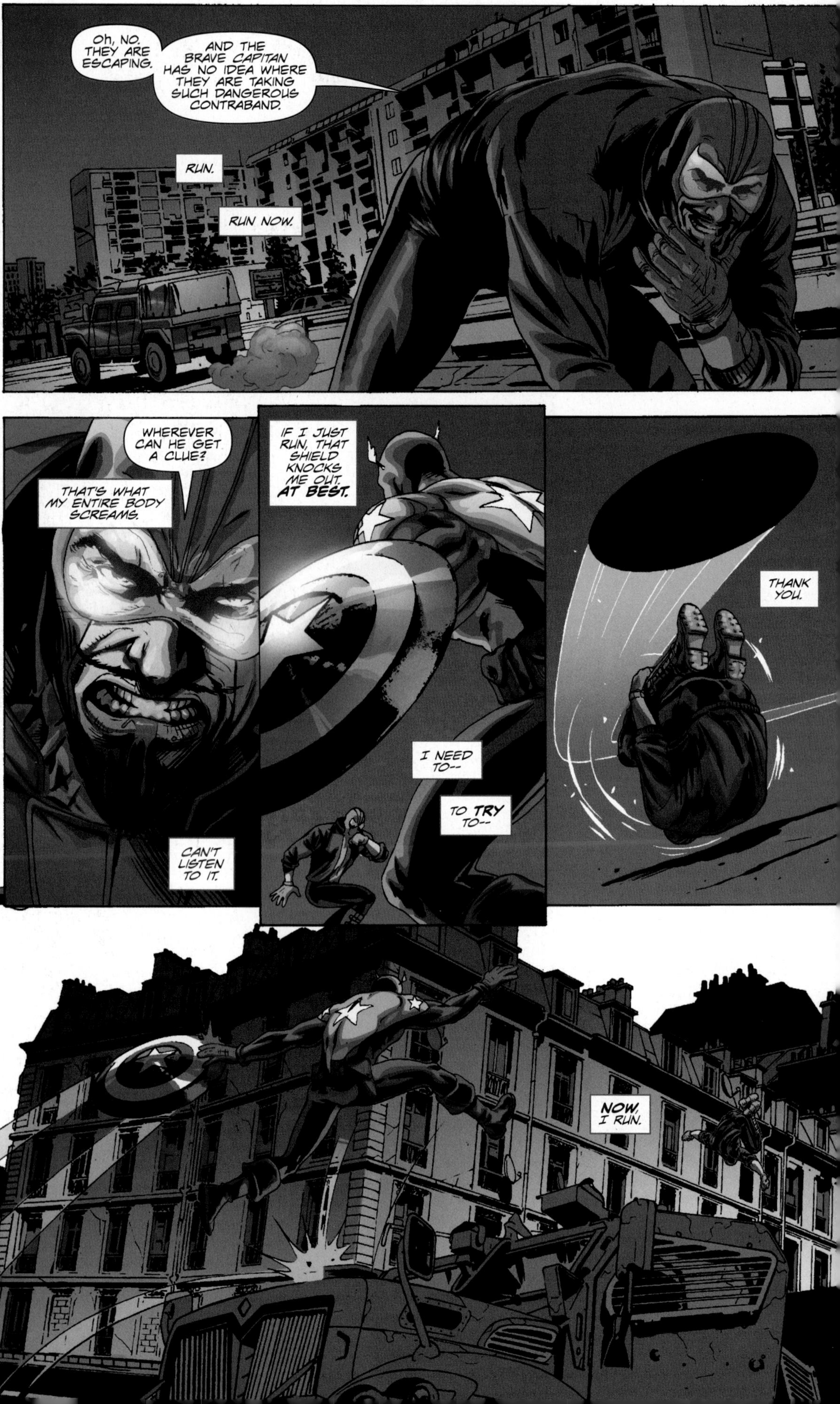
Oh, NO. THEY ARE ESCAPING.
AND THE BRAVE CAPITAN HAS NO IDEA WHERE THEY ARE TAKING SUCH DANGEROUS CONTRABAND.
RUN.
RUN NOW.
WHEREVER CAN HE GET A CLUE?
THAT'S WHAT MY ENTIRE BODY SCREAMS.
CAN'T LISTEN TO IT.
IF I JUST RUN, THAT SHIELD KNOCKS ME OUT. AT BEST.
I NEED TO--
TO TRY TO--
THANK YOU.
NOW, I RUN.

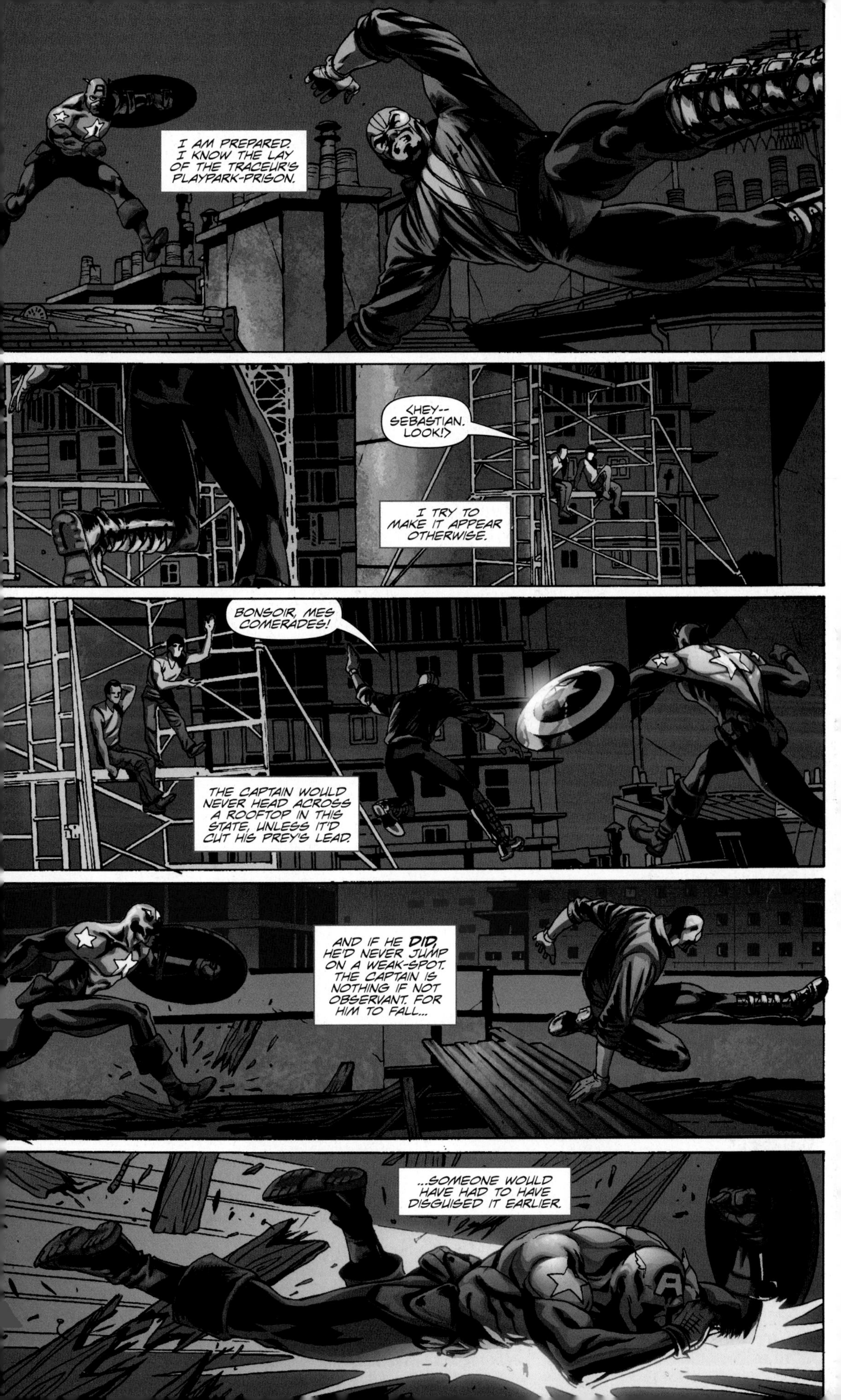
I AM PREPARED. I KNOW THE LAY OF THE TRACEUR'S PLAYPARK-PRISON.
<HEY-- SEBASTIAN. LOOK!>
I TRY TO MAKE IT APPEAR OTHERWISE.
BONSOIR, MES COMERADES!
THE CAPTAIN WOULD NEVER HEAD ACROSS A ROOFTOP IN THIS STATE, UNLESS IT'D CUT HIS PREY'S LEAD.
AND IF HE DID, HE'D NEVER JUMP ON A WEAK-SPOT. THE CAPTAIN IS NOTHING IF NOT OBSERVANT. FOR HIM TO FALL...
...SOMEONE WOULD HAVE HAD TO HAVE DISGUISED IT EARLIER.

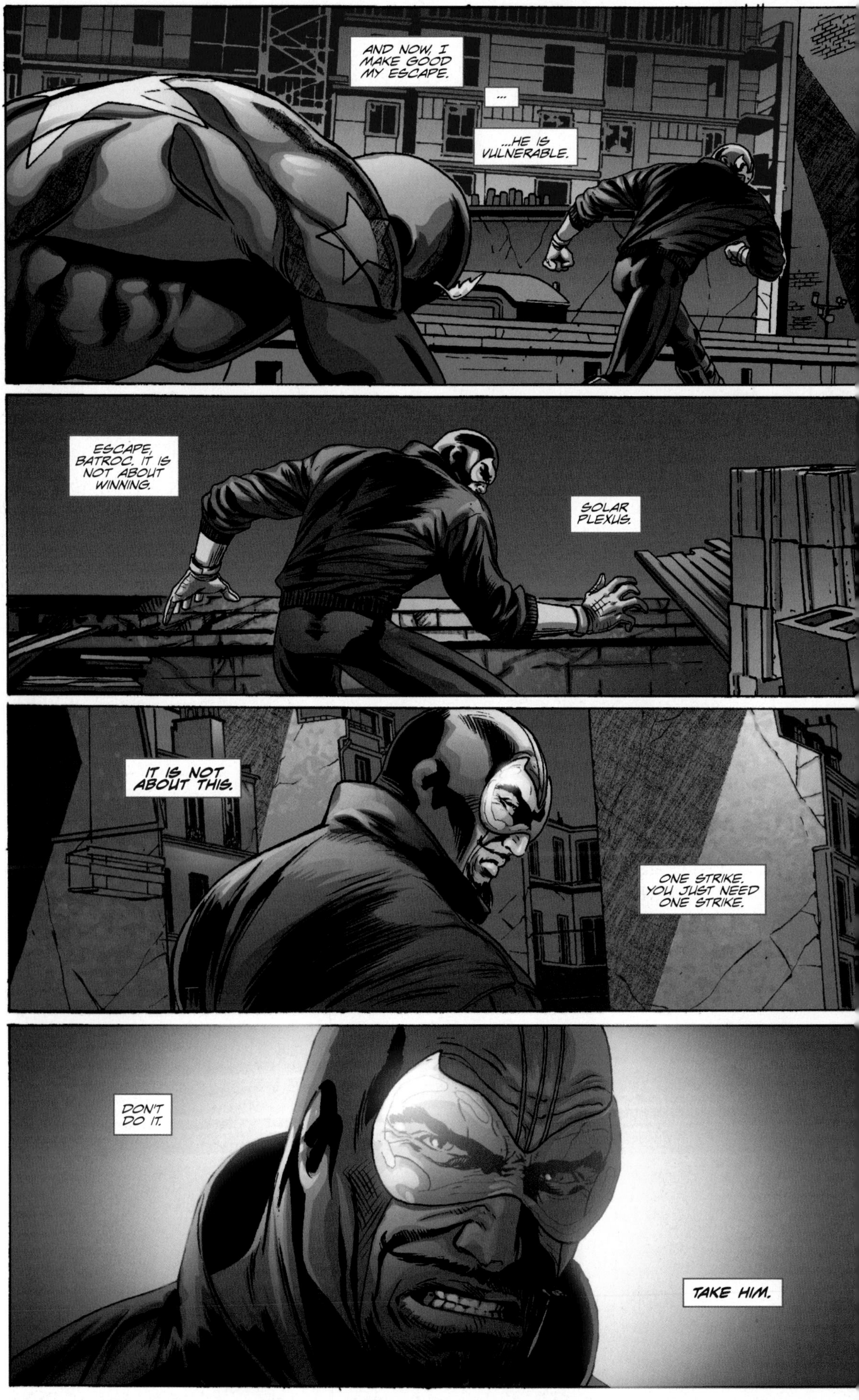

AND NOW, I MAKE GOOD MY ESCAPE.
...
...HE IS VULNERABLE.
ESCAPE, BATROC. IT IS NOT ABOUT WINNING.
SOLAR PLEXUS.
IT IS NOT ABOUT THIS.
ONE STRIKE. YOU JUST NEED ONE STRIKE.
DON'T DO IT.
TAKE HIM.

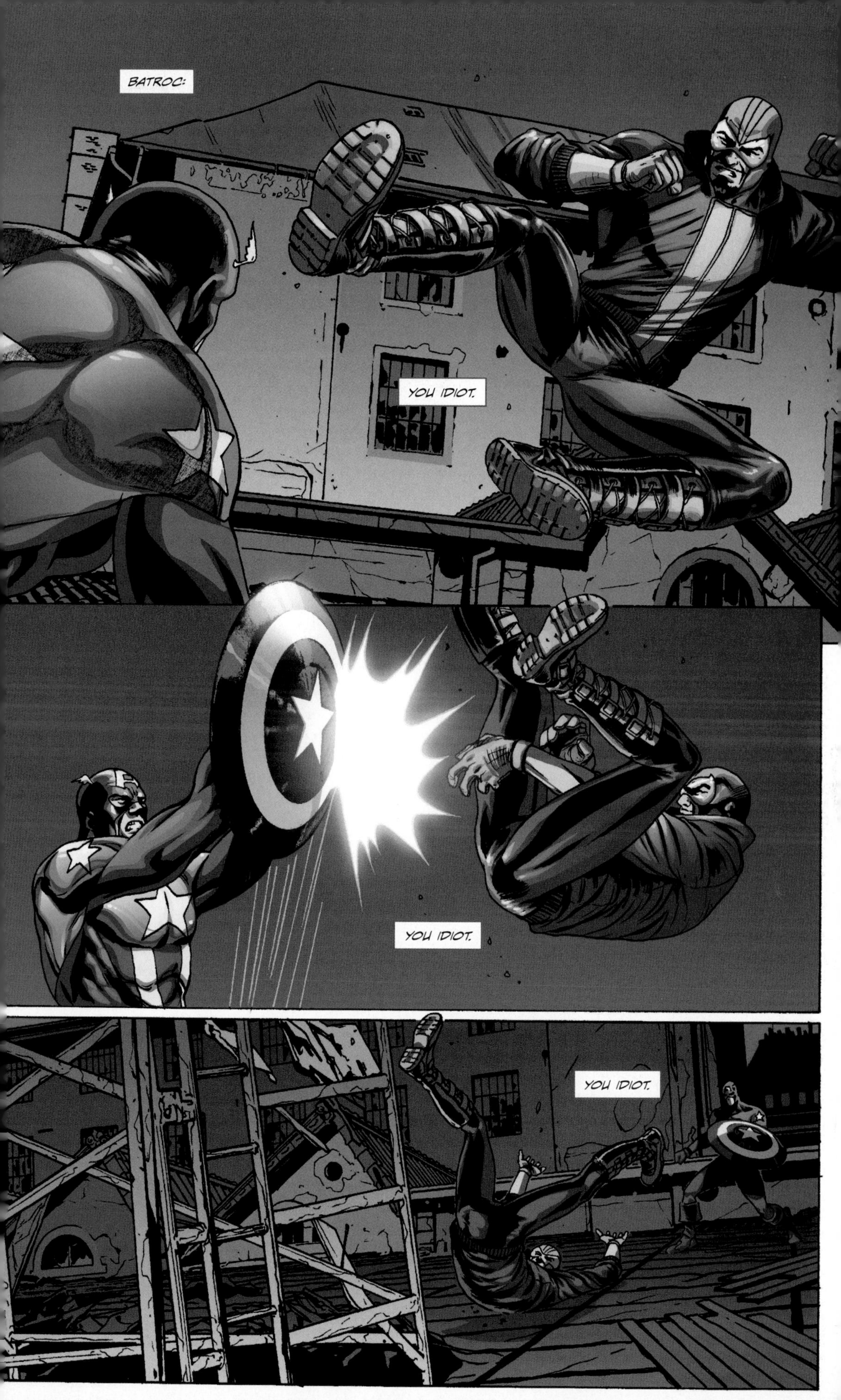
BATROC:
YOU IDIOT.
YOU IDIOT.
YOU IDIOT.

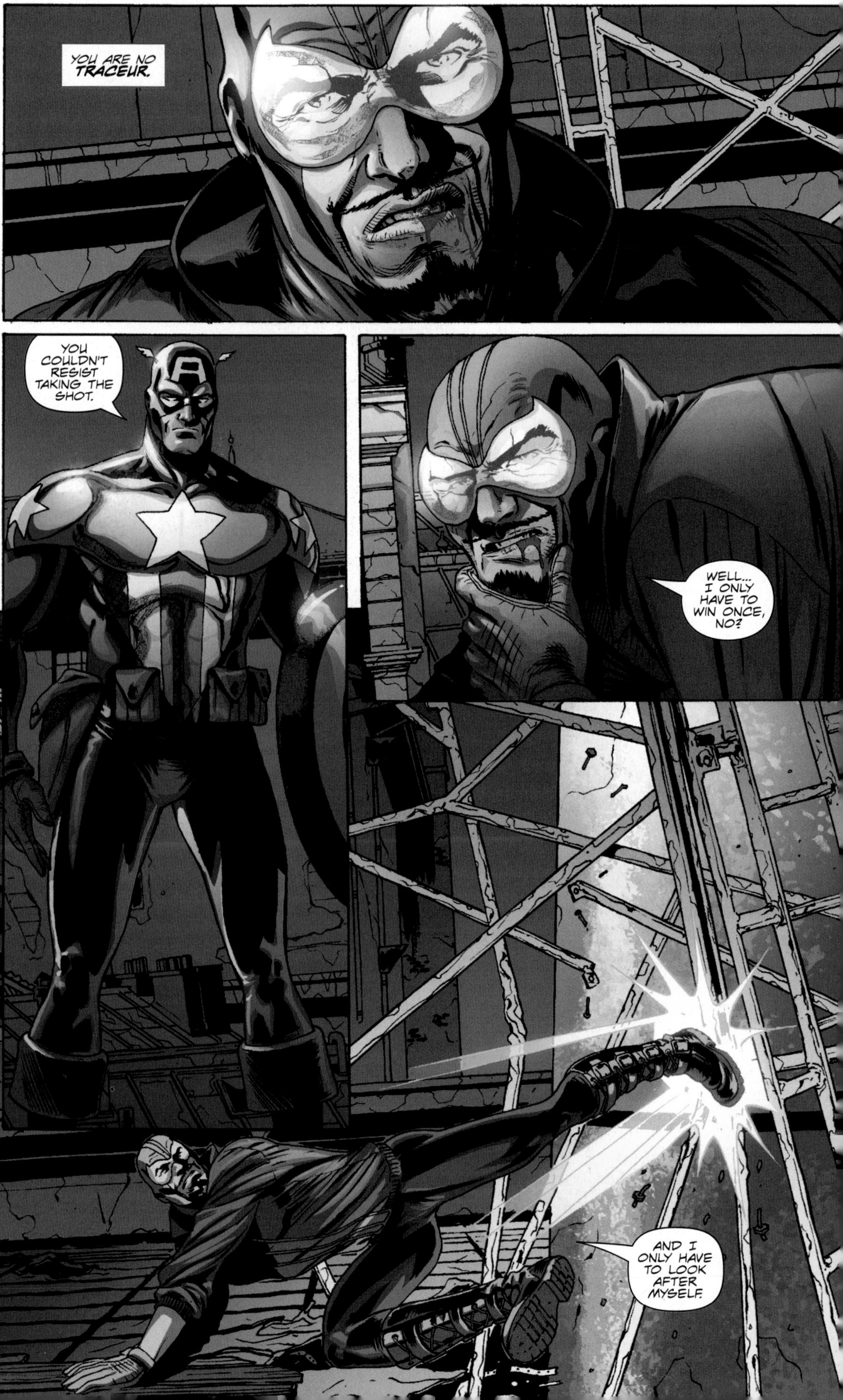
YOU ARE NO TRACEUR.
YOU COULDN'T RESIST TAKING THE SHOT.
WELL... I ONLY HAVE TO WIN ONCE, NO?
AND I ONLY HAVE TO LOOK AFTER MYSELF.

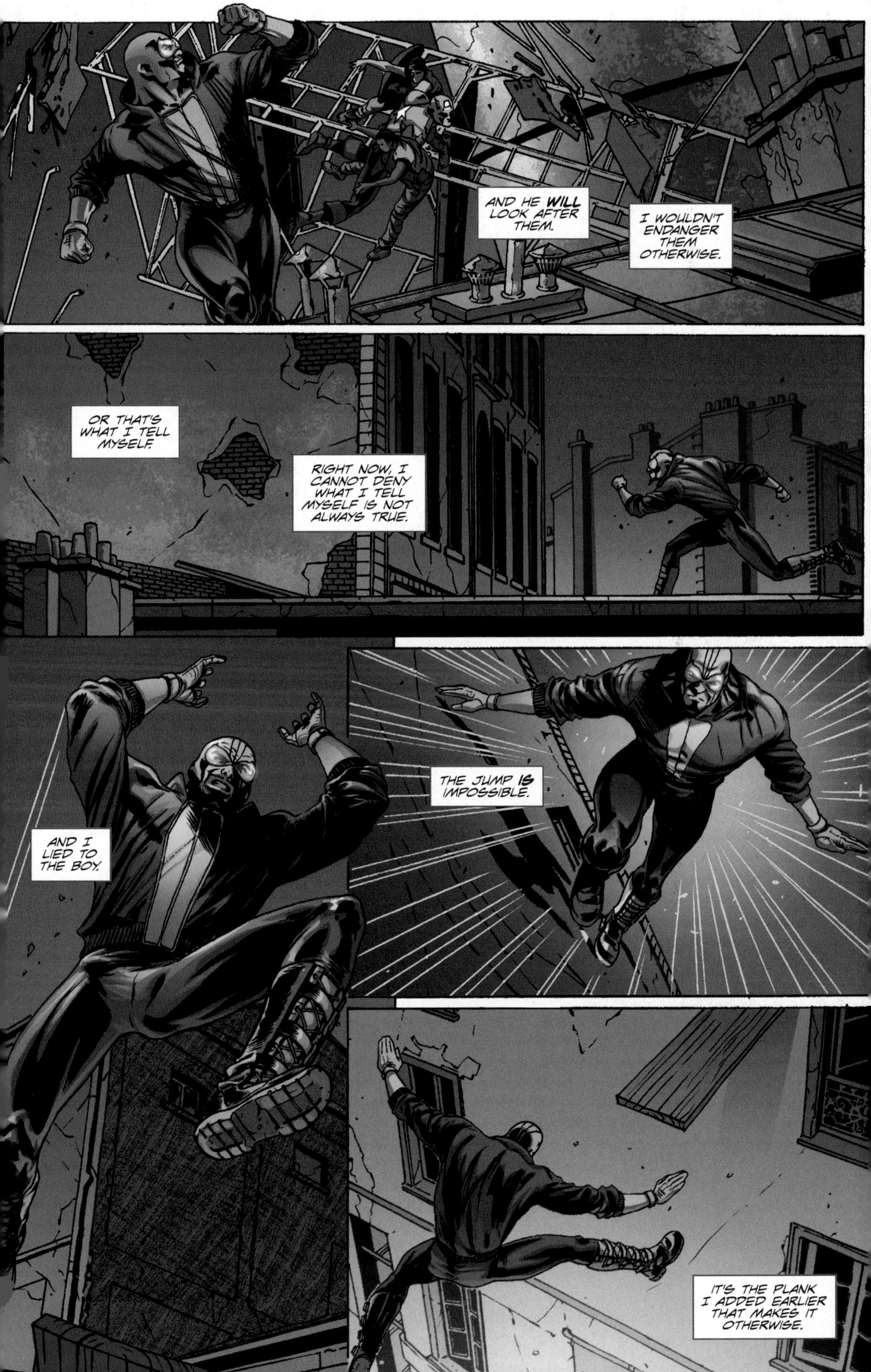
AND HE WILL LOOK AFTER THEM.
I WOULDN'T ENDANGER THEM OTHERWISE.
OR THAT'S WHAT I TELL MYSELF.
RIGHT NOW, I CANNOT DENY WHAT I TELL MYSELF IS NOT ALWAYS TRUE.
AND I LIED TO THE BOY.
THE JUMP IS IMPOSSIBLE.
IT'S THE PLANK I ADDED EARLIER THAT MAKES IT OTHERWISE.

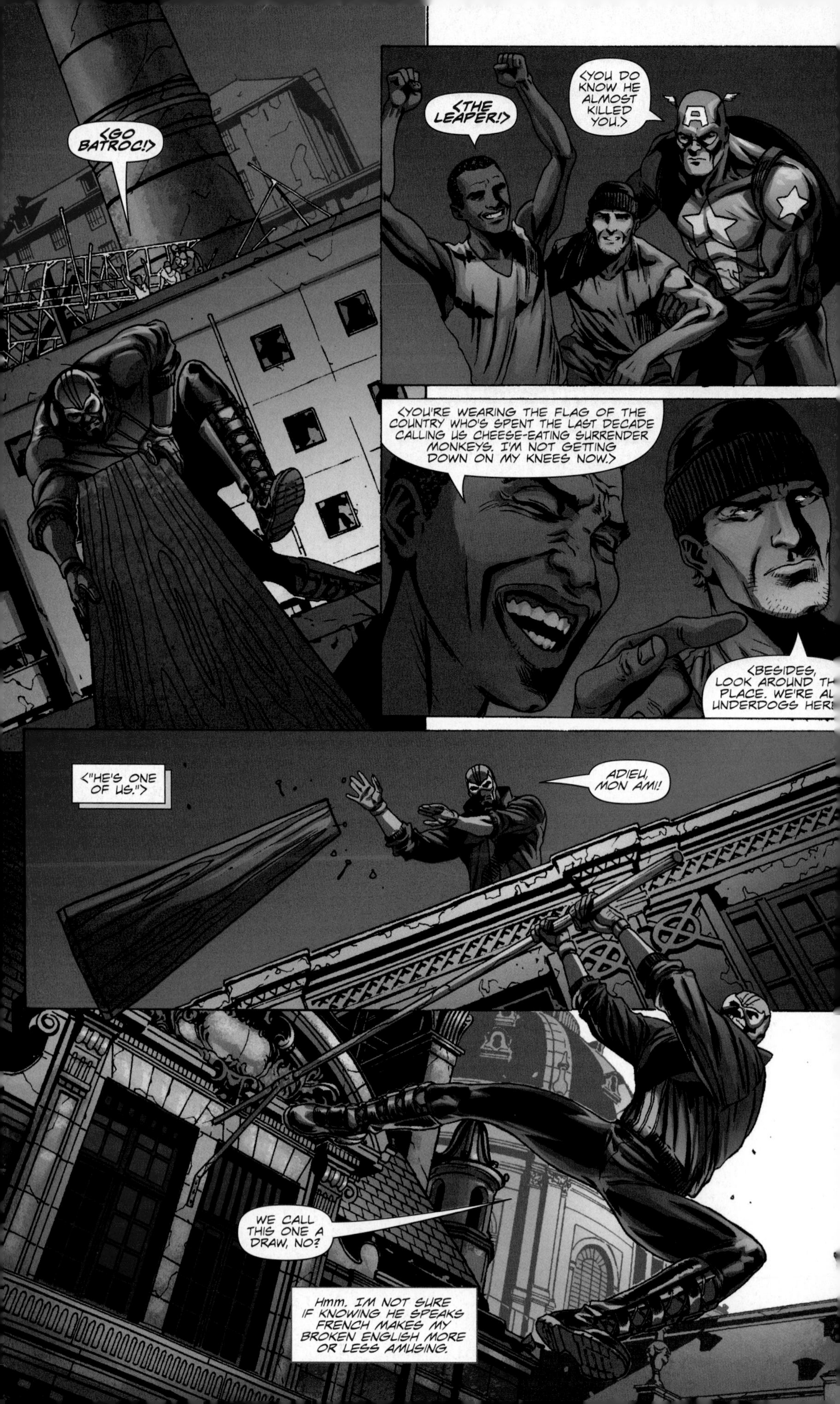
<GO BATROC!>
<THE LEAPER!>
<YOU DO KNOW HE ALMOST KILLED YOU.>
<YOU'RE WEARING THE FLAG OF THE COUNTRY WHO'S SPENT THE LAST DECADE CALLING US CHEESE-EATING SURRENDER MONKEYS. I'M NOT GETTING DOWN ON MY KNEES NOW.>
<BESIDES, LOOK AROUND TH PLACE. WE'RE AL UNDERDOGS HER
<"HE'S ONE OF US.">
ADIEU, MON AMI!
WE CALL THIS ONE A DRAW, NO?
Hmm. I'M NOT SURE IF KNOWING HE SPEAKS FRENCH MAKES MY BROKEN ENGLISH MORE OR LESS AMUSING.

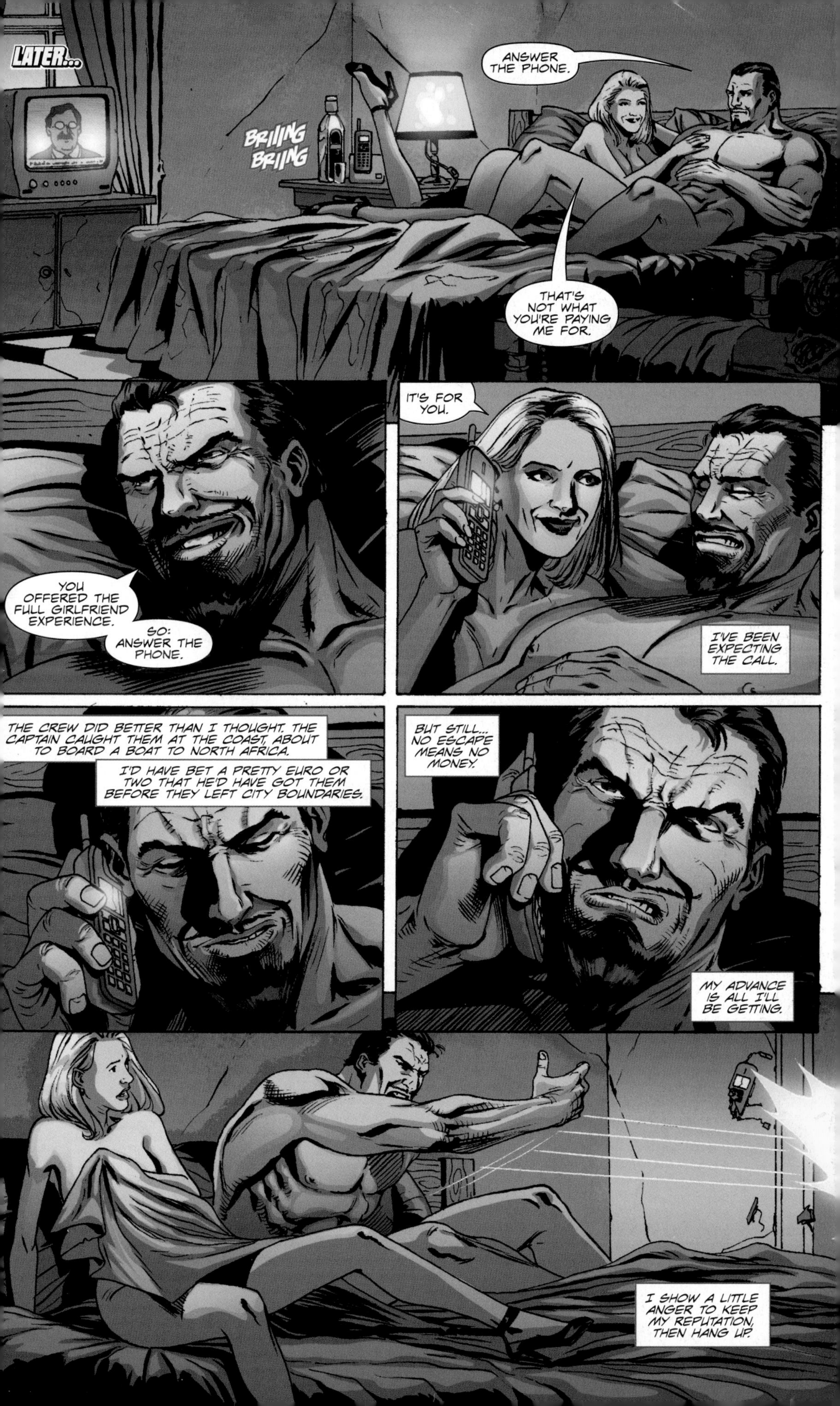
LATER...
ANSWER THE PHONE.
BRIIING BRIING
THAT'S NOT WHAT YOU'RE PAYING ME FOR.
YOU OFFERED THE FULL GIRLFRIEND EXPERIENCE.
SO: ANSWER THE PHONE.
IT'S FOR YOU.
I'VE BEEN EXPECTING THE CALL.
THE CREW DID BETTER THAN I THOUGHT. THE CAPTAIN CAUGHT THEM AT THE COAST, ABOUT TO BOARD A BOAT TO NORTH AFRICA.
I'D HAVE BET A PRETTY EURO OR TWO THAT HE'D HAVE GOT THEM BEFORE THEY LEFT CITY BOUNDARIES.
BUT STILL... NO ESCAPE MEANS NO MONEY.
MY ADVANCE IS ALL I'LL BE GETTING.
I SHOW A LITTLE ANGER TO KEEP MY REPUTATION, THEN HANG UP.

GO.

NOW.

I WAIT FOR HER STEPS TO DISAPPEAR, THEN COUNT TO THREE...

AND THEN I LAUGH.

A DRAW. OR, AS GOOD AS. OR NEAR ENOUGH.

WITH "MON CAPITAN", IT'S NEVER ABOUT THE MONEY.

IT'S ABOUT HAVING ANOTHER CHANCE TO BE THE BEST A MAN CAN BE.

AND THE HOPE THAT MAYBE TODAY IS THE DAY WHEN I CAN BE A LITTLE BIT MORE.

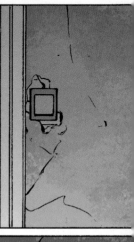

Fin.